Victorian demons

Victorian demons

Medicine, masculinity and the Gothic at the *fin de siècle*

Andrew Smith

Manchester University Press
Manchester and New York
distributed exclusively in the USA by Palgrave

Copyright ©Andrew Smith 2004

The right of Andrew Smith to be identified as the author of this work has been asserted by him in accordance with the Copyright, Designs and Patents Act 1988.

Published by Manchester University Press
Oxford Road, Manchester M13 9NR, UK
and Room 400, 175 Fifth Avenue, New York, NY 10010, USA
www.manchesteruniversitypress.co.uk

Distributed exclusively in the USA by
Palgrave, 175 Fifth Avenue, New York NY 10010, USA

Distributed exclusively in Canada by
UBC Press, University of British Columbia, 2029 West Mall,
Vancouver, BC, Canada V6T 1Z2

British Library Cataloguing-in-Publication Data
A catalogue record for this book is available from the British Library

Library of Congress Cataloging-in-Publication Data
A catalog record for this book is available from the Library of Congress

ISBN 13: 978 0 7190 6357 2

First published 2004 by Manchester University Press

First digital paperback edition published 2008

Printed by Lightning Source

Acknowledgements

A variety of people commented on this project at certain stages of its development. I am very grateful for the initial support which came from Professor Jane Aaron and Martha Stoddart Holmes when I was planning this book. Friends and colleagues who provided extremely helpful and detailed readings of parts of this book include Jeni Williams, William Hughes, Diana Wallace and Gill Plain, and because of their comments it is a much better book than it might otherwise have been. Some of my early findings were delivered as conference papers at the International Gothic Association conference, hosted by Mount Saint Vincent University in Halifax, Nova Scotia in 1999, and at the INCS annual conference held at Yale University in 2000. I am grateful for the helpful and supportive comments made by delegates at those conferences. I would also like to thank the staff at Manchester University Press for their encouragement and support. This book was completed during a period of sabbatical leave from the University of Glamorgan during the Spring term 2003, and I am very grateful to the English Department in making this possible, especially to my Head of Department, Jeff Wallace, and to Meredith Miller, who kindly took over my administrative duties during my absence. I would also like to thank Frances Hackeson for her copy-editing of the final manuscript. Finally, as always, I would like to thank Joanne Benson for her love, support, and copy-editing skills during the period it took me to write this book.

An earlier, shortened version of Chapter 2 was published as 'Pathologising the Gothic: The Elephant Man, the Neurotic and the Doctor' in *Gothic Studies* (published by Manchester University Press), vol. 2, no. 3, (2000).

Introduction

This book is a study of constructions of masculinity in a range of medical, cultural and Gothic narratives at the *fin de siècle*. My principal argument is that the final decades of the nineteenth century provide a particularly complex set of examples of how the dominant masculine scripts came to be associated with disease, degeneration and perversity. By exploring theories of degeneration, sexological writings, and medical writing on syphilis at the time, it is possible to see how such a pathologisation of the ostensibly dominant masculine scripts becomes developed in scientific, quasi-scientific, and literary contexts.

Gender and the fin de siècle

It has become somewhat of a commonplace to argue that the *fin de siècle* was characterised by crisis, and I want to pursue a different line of enquiry by suggesting that, in part, this notion of crisis was staged within the dominant masculinist culture, rather than that this culture was thrown into crisis by external threats to it. This case could be overstated and the contribution that, for example, the women's movement made at the time to debates about the constructions of masculinity cannot be ignored. Both Judith R. Walkowitz and Elaine Showalter, for example, have persuasively argued that the *fin de siècle* was dominated by a series of debates about gender prompted by the emergence of a range of women's pressure groups which militated for social change.[1] Further, Bram Dijkstra in *Idols of Perversity: Fantasies of Feminine Evil in Fin-de-Siècle Culture* (1986) examines the presence of a reactionary response to images of projected women's emancipation.[2] His argument convincingly emphasises how certain paintings, literary forms, and theories of degeneracy indicate the presence of a cultural tendency to associate women with physical disease and sexual immorality.

In some respects the critical debate about masculinity has been conditioned, both then and now, by a response to these issues. James Eli Adams, for example, in *Dandies and Desert Saints: Styles of Victorian Masculinity* (1995) argues that 'Reconfigurations of masculinity compensated for the loss of traditional, more assured forms of masculine identity and authority; they endeavoured to restore the prerogatives of a "manhood" – as distinct from mere "maleness" – that had severely been eroded by the pressures of modernity'.[3] For Adams, such pressures meant that men sought to establish new masculine identities which operated beyond the traditional, patriarchal domestic spaces. A new form of masculinity, one associated with Empire, for example, therefore became constructed during the period. A change in attitude towards 'manhood' was thus, to some extent, prompted by a reassessment of traditional models of masculinity. In part this was also a consequence of the emergence of the women's movement and the appearance of the New Woman in the 1890s. Such changes were also dependent upon the erosion of paternal authority within the middle-class home. This revolt against domesticity was therefore predicated on an emerging social and cultural critique of fatherhood. John Tosh in *A Man's Place: Masculinity and the Middle-Class Home in Victorian England* (1999), argues that 'Middle-class domesticity in Victorian England could hardly be described as an unqualified endorsement of patriarchal privilege', because:

> For the first time the legal *carte blanche* of the paterfamilias was subjected to significant inroads, by parliamentary legislation as well as judicial pronouncement. Male sexuality was the subject of unprecedented critique. The writers of advice books demanded higher standards of behaviour from husbands and tended to blame them when marriages came unstuck. The role and capacities of fathers were widely disparaged, and children of both sexes were less inclined to accept paternal authority.[4]

Such a marginalisation, and the anxiety with which it is associated, is one of the subjects of this book. However, my principal focus is on how this new, non-domestic masculinity is accounted for in scientific and literary contexts. Although reassessments of masculinity at the time provoke this marginalisation, nevertheless there is also a sense in which the dominant masculine gender scripts are pathologised from within that masculine culture. An example of this, which I discuss at length, concerns the relationship between theories of degeneration and sexology.

Degeneration and sexology

Max Nordau is the central figure here because his *Degeneration* (1892) provides a way of reading *fin de siècle* decadence which is based on a model of a dangerous, potentially perverse and possibly infectious version of male effeminacy. Wilde is to some degree his key target, but his argument is more broadly developed as a critique of an artistic amorality which, for Nordau, threatened the fundamental social contracts that maintained a well regulated, organically modelled version of society. However, Nordau argues that all is not lost because the very philistinism of the middle classes renders them immune from the pernicious influence of decadent Art. Nordau's critique rather overlooks the fact that such a challenge to the middle class had, as Tosh claims, already spread to the family, and his is a misdirected attempt at blaming various male writers for such developments. However, it also indicates the presence of a curious strategy in which men (including writers as diverse at Wilde, Zola and Ibsen) are held responsible for undermining masculine authority. The pathologisation of such men through a quasi-scientific argot (Ibsen is defined as an 'egomaniacal anarchist'[5]) indicates Nordau's policy of identifying certain 'aberrant' types which threaten the status quo. However, this language of Type and Symptom, while suggesting that one can easily discern the perverse and culturally anomalous, rests on an assumption that the masculine 'norm' is itself stable and coherent.

This model of stability was challenged in sexological writings which attempted to explore the relationship between gender and sex in a more rigorously scientific way. Nordau attempts to apply a theory of degeneration to writers, because writers, by definition, are not part of the mass and their very sense of intellectual detachment could be used to both marginalise them and to link them with deviancy. However, sexologists tended to examine the apparently commonplace experiences of 'ordinary' individuals and consequently developed a critique of supposedly 'normal' gender scripts. Havelock Ellis in *Studies in the Psychology of Sex* (1897–1928) and Edward Carpenter in *The Intermediate Sex* (1908) radically problematised the relationship between gender and sex designation by suggesting that a subject's adherence to the dominant masculine script was no guarantor of that subject's sexual preferences. The presence of masculine homosexuals and feminine heterosexuals, for example, challenged any notion of a fundamental or 'natural' link between gender and sex; indeed, it implied that any such link would be ideological. The coherent masculine script that ghosts Nordau's writing is therefore undermined in sexology.[6]

What all of this suggests is in some sense obvious: that gender scripts are performative. However, I also want to argue, in Chapter 1, for a British context which parallels mainstream models of degeneracy, but which also incorporates a particular reading of gender which would later be echoed by sexologists. Samuel Smiles's *Self-Help* (1859) is the key text in this British tradition because it articulates an anxiety relating to national, Imperial decline which is associated with a threatened masculinity, but suggests that social, cultural and personal revitalisation is made possible by performing the role of the gentleman. As we shall see, Smiles acknowledges that this particular model of masculinity is contrived, but that an agreement to perform the role enables the male subject to overcome his base, lower urges and so reaffirm a set of middle-class values which ensures the political and economic continuance of the nation. This is a position also echoed, in a slightly different way, by Charles Kingsley, who also asserts the notion that an adherence to gentlemanly, Christian behaviour enables the subject to transcend biological, sexual impulses.

Neither Smiles nor Kingsley attempt to reaffirm a natural link between gender and sex, although they do stress its social necessity. Nevertheless they both constructed a model of a divided male subject, one who asserts a social role in order to overcome a distracting biological presence, and this image of the divided male subject is central to much discussion in this book. It is also an issue that helps to move the debate beyond readings of masculinity in the period which have attempted to account for 'crisis' in terms of either a reactionary response to the women's suffrage movement, or due to associated changes in domestic relations. Rather, I want to stress the presence of an alternative history which suggests that a bifurcated model of masculinity, one that in its own way constitutes a crisis, is generated out of a male tradition of writings on degeneracy, sexology and self-help. Such a model of masculinity also appears in a medical context which uses images of disease in order to pathologise the ostensibly respectable middle-class male. This is a topic I address directly in Chapter 4 in my account of medical textbooks on syphilis and how they came to apportion blame to the client rather than the prostitute. In some respect this is to get ahead of my argument, but what I want to stress is that this notion of a masculinity in crisis can be accounted for by debates at the time concerning the relationship between gender and sex, and that these debates are, at least in substantial part, staged within a tradition of male writing about gender. This book therefore attempts a reassessment of the *fin de siècle*, one which argues for a reconsideration of the origins of such a notion of crisis.

However, this book is not solely about how medical texts and contexts construct problematic models of pathologised masculinity, it is also about how the Gothic stages a very similar debate about disease and 'maleness' at the time.

The Gothic

One danger in assessing the relationship between literary and scientific contexts is that they could become crudely mapped on to each other. However, the literary texts explored here, which includes an extensive analysis of R.L. Stevenson's *The Strange Case of Dr Jekyll and Mr Hyde* (1886), Stoker's *Dracula* (1897) and Doyle's Sherlock Holmes tales, can not simply be read as fictional reformulations of scientific debates. Science does not articulate a view of masculinity which directly recrudesces elsewhere, because literary texts and scientific discourse are different in kind. It is important to note this difference between the Gothic and science at the time, and in this respect I support Robert Mighall's view that 'Novelists, Scientists, criminologists, and even polemicists have different professional and epistemological agendas and obligations. To subsume all utterances produced at a given time into a monolithic cultural "context" suppresses these important differences'.[7] This is especially relevant to the Gothic because, as Mighall claims, the danger is that 'a fiction of monsters and supernatural threats is reduced to a covert articulation of ideology, while science appears to function principally as an arbiter or shaper of "fear"' (p. 167). This is to acknowledge that science, especially that science associated with theories of degeneration, relied on models of otherness and abnormality in order to generate knowledge of the 'norm'. This process is not immune from ideological considerations because, as Mighall points out, it tends to support bourgeois, patriarchal interests. However, science as a creator of epistemology (no matter how nefarious its origins) tells us something about models of truth in the period because the norm requires the abnormal in order to situate itself. This caveat about the relationship between science and the Gothic aside, it is also the case that we need to understand how literature represents gender, often in ways which echo (in transformed ways) how it is represented in certain scientific contexts.

Cyndy Hendershot in *The Animal Within: Masculinity and the Gothic* (1998) argues that 'the Gothic exposes the others within and without that give the lie to the notion of such a category as stable masculinity'.[8] I would support this claim and also acknowledge that to an extent science and the Gothic, although the product of very different intellectual and aesthetic traditions, nevertheless possess a shared fascination with the collapse of dominant gender scripts. A 'scientific' interpretation of this collapse is, of course, quite different to a literary representation of it, and although I follow Mighall's view on the dangers of simplifying or rendering 'monolithic' the cultural context, I do feel that it is necessary to move beyond this claim by acknowledging that theories of degeneration, sexology and certain types of medical discourse are not particularly 'scientific'. Certainly it is important to acknowledge, for example, that the claims for scientific objectivity are working at a different level in Sir Jonathan Hutchinson's medical textbook *Syphilis* (first published in 1887) than they are in Nordau's *Degeneration*. Also, theories of degeneration which rely on images of perversion, atavism and forms of monstrosity suggest an already Gothicised presence which inhabits such theories. Even in the more sophisticated deliberations of sexology there is an image of the unstable, divided self which is echoed in the Gothic instabilities of the seemingly bifurcated subject suggested in *Jekyll and Hyde*. Hendershot claims that 'One area that has served a crucial site for defining modern masculinity has been science. As the Gothic troubles stable notions of the body, so it invades the objective discourse of science' (p. 69). Science and the representation of science in the Gothic is not the same thing, but they do touch on a shared debate concerning the function and status of prevailing models of masculinity.

Hendershot makes many relevant and interesting points although I find her argument concerning the vestigial presence of an older one-sex (undifferentiated) body which haunts accounts of Victorian two-sex (male/ female) bodies, overly schematic as it tends to ignore the often highly specific way in which gender and class are related. It also tends to overlook the often problematic relationship which exists between models of deviancy and apparently 'normative' gender scripts. Adams addresses this and argues for the peculiar proximity of 'abnormal' to 'normal' in the period, claiming that there exist 'unexpected points of continuity and contact between normative and transgressive masculinities' (p. 19). A good example of this, and one that is referred to in a variety of related contexts in this book, is *Jekyll and Hyde*.

Stevenson's novella implicitly demonises the notion of the respectable middle-class professional (including doctors and lawyers) and suggests that true horror is not reflected in Hyde but through the fragile, because empty, world inhabited by the bourgeois professional. In this way the normative becomes demonised, while in the figure of Hyde, who at some level represents a distorted model of the 'gentleman', the deviant becomes normalised. This specific critique of the middle class is also, as we shall see, reflected in medical textbooks on syphilis and permeates newspaper speculation that the Whitechapel murderer could have been an ostensibly respectable doctor.

The Gothicisation of a certain kind of medical practice is in some way conditional upon a technical rather than a specifically ideological consideration. After all, medicine's association with disease does not mean that medicine is itself diseased. However, in the case of syphilis, for example, the disease is discussed in such a coy way that medicine functions as a means of concealing the role played by the middle-class client in the spread of the disease (even while there is a grudging acknowledgement that this is the case). In this way medicine reveals a certain political partiality.

Medicine

That the medical profession was perceived in a sinister light is clear from an examination of press reports at the time of the Whitechapel murders. The image of the 'mad' doctor discussed in the press emerges from pre-existing anxieties relating to the conduct of medicine in general and journalistic anxieties about middle-class men in particular. Popular concern that the wealthy, fashionable West End of London was preying upon the working class East End is evidenced by contemporary newspapers reports such as those in W.T. Stead's *The Pall Mall Gazette*. However, that medicine, as a profession, was itself concerned with how it was perceived is illustrated by medical memoirs written by doctors who worked during the period. Such reflections are not gender neutral, and they often specifically address the role that masculinity plays in the medical profession.

Sir Wilfred Grenfell in *A Labrador Doctor* (1920) and D.G. Halstead in *Doctor in The Nineties* (1959) both discuss their experiences of working at the London Hospital in Whitechapel in the 1880s.[9] Both argue that by setting up Boys Clubs for the poor of the East End (which encouraged sporting activities) it would be possible to inculcate a set of moral values that could help to rejuvenate, morally and physically, the next generation. Such a medical model of muscular Christianity implies that medicine has a social mission to generate normative models of masculine behaviour. However, their tutor at the London Hospital, Sir Frederick Treves, gives a very different account of masculinity in his *The Elephant Man and Other Reminiscences* (1923).[10] Treves uses a Gothic language in his discussion of medical cases which I discuss at length in Chapter 2. This use of the Gothic frames his account of Joseph Merrick (aka 'The Elephant Man') and evidences an anxiety relating to the proximity of the normal and the pathological, within what is a covert debate about masculinity. Also, in his account of a female hysteric, the medical profession is represented as resembling a gentleman's club which has very little interest in supposedly female maladies. Indeed doctors become perceived by the hysteric as Gothic figures, inflicting pain and distress either through neglect or through a misplaced sense of surgical bravado. The role that the Gothic plays therefore provides us with an insight into how this process of pathologising the 'normal' becomes staged within accounts of medicine.

My broader argument is that the *fin de siècle* Gothic uses a language of othering in order to emphasise difference. This type of othering appears to suggest the presence of a conservative agenda which is shared by medicine at this time (with its fascination with the physically and socially 'abnormal'). However, I will argue, this process is much more complex than this because, as in the case of Treves, there is a sense that masculinity is in crisis and that this crisis is inherent to medical practice.

Performing gender and the urban jungle

One key issue is that of visibility and invisibility. Medical textbooks on syphilis, for example, have a tendency to conceal the reasons for the spread of the disease even as they attempt a discussion of its modes of transmission. This notion of visibility is also central, in a related way, to sexological readings of gender that argue for a disjunction between sexual orientation and gender performance. The figure of the masculine homosexual, for example, appears to conceal same-sex desire and this is an issue which played an important role in the trials, and indeed in the writings, of Oscar Wilde which are discussed in Chapter 6. As we shall see, Wilde's camp performance covertly developed a gay identity which was not interpreted as such by the dominant heterosexual culture, because it was invisible to it. Wilde's writings, such as *The Picture of Dorian Gray* (1891), *De Profundis* (published in 1905) and *The Ballad of Reading Gaol* (1898) also suggest the presence of a secret gay identity, one that emphasises the fundamentally performative nature of gender scripts. At some, perhaps obvious, level Wilde's trials scrutinised what was meant by 'masculine', but they also, more problematically, attempted to account for the presence of a homosexual identity which, hitherto, had not been made visible to the dominant, supposedly normative, culture. Wilde's trials therefore raised troubling questions at the time about how a homosexual identity could be developed within apparently normative gender scripts (Wilde as an Oxford educated club-land gentleman and married father of two).[11]

The narratives considered here are also related to London and debates about the economic and class characteristics of the city have an important place in accounts of degeneracy and speculation relating to the Whitechapel killings. London appears as a class-bound, gendered space, and this is an issue in *Jekyll and Hyde* but also in Stoker's *Dracula* which attempts to purify the city of dangerous, diseased, foreign (vampiric) invaders. However, that the city was a gendered space is also clear from Doyle's Sherlock Holmes tales, discussed in Chapter 5, which indicate that Holmes's frequent inability to exert mastery within the city (many of the tales are set outside London in the Home Counties) can be explained as a reaction to certain gender debates at the *fin de siècle*. London becomes a site of gender contestation at the *fin de siècle*, and the sense that it becomes an increasingly female-controlled public sphere (largely associated with the female shopper) also led to a reassessment of the now compromised dominant masculine scripts.

Masculinity, 'manhood' and 'manliness' became synonymous at the time and when I make occasional reference to 'male' culture this is to acknowledge that 'maleness' was itself subject to much debate and interrogation during the period. This book attempts a reassessment of masculinity at the *fin de siècle* by exploring how a sense of crisis is generated within the dominant culture. Medicine, a definitively male, white, middle-class profession provides a good example of how such a crisis is developed within this culture. This book also examines how, and why, the Gothic frequently states the case, as in *Dracula* for example, for the need to re-establish a link between gender and sex. However, once the gender scripts have become detached from sex, it is difficult to get back to some prelapsarian state. This book is therefore about medicine and the Gothic and the wider culture which, in different but related ways, they share. I should also emphasise that this is not a revisionist account of the period. While models of masculinity may be in crisis, this does not mean that true political and economic power was anything other than a male preserve, even if debates on that authority were taking place at the time.

Chapter 1 is an outline of theories of degeneracy and how they relate to masculinity. It also charts an alternative British tradition of degeneracy which is developed in the work of Smiles, Kingsley and Lankester, as this British context provides a more immediate background to the case histories that follow (although Nordau is still to some significant extent a key figure here). Theories of sexology constructed by Ellis, Carpenter, and Weininger are also discussed in order to indicate how they unsettle the relationship between gender and sex, an argument which is also to be found in the work of Smiles and Kingsley (and which suggests a subtle way of bridging the apparently incompatible worlds of degeneration and sexology). Finally a reading of *Jekyll and Hyde* and *Dracula* is made which indicates how such images of gender are developed and debated in a literary context which in its own way is responding to contemporary 'scientific' debates about gender.

Chapter 2 is a close reading of Treves's *Reminiscences*. Treves's memoirs focus on the issues confronted by doctors working in the late Victorian period. I explore three of Treves's narratives; one on Merrick, one on hysteria, and one on a peculiar dream that he has during a visit to India.

Treves's account of Merrick is edged by a discourse of degeneracy that he fails to properly apply. For Treves the cause of Merrick's illness remains a mystery, but he identifies Merrick's apparently troubling sexuality as something which needed to be controlled. After applying a failed scientific and Gothic language to Merrick he applies a model of literary romance which mockingly dandifies Merrick but which also, ambiguously, feminises him. This failure of science is also emphasised in Treves's narrative attempt at impersonating a female hysteric, one in which the 'patient' comes to associate doctors with specifically Gothic horrors. The failure of science and its subsequent demonisation is also developed in an Imperial context when Treves recounts a dream in which he imagines, during a trip to India, being attacked by an allegedly ungrateful Indian patient who blames his blindness on the medical profession. Treves, in the dream, attacks and escapes from the Indian in what is a highly ambiguous expression of a 'superior' masculine control that is also apparent in the accounts of Merrick and hysteria. Treves's *Reminiscences* thus bring together masculinity, medicine and the Gothic, and creates a set of connections between them that are made clear through an examination of deformity, gender and race.

The Whitechapel murders of 1888 are discussed in Chapter 3. Media speculation demonised different versions of masculinity: the West End aristocrat, the doctor, and the working class 'Jack'. The focus in this chapter is on how and why the medical profession became implicated in the murders. The autopsy reports on the victims, for example, suggested that the murderer was a 'mad' doctor and this process of pathologisation began to spread to the supposedly normative practices of medicine. Medicine's fascination with disease, pathology and death suggested to the press that medicine was inherently perverse and dangerous, and *Jekyll and Hyde* was repeatedly referred to by the press as an example of how medicine represented conflicting impulses: the desire to help, but also the desire to do harm. This idea of a divided subject is also apparent from contemporary accounts of London which emphasised the relationship between the wealth of the West End and the poverty of the East End. This Gothic London functioned as a backdrop against which the murders occurred even while such murders suggested that the bourgeois professional (the doctor) might be responsible for them.

One of the issues raised by the killings concerned the conditions under which prostitution could flourish. Prostitutes had been held principally responsible for the spread of syphilis, however by the end of the century this view had changed. The Contagious Diseases Acts of 1864, 1868 and 1869 had meant that any woman could be forced to undergo a medical examination in a search for symptoms of sexually transmittable disease. However, largely as a result of the efforts of Josephine Butler, the Acts were repealed in 1886 and after this there was a shift in attitude towards attributing responsibility for the spread of syphilis, as the middle-class client was now held responsible for transmitting the disease to the bourgeois family. In Chapter 4 I discuss medical textbooks on syphilis from the period and how they responded to these developments. A reading of Sir Jonathan Hutchinson's *Syphilis* and Alfred Cooper's *Syphilis* (1895) indicates how the medical profession sought to conceal this now pathologised middle-class male, even within the context of apparently apolitical discussions relating to health. That such textbooks reveal a specifically male strategy of reading the disease is also underlined by an examination of Nordau's account of Ibsen's representation of syphilis in *Ghosts* (1881). Nordau, like Hutchinson and Cooper, plays down the significance of the disease in the interests of reasserting the importance of the family ties which the disease so clearly threatened. This chapter is therefore concerned with how male readings of the disease operated along a precarious line of disclosure and concealment concerning the activity of the middle-class client.

London provides the context for all of the issues and case histories explored here. In Chapter 5 an examination is made of how London appears as a gendered space in the work of male authors. De Quincey, Wilkie Collins and Dickens all represent London in terms of gender and this constitutes a particular literary history of London to which later writers such as Doyle and Stoker responded and contributed. The main focus in this chapter is on how Doyle's Sherlock Holmes tales suggest that Holmes is a comparatively disempowered figure when he works within London, and that his assertion of order and rationality is often more apparent in cases that are set in the Home Counties. The reasons for this displacement of Holmes are due to the economic and cultural changes in London (specifically in the area around Baker Street) which were related to the debates about gender and economic ownership of the city at the time. Stoker's *Dracula* also represents an image of a threatened London, one seemingly subject to assault from outsiders. The novel also represents an attempted assertion of a masculine control over the city that Holmes is not able to produce: an issue about control which in the case of the Whitechapel murders suggested the presence of a demonic, criminalised form of masculine control over the East End. London therefore functions as a space in which mastery over it is related to contemporary debates about masculinity.

In Chapter 6 some aspects of Oscar Wilde's trials are examined as well as a range of his writings. Wilde constructed a new Camp identity within the space between gender performance and sexual orientation. Wilde's theatrical performance in the witness box implies the performative element of gender. It is important to emphasise that Wilde not only subverted models of gender but also subverted notions of degeneracy: his theory of aesthetics is, as we shall see, predicated on a model of immanence drawn from Aristotle but it is also one which parodies the idea of biological immanence to be found in theories of degeneracy. Ultimately in Wilde's trials masculinity is put on trial.

All of the chapters in this book concern narratives about masculinity. What also brings these narratives into alliance is the convergence between them. I do not intend to indulge a biographical fallacy here, but it is noteworthy that Wilde knew Stoker (Wilde had in fact courted Florence Balcombe, who later became Stoker's wife). Also, both Sir Henry Irving (the leading actor of the period whom Stoker worked with at the Lyceum Theatre) and R.L. Stevenson had been treated for medical problems by Sir Frederick Treves. In addition Doyle made some observations on the likely identity of Jack the Ripper (that 'Jack' was a midwife, or a man disguised as such), and Wilde's father had also written about syphilis in a paper published in 1858.[12] In other words this book is a history of a middle class, white, male, cultural and intellectual elite *and* a history of how their power became challenged from within.

Notes

1   See Judith R. Walkowitz, *City of Dreadful Delight: Narratives of Sexual Danger in Late-Victorian London* (London: Virago [1992] 1998) pp. 73–80

and p. 141. Elaine Showalter, *Sexual Anarchy: Gender and Culture at the Fin de Siècle* (Harmondsworth: Viking, 1990) pp. 33–58.

2 Bram Dijkstra, *Idols of Perversity: Fantasies of Feminine Evil in Fin-de-Siècle Culture* (Oxford: Oxford University Press, 1986).

3 James Eli Adams, *Dandies and Desert Saints: Styles of Victorian Masculinity* (Ithaca, NY and London: Cornell University Press, 1995) p. 5. All subsequent references are to this edition, and are given in the text.

4 John Tosh, *A Man's Place: Masculinity and the Middle-Class Home in Victorian England* (New Haven, CT and London: Yale University Press, 1999) p. 145.

5 Max Nordau, *Degeneration* (Lincoln, NE and London: University of Nebraska Press [1895] 1993) p. 357.

6 *The Intermediate Sex: A Study of Some Transitional Types of Men and Women* (London: Swan Sonnenschein, 1908) contains a chapter 'The Intermediate Sex' which was first published in the fifth edition of Carpenter's *Love's Coming of Age* (London: Swan Sonnenschein, 1906). In turn the chapter was based on an earlier article 'An Unknown People' which was published as *An Unknown People* (London: A. and H.B. Bonner, 1897).

7 Robert Mighall, *A Geography of Victorian Gothic Fiction: Mapping History's Nightmares* (Oxford: Oxford University Press, 1999) p. 167. All subsequent references are to this edition, and are given in the text.

8 Cyndy Hendershot, *The Animal Within: Masculinity and the Gothic* (Ann Arbor, MI: University of Michigan Press [1998] 2001) p. 1. All subsequent references are to this edition, and are given in the text.

9 Sir Wilfred Grenfell, *A Labrador Doctor: The Autobiography of Sir Wilfred Grenfell* (London: Hodder and Stoughton [1920] 1931). D.G. Halstead, *Doctor in The Nineties* (London: Christopher Johnson, 1959).

10 Sir Frederick Treves, *The Elephant Man and Other Reminiscences* (London: Cassell, 1923).

11 Wilde's camp performance does not quite accord with this image, and yet one of the oddities is that it did not necessarily compromise his apparent heterosexuality.

12 W.R. Wilde, 'Medico-Legal Observations upon the Case of Amos Greenwood', *Dublin Quarterly Journal of Medicine & Science*, 27 (1858), 51–87.

1

Degeneration, masculinity, nationhood and the Gothic

Understandings of human identity underwent a radical transfiguration at the *fin-de- siècle* as new modes of imagining and narrativizing the (ab)human subject became available.

(The Gothic Body)[1]

Though so profound a double-dealer, I was in no sense a hypocrite: both sides of me were in dead earnest: I was no more myself when I laid aside restraint and plunged in shame, than when I laboured, in the eye of day, at the furtherance of knowledge or the relief of sorrow and suffering.

(The Strange Case of Dr Jekyll and Mr Hyde)[2]

Daniel Pick's authoritative study of theories of degeneration and their historical contexts, *Faces of Degeneration* (1989) charts the development of such theories from the 1840s to the end of the First World War.[3] Degeneration had its roots in the work of Bénédict Augustin Morel, who in the 1840s and 1850s attempted to explain psychological abnormalities through a theory of mental decline that was to influence the later work of criminologists, sociologists, psychologists and, towards the end of the nineteenth century, cultural commentators. Pick rightly sees such theories as constituting a fundamentally European movement which in part developed out of the political and social turmoil of the period. Such theories attempted to account for popular anxieties about national decline by exploring its alleged causes within particular nations. Early accounts of degeneration were written by specialists, while by the end of the century the debate had taken on a wider cultural dimension. From the work of Morel on cretinism in France in the 1850s, to the criminological writings of the Italian Cesare Lombroso in the 1870s, degeneration crossed national and scientific boundaries; culminating in the 1890s with Max Nordau's attack on *fin de siècle* decadence written for a general, popular audience.[4] Indeed, the ease with which the theory crossed the borders of various disciplines, with their different readerships, suggests that the theory was always, in essence, a cultural narrative. This is a cultural narrative which can also be discerned in *fin de siècle* Gothic, a literary form discussed at the end of this chapter, which both draws on images of the degenerate in its construction of monstrosity, and suggests that such theories constitute a Gothic narrative concerning individual pathology and national decline.

Pick's study explores how ideas of heredity and pathology were used to diagnose what were political problems concerning Empire and the status of various European nations. The mentally ill, the gambler, the alcoholic, the criminal and the artist were just some of the characters who, at various times, composed a pantheon of degenerate figures. It is, however, the idea of masculinity and its susceptibility to pathologisation which concerns us here, and it was an issue given particular prominence by Max Nordau in *Degeneration* (1892), a book which is also, in part, a summation of earlier accounts of degeneracy.

The publication of *Degeneration* introduced the theory of degeneration to a wide, popular audience. Nordau, a journalist, novelist and a playwright rather than a scientist, refashioned a quasi-Darwinian notion that the human species could, under certain circumstances, *de*volve and argued that this was evidenced by the presence of particular literary and cultural trends. For Nordau the symptoms of degeneration were manifested in the amoral artistic posturing of a dramatist such as Ibsen and through the quite different writings of Zola and Wilde. Nordau also claimed that degeneration was revealed through 'diseased' art; such art indicated the presence of corruption, and was itself potentially corrupting. What was reassuring, according to Nordau, was the immunity of the philistine middle classes from the damaging influence of such artistic practice, and it was through the middle class, specifically through their supposed diligence, level-headedness, and capacity for hard work, that society could be revitalised. Indeed, it was the bourgeoisie who would ensure that *fin de siècle* decadence would be marginalised and so devolve and disappear. This was a conclusion seemingly literalised in Oscar Wilde's marginalisation when, in 1895, he was imprisoned for 'gross indecency', and by his subsequent exile to mainland Europe.

If at one level Nordau had in mind the apparently corrosive aspects of art, at another level he had tied this to an idea of masculinity. For Nordau, Wilde's art was simply perverse because it was the product of perversity. A principal target of Nordau's was what he saw as an effeminate 'emotionalism' which constituted a key aspect of the 'mental stigma of degenerates', of whom he writes:

He laughs until he sheds tears, or weeps copiously without adequate occasion; a commonplace line of poetry or prose sends a shudder down his back; he falls into raptures before indifferent pictures of statues; and music, especially, even the most insipid and least commendable, arouses in him the most vehement emotions. He is quite proud of being so vibrant a musical instrument, and boasts that where the Philistine remains completely cold, he feels his inner self confounded, the depths of his being broken up, and the bliss of the Beautiful possessing him to the tips of his fingers.[5]

In other words it is not just art which is the problem but also the way that it is consumed. Nordau regards this unmanly emotionalism as a key indicator of a society's ill health. At stake therefore is the link between masculinity and nation. The decline of the nation is intimately connected with the future of masculinity, the prevailing model of which, for Nordau, appeared to be challenged by the decadent, and culturally symbolic Oscar Wilde.

Nordau's views were largely directed towards a generalised portrait of Europe, and his principal concern is with an alleged European decadence. However, this chapter will move beyond Nordau and explore how British commentators responded to some of these ideas about masculinity and nation. This debate about decline is given a particular local inflection in a British context, one which enables us to see how a specific construction of masculinity was mobilised in order to adapt Nordau's claims. In Britain, for example, Nordau's book inspired Egmont Hake in *Regeneration: A Reply to Max Nordau* (1895) to claim that, 'In some countries the cry is for leaders; but the old faith that the situations will bring out the men seems to have been utterly falsified: for everywhere mediocrity, prejudice, and corruption, hold the helm'.[6] Elsewhere Egmont claims that Britain may need to go through a period of degeneration in order for a stronger revitalised nation to emerge. What is clear in these accounts of degeneration is the claim that there existed a relationship between the unhealthy male body and the wider body politic, and it is this specific claim which will be developed after briefly discussing how Nordau's book was received by cultural and social critics at the time.

Typically for a British commentator, Hake makes associations between Nordau's idea of degeneration and a threatened Imperial decline although one which can, as Nordau claimed, be obviated by hard work: 'Degenerate Englishmen may still wish to meekly follow other nations, but our mission is to be practical, energetic, daring pioneers heading the march of progress' (p. 18).[7] Hake's nationalistic twist to the debate indicates how a (very conservative) British commentator was prepared to adapt these ideas to the specific context of Britain in order to claim that Britain, and specifically England, was in the vanguard of this movement towards change:

> By using its great power and influence, the British nation can render invaluable service to humanity in the present crisis. On England must therefore rest our hopes for the practical solution of the grave questions on which progress and retrogression depend. From England alone can proceed that electrifying impulse of which the bewildered nations stand in need, that they marshal the forces and focus the goal of progress. (p. 19)

Nordau's book was not greeted with universal acclaim. William James, for example referred to it as 'A pathological book on a pathological subject', and George Bernard Shaw lampooned the catch-all term of degeneration in his tellingly entitled *The Sanity of Art: An Exposure of the Current Nonsense About Artists Being Degenerate* (1908).[8] Nevertheless what is revealing in such accounts of degeneracy is the links made between masculinity and nation. These links will be developed here before exploring how sexology critiqued the links between maleness and masculinity that commentators such as Nordau and Hake attempted to establish. The British response to theories of degeneration was not simply an adaptation of existing European ideas, they were also a culmination of a peculiarly British tradition of self-help, an examination of which helps us to situate these concerns about masculinity within a specific national context.

First it is necessary to explore the roots of this British context. If Morel inaugurates the debate about degeneration in a medical context during the 1850s, then this is paralleled by an alternative point of origin in a British, non-medical context: that of Samuel Smiles's *Self-Help: With Illustrations of Conduct and Perseverance* (1859).

Smiles and character

Smiles's book is largely composed of a series of biographical vignettes designed to provide moral instruction to an essentially middle-class readership. Throughout, Smiles emphasises the importance of hard work, a practice which would not only facilitate a personal sense of moral well-being and guarantee one's social and economic 'success', but would also, and more importantly, ensure the continued vitality of the nation. What is required are some energetic (and heroic) role models. Smiles notes in his chapter 'Energy and Courage' that 'A fine and just appreciation of character' will indicate to the 'thoughtful observer' the 'strikingly illustrative … fact that it is the energy of the individual men that gives strength to a

State, and confers a value even upon the very soil which they cultivate'.[9] The future of the 'State' is thus linked to the vitality and courage of the individuals which compose it. However in order to revitalise the nation it also becomes necessary to revitalise masculinity. According to Smiles, energy and a steadfastness of purpose are essential elements of the vital activities of the productive middle classes, claiming that 'energy of will may be defined to be the very central power of character in man – in a word it is the Man himself' (p. 224). The idea of character and vitality is central to Smiles's project of constructing a dynamic, and highly specific, version of middle-class masculinity. This is because Smiles claims that by the mid-nineteenth century it is the middle class, rather than the aristocracy, who have responsibility for the credibility and maintenance of public office. Self-help and the self-made are key elements in this character formation. He approvingly notes, for example, how the explorer David Livingstone supported his medical studies 'entirely by his own earnings as a factory workman' (p. 243). Such self-sufficient masculine individualism militates against disease and degeneration and is therefore a component part in developing a strategy which guarantees the health of the nation. For Smiles this masculinity is forged through a balance of physical and intellectual abilities.

That this is all a matter of balance is also suggested in his account of the relationship between work and leisure. The implication is that character may become dissipated through extreme play or leisure, so that '"Fast" men ... Having forestalled their spring ... can produce no healthy growth of either character or intellect' (p. 334). What is implied here is the importance of reproducing a version of yourself through self-development (or 'self-help'). The dissipated man foregoes his 'spring' and is not revitalised, and the dangerous consequence is that this has an effect on the future of the State and the Nation. This concern about growth represents an anxiety about the future generation (as it would in theories of degeneration), and this is underlined by the closing lines from his chapter on 'Self-Culture' which are specifically aimed at parents who need to provide a context in which manly self-reliance can be developed:

> Let them see to it that the youth is provided, by free exercise of his bodily powers, with a full stock of physical health; set him fairly on the road of self-culture; carefully train his habits of application and perseverance; and as he grows older, if the right stuff be in him, he will be enabled vigorously and effectively to cultivate himself. (p. 359)

The point for Smiles is that it will also be necessary to turn the youth into a man, specifically a gentleman.

It is in his final chapter, 'Character – the True Gentleman', that Smiles moves his argument beyond some of these earlier claims about the need to cultivate moral character. This is because he now argues that the character of the 'True Gentleman' contrasts with the base, potentially degenerate, demands of the male body. He argues that, 'Character is human nature in its best form. It is moral order embodied in the individual. Men of character are not only the conscience of society, but in every well-governed State they are its best motive power; for it is moral qualities in the main which rule the world' (p. 383). The crucial claim is that character is *acquired* rather than innate and Smiles argues, unironically, that this desire to acquire character represents the noblest aspects of 'human nature'. He refers to the late MP Francis Horner (who died aged 38) and how he was remembered by one of his parliamentary colleagues, Lord Cockburn. Cockburn says that what was remarkable about Horner was his force of character and that 'this character [was] not impressed upon him by nature, but formed out of no peculiarly fine elements by himself' (p. 384). Horner therefore represents the triumph of acquisition over heredity. The point is that one should not give in to biology or disposition, but rather struggle against these in order to fabricate a version of the self *and* that it is through the subject's very allegiance to this process (through hard work and persistence) that moral character is developed.

The subject needs to be truly self-effacing because they leave behind the demands of baser, biological needs in order to enter into a chaste, but morally meaningful world of public office. This allegiance to a covert artificiality for the greater good is one also associated with a model of masculinity, and so gentlemanly conduct. For Smiles, 'Every man is bound to aim at the possession of a good character as one of the highest objects of life. The very effort to secure it by worthy means will furnish him with a motive for exertion; and his idea of manhood, in proportion as it is elevated, will steady and animate his motive' (p. 386). The essentially artificial aspects of this do not appear to have troubled Smiles. Indeed the impetus is on how one leaves behind a certain type of character (a potentially 'low' one) in order to embrace a higher ideal. This would enable the subject to move beyond what would later in the century be understood as degenerate traits and fashion a new sense of self that is inherently social because it indicates an allegiance to moral value which can only benefit everyone. For Smiles, all that is necessary is the ability to put on a convincing performance: 'A man must really be what he seems or purposes to be' (p. 387). Smiles then quotes approvingly from the abolitionist Granville Sharp who claimed that his family's maxim was '*Always endeavour to be really what you would wish to appear*' (p. 387, emphasis in Smiles). Smiles suggests that the theatrical dimensions of gentlemanly behaviour are therefore necessary in order to quell the insistent, baser demands of the body's appetites.

Taking on the character of a gentleman seems to suggest a curious double life, but Smiles emphasises that by becoming a gentleman one is able to overcome internal division. Smiles claims that a moral commitment to acquire character is a vital component in playing the role, arguing that:

> Without this dominating influence, character has no protection, but is constantly liable to fall away before temptation; and every such temptation succumbed to, every act of meanness or dishonesty, however slight, causes self-degradation. It matters not whether the act be successful or not, discovered or concealed; the culprit is no longer the same, but another person; and he is pursued by a secret uneasiness, by self-reproach, or the workings of what we call conscience, which is the inevitable doom of the guilty. (p. 388)

So, base conduct transforms the subject. However, the problem for Smiles is how the subject can maintain a sense of character when confronted by temptation. Ultimately the solution is to be found within a model of virtuous manliness that evokes a world of chivalrous behaviour. It is one of the few passages in *Self-Help* where the threat of degeneration (and its refutation) are explicitly referred to:

> Notwithstanding the wail which we occasionally hear for the chivalry that is gone, our won age has witnessed deeds of bravery and gentleness – of heroic self-denial and manly tenderness – which are unsurpassed in history. The events of the last few years have shown that our countrymen are as yet an undegenerate race. On the bleak plateau of Sebastopol, in the dripping perilous trenches of that twelvemonth's leaguer, men of all classes proved themselves worthy of the noble inheritance of character which their forefathers bequeathed to them. (pp. 403–4)

Smiles's resurrection of a manly Britain, here at war, is always tinged (indeed compromised) by a sense of its passing.

Masculinity and character are closely related in Smiles's social philosophy; he at once points both to its contrivance and its absolute necessity. The virtuous body is only seen in action when it is working, exercising, or fighting. It is never a private body, because for Smiles the gentleman must never be off-script even during unwitnessed moments.

Masculinity as a means of moral and physical control is precariously defined here because the body is also a dangerous, private place through which all kinds of (largely unspoken) desires are manifested. Self-help is really self-denial. The image of the male subject battling against his own base instincts suggests that what really is at issue is Britain's future. The failure of masculinity becomes a *national* failure, but the suggestion that men are required to overcome their 'natural' propensity to degenerate is not specific to Smiles. Although it is an idea found in Morel's 'scientific' work of only a few years earlier, it is also to be found in the social and theological writings of another British commentator, the novelist, clergyman, and early proponent of muscular Christianity, Charles Kingsley.

Kingsley's fallen man

Kingsley, in a speech delivered at the Midland Institute in Birmingham in 1872, suggested a very different interpretation of the effects of war than that suggested by Smiles. For Kingsley:

> War is, without doubt, the most hideous physical curse which fallen man inflicts upon himself; and for this simple reason, that it reverses the very laws of nature, and is more cruel even than pestilence. For instead of issuing in the survival of the fittest, it issues in the survival of the less fit: and therefore, if protracted, must deteriorate generations yet unborn.[10]

An additional problem is that those who did not fight (because they were unfit for active service) are the weakest group of the nation and so least likely to survive, even if the war had not have taken place. Kingsley, like Smiles, sees the solution in health education. Kingsley comments that 'We must teach men to mend their own matters, of their own reason, and their own free-will' (p. 29). Kingsley's blend of theology, 'free-will' and sociology, and his concern about the health of the nation constructs an alternative view of moral value to that of Smiles. The subject is free to choose health or ill health and that choice is not linked to a concept of the gentleman even though it has some associations with the notion of character. What concerns Kingsley (and indeed Smiles) is the issue of descent. Men need to be taught 'that they are the arbiters of their own destinies; and, to a fearfully large degree, of their children's destinies after them' (p. 29). For Kingsley the solution is to be found through an adherence to a manly life of healthy living without which there would be a 'tendency to sink into effeminate barbarism' (p. 31). Instead we need to be attentive to the 'divine voice' that tries to guide us towards a more meaningful, masculine world.

That masculinity is the key to this regeneration is, paradoxically, indicated by the emphasis that Kingsley placed on the role of women in developing men's finer sensibilities. What is perhaps remarkable, in what is otherwise a conservative claim about the higher purity of women, is that it required Kingsley to rewrite his own Christian theology. In 'The Tree of Knowledge' (published in 1880) he rewrites the Fall claiming that Eve was not to blame because although the Fall 'represents the woman as tempted' she must have been 'tempted seemingly, by a rational being, of lower race, and yet of superior cunning; who must, therefore have fallen before the woman'.[11] This 'rational being' of a 'lower race' represents, for Kingsley, an image of predatory male desire. Women come to symbolise a chastity, an inherent purity, that male desire needs to defile in order to assert both its difference and physical, mental and sexual superiority. Central to this is a theory of objectification although one which is, inevitably, circumscribed by a model of female passivity. The aim of Kingsley's argument is to shift the emphasis within the narrative of the Fall, by claiming that it represents the depraved, bestial and yet 'normal' traits of male sexuality. It is the very purity of women, which, for Kingsley, incites the baser urges of the male and so illustrates the real moral 'fall' of the male. This is hardly a liberal theology as in trying to avoid an image of demonised female sexuality it merely replaces it with a mute passivity, but it does suggest that what is significant is the attribution of moral culpability. The argument is that men inhabit their bodies, are defined by them, whereas women transcend their biology and are consequently able to assert a moral superiority (although one reliant on a strictly male construction of a 'chaste' female identity):

> the woman's more delicate organisation, her more vivid emotions, her more voluble fancy, as well as her mere physical weakness and weariness, have been to her, in all ages, a special source of temptation; which it is to her honour that she has resisted so much better than the physically stronger, and therefore culpable, man. (p. 171)

Kingsley's view of male biology suggests the inherent presence of competition and conflict. For Kingsley the problem is that men have never managed to leave their bodies behind in order to embrace a higher, spiritual, Christian truth, whereas women have. In effect this represents a failure on the part of masculinity to provide an alternative to the supposedly biological demands of the male body. If for Smiles men need to act the gentleman in order to transcend the biological, for Kingsley the biological reigns because masculine gender scripts are no longer operative, and this failure of masculine scripts becomes a key indicator of a degenerative age.

Kingsley's contribution to the notion of degeneration lies in the suggestion that modern, urban society generates an array of temptations that men are unable to resist. For Kingsley the city caters for the indulgence of a range of moral vices designed to offer a means of, falsely, escaping the effects of urban squalor. Kingsley asks of this urban male population, 'Can they live and toil there without contracting a probably diseased habit of body; without contracting a certainly dull, weary, sordid habit of mind, which craves for any pleasure, however brutal, to escape from its own stupidity and emptiness?' (p. 175). This leads to 'the growing degeneracy of a population', one which uses 'stimulants and narcotics' in order to temporarily escape from the 'greedy barbarism' of 'miscalled civilisation' (p. 176). The problem, according to Kingsley, is therefore two-fold. Men are naturally degenerate, and they can only transcend this degeneracy through the kind ministrations of women who can enlighten the degenerate male about the existence of a higher form of moral conduct. However, the modern world, with its cities and forms of labour, creates the possibility of barbarism by awakening in men their debased appetites for certain types of bodily stimulation.[12]

Both Smiles and Kingsley construct versions of the male subject which suggest that subject's inability to resist the temptations of a range of moral vices including sex, alcohol and gambling. What also unites these two otherwise quite different commentators is the link between the health of the male subject and the health of the nation. Masculinity as a social script tied, in the case of Smiles, to a version of the greater good that enables the male subject to transcend their baser desires, articulates an abstract (and highly politicised) notion of moral rectitude. What is revealing is the acknowledgement that the link between masculinity and maleness is not an inevitable one. That particular ideological claim is undermined in the emphasis given both to the essentially cultural standing of the idea of the 'gentleman' (Smiles) and in the notion that all men will revert to bestial type due to the pressures of the modern, urban age (Kingsley). So far, these British examples indicate how arguments about masculinity were staged within debates about politics, culture, religion and health. Although both Smiles and Kingsley refer to the 'corrupt' male body, it is not explained in 'scientific' terms. Edwin Lankester, however, was to take up this challenge in *Degeneration: A Chapter in Darwinism* (1880), a book that makes explicit the links between culture, politics, biology, health and degeneration. Lankester does not specifically address the status of the male subject as

Smiles and Kingsley do, but nevertheless his book provides a good example of how theories of degeneration became mapped onto what ostensibly appear to be unrelated areas. It is in this application that versions of culture and society are addressed, ones which have implications for a reading of British anxieties of national decline during the period.

Lankester's fallen empires

Lankester defines degeneration as a movement from more complex to less complex forms; he argues that this is a theory that has only been applied to 'a few exceptional animals', but which may also be applied to a range of knowledges.[13] The conditions under which degeneration could occur conflate the biological with the historical and cultural:

> Any new set of conditions occurring to an animal which render its food and safety very easily attained, seem to lead as a rule to Degeneration; just as an active healthy man sometimes degenerates when he becomes suddenly possessed of a fortune; or as Rome degenerated when possessed of the riches of the ancient world. The habit of parasitism clearly acts upon animal organisation in this way. Let the parasitic life once be secured, and away go legs, jaws, eyes, and ears; the active, highly-gifted crab, insect, or annelid may become a mere sac, absorbing nourishment and laying eggs. (p. 33)

What is lost in degeneration is kinetic rather than potential energy. Lankester's notion of energy corresponds to Smiles's idea that the subject needs to replicate themselves through productive labour. For Smiles the issue of production is not just confined to activity in the workplace, it is also related to the idea of working upon the self in order to ensure its reproduction. For Kingsley, the subject needs to guard against the demands of the body. If Kingsley represents an emerging pessimism about the possibility of exercising this necessary vigilance, by the time we get to the 1880s there are only the most vestigial traces of a Smilesean optimism left. What Lankester suggests in the above quotation is that degeneration occurs when subjects or societies no longer have to strive for self-development. The passing of species is made to correspond to the passing of dynasties. Lankester explicitly argues that this model of degeneracy does not solely apply to traditional areas of scientific enquiry: 'Though we may establish the hypothesis most satisfactorily by the study of animal organization and development, it is abundantly clear that degenerative evolution is by no means limited in its application to the field of zoology' (p. 57). Lankester extends his argument about decline in order to account for the disappearance of certain societies, such as the natives of Central America and Ancient Egyptians. However, he is quick to counter any suggestions that these declines were the consequence of racial inferiority: rather it is the case that all complex societies can be become more simple, degenerate societies. In this way Lankester strikes a pessimistic note about the possibility of progress, by suggesting that 'the white races' of imperial standing may degenerate and therefore this possibility becomes a precautionary warning about the potential for Britain's decline because:

> In accordance with a tacit assumption of universal progress – an unreasoning optimism – we are accustomed to regard ourselves as necessarily progressing, as necessarily having arrived at a higher and more elaborated condition than that which our ancestors reached, and as destined to progress still further. On the one hand, it is well to remember that we are subject to the general laws of evolution and are as likely to degenerate as to progress. (pp. 59–60)

Also Lankester suggests that the presence of degeneration is already to be witnessed in the signs of superstition, irrationality and moral perversity that, for him, characterise modern Britain. Lankester, however, also argues that a solution exists in our ability to rationalise because 'To us has been given the power to *know the causes of things*, and by the use of this power it is possible for us to control our destinies' (p. 61, emphasis Lankester's). His concluding words are a *cri de coeur* for the scientific imagination: 'The full and earnest cultivation of Science – the Knowledge of Causes – is that to which we have to look for the protection of our race – even of this English branch of it – from relapse and degeneration' (p. 62).

Lankester's account of degeneracy therefore runs together a range of different issues, and this is typical of such accounts because potentially so many diverse types of behaviour, and forms of knowledge, were read as indicating the possibility of decline. As with Nordau, such claims did not go unchallenged. H.G. Wells in 'Zoological Retrogression' (1891), for example, claimed that theories of degeneration were constituted through a crude quasi-Darwinian 'Excelsior biology', which overlooked the complex, because non-linear, process of biological development.[14] Wells's assault on degeneration (which was also a specific attack on Lankester), was an attack on what he regarded as the false scientific principles which underpinned theories of degeneration. Wells mocks the idea of the superiority of *homo sapiens* in order to challenge the notion of a quasi-Darwinian mode of progression which places the human subject at the pinnacle of evolutionary development because more properly, for Wells, the human subject could be regarded as merely a consequence of an earlier inability to adapt to physical surroundings, so that: 'The whirligig of time brings round its revenges; still, in an age of excessive self-admiration, it would be well for man to remember that his family *was* driven from the waters by the fishes, who still – in spite of incidental fish-hooks, seines, and dredges – hold that empire triumphantly against him' (253). Wells's point is not just that the science is wrong, but also that the rhetoric employed in accounts of degeneration constructs false analogies between animal and cultural worlds. Lankester's chief example of degeneration is the Ascidian, a marine animal that degenerates in its lifecycle from a complex tadpole-like form into a less complex sucker attached to a rock from which it simply becomes a mouth that feeds. Wells transforms this image of the degenerating Ascidian into a playful image of bourgeois domesticity (an image central to Nordau's claims for middle-class probity) in order to mock the rhetorical leap from the animal to the human. He registers the development from tadpole to sucker as one from child to adult, where in the beginning:

> He shocks his aunts. Presently, however, he realizes the sober aspect of things. He becomes dull; he enters a profession; suckers appear on his head; and he studies. Finally, by virtue of these he settles down – he marries. All his wild ambitions and subtle aesthetic perceptions atrophy as needless in the presence of calm domesticity. (p. 250)

Ultimately 'His Bohemian tail is discarded' and 'in the tranquillity of his calling [he] finds that colourless contentment that replaces happiness' (p. 250). Wells's jibe at degenerationist rhetoric is not as innocent as the humour might suggest because it highlights one of the fundamental failings of this rhetoric. J. Edward Chamberlain has noted that the term degeneration 'was a particular item of rhetoric, and a general type of image'.[15] That is, its meaning was partially understood by its use in particular scientific or cultural contexts, but also it was a very general term which enabled these different, often incompatible contexts, to be bridged. Chamberlain also notes that the use of the term in these different contexts 'tended to implicate the figures of speech in the meanings of degeneration', which is also, of course, the point made by Wells.[16] Degeneration is not just a trick of rhetoric, but such theories illustrate how an apparently essentialist discourse, such as biology, was brought to bear on cultural, and therefore provisional, debates such as those on gender.

In the work of Smiles and Kingsley there is an explicit debate about the function and status of masculinity. Smiles acknowledges that it is the role of the gentleman to regulate what would otherwise be dangerous biological impulses. Kingsley states this problem in a slightly different way by emphasising that men are fundamentally too weak to resist the dangerous, sensuous temptations of urban life, which place men on the road to physical degeneration and moral perdition. Kingsley sees women as providing a way of overcoming this decline, as it is their alleged moral superiority that can correct these moral, male failings. Although Smiles and Kingsley see slightly different problems and advance different solutions, both are focused on the effect that degeneration would have on the nation as a whole. This link between nationality and masculinity suggests just how far the nation is conceived in gendered terms, indeed Ania Loomba has explored how 'from the beginning of the colonial period till its end (and beyond), female bodies symbolise the conquered land'.[17] However both Smiles and Kingsley testify to just how weak this relationship can become when the prevailing models of masculinity are compromised. Lankester also implicitly develops this anxiety in his account of the fall of empires.

In Smiles and Kingsley masculinity is conceived of as a dynamic force which needs to express itself through action and through the expenditure of energy; whereas for Nordau the Decadents seemed to cultivate a studied inertia that implicitly challenged the credibility of the hard-working middle classes. However, as we saw with Smiles, there is also an admission that the link between maleness and masculinity is arbitrary and therefore potentially unstable. Kingsley also acknowledges the need for men to transcend the biological in order to follow a more spiritual path. For Lankester, there is no escaping biology, other than through the exercise of a rational inquiry that distances us from the animal world. The suggestion is that the model of a virtuous, public-spirited masculinity is compromised by the presence of atavistic biological needs (which are very loosely defined). However this is also an issue addressed in a rather different way by the sexologists whose version of masculinity has more in common with the concerns of Smiles, Kingsley and Lankester than it might initially appear.

Sexology

Siobhan B. Somerville has recently argued that in sexology racial identifications were mapped on to sexual orientation, so that the 'blackness' or 'whiteness' of a subject was correlated to the levels masculinity or femininity exhibited by the subject.[18] This bears an obvious link with the concerns about nation which characterise the work of Smiles, Kingsley and Lankester. For these commentators a threatened loss of masculinity implies a national and racial decline. This is just one historically conditioned link which exists between sexologists and degenerationists, although critics have often claimed that the sexologists sought to refute the biological essentialism of the degenerationists.[19] However, it would appear to be more legitimate to claim that sexological critiques of degeneration have in mind the broad work of Nordau and Lombroso rather than a covert British tradition that includes Smiles and Kingsley. A further difference is that sexology provides an analysis of the instability in dominant gender models whereas Nordau is content to take them as given and to draw moral conclusions from them. Even in the case of Smiles and Kingsley gender instability is represented rather than discussed. Also, a more explicit difference is that the theoretical ambitions of the sexologists are scientific and are focused on the idea of gender, sex and desire. Their findings are not then extrapolated in cultural terms: in other words they do not build the same analogous bridges or rhetorical constructions which mark the work of the degenerationists. The central figure in this British tradition is Havelock Ellis whose principal theoretical tract was *Studies in the Psychology of Sex* (1897–1928) although his arguments in *Man and Woman* (1894) are also relevant to this debate about the instability between masculine gender scripts and biology.

These concerns about the unstable subject were also developed in a range of Gothic texts at the time, including Stevenson's *Dr Jekyll and Mr Hyde* (1886) and Stoker's *Dracula* (1897), as well as H.G. Wells's *The Island of Dr Moreau* (1896) and Wilde's *The Picture of Dorian Gray* (1891). Such Gothic narratives debated what was meant by 'nature' and the 'human' by reworking the instability that characterised the prevailing notions of (masculine) subjectivity at the time. The precarious nature of this subjectivity is also related, in these Gothic texts (with, perhaps, the exception of *Moreau*) to gender, biology, and desire. The analysis of *Dracula* and *Jekyll and Hyde* which concludes this chapter will address the permeability that existed between fictional, and supposedly 'scientific' notions of the unstable, often hybrid, male subject.

Havelock Ellis

Ellis in *Man and Woman* implicitly refutes Nordau by suggesting that an artistic temperament is fundamentally masculine. Ellis rests this claim on the idea that there are more successful male artists than female ones because men have a greater emotional and psychological complexity than women and consequently are able to establish a more complex artistic practice.[20]

For Ellis 'the artistic impulse is vastly more spontaneous, more pronounced, and more widely spread among men than among women' (p. 23). For Ellis, men represent Art whereas for men women are, because of their potential role as mothers, associated with Nature. Ellis's speculation on this leads him to the view that men's commitment to Art is predicated on this denial of biology. This means 'that the subjugation of Nature by Man has often practically involved the subjugation, physical and mental, of women by men' (p. 24). Therefore 'The lust of power and knowledge, the research for artistic perfection, are usually masculine characters; and so most certainly are the suppression of natural emotion and the degradation of sexuality and maternity' (p. 24). Ellis's model of male desire is not confined to heterosexuality, and although he does not explicitly introduce homosexuality into this argument it is still the case that Ellis promotes a model of masculinity which transcends sexual orientation. Art for Ellis is based on a repudiation of the instincts, a claim which paradoxically aligns him with critics such as Smiles, Kingsley and Lankester, who also sought to transcend the demands made by the body. This is to suggest that Ellis can be read as part of an ongoing British tradition of debates concerning masculinity and desire, even though he tried to move beyond the more explicit condemnations of certain types of male behaviour made by their European counterparts: Nordau and Lombroso.

Ellis claims that one of the central problems in defining the place of male desire is because of its strange mobility; whereas women's desires are largely associated with procreation, 'In men the sexual instinct is a restless source of energy which overflows into all sorts of channels' (p. 23). Ellis suggests that this restlessness means that desire cannot be circumscribed by gender. For Smiles men could transcend desire by taking on the acquired, masculine traits of the gentleman. Implicit to this is the model of a bifurcated subject who performs a gender role in order to suppress a more dangerous, and dangerously insistent, biological identity. Ellis's exploration of this is focused specifically on how gender associations fail to provide the kind of corrective that degenerationists were looking for. Smiles may acknowledge that there is no natural link between maleness and masculinity, but Ellis underlines this separation by his claim in *Studies in the Psychology of Sex,* Vol. II: *Sexual Inversion* (1897) that there is no necessary link between sexual orientation and gender.

In *Sexual Inversion* Ellis sets out a series of case histories in which homosexual subjects (both male and female) discuss their development, and reflect on their desires. These histories indicate that the link between masculinity and heterosexuality was not a necessary or inevitable one. In

History VII the male middle-class subject, after reflecting on some of his earlier, defining experiences states that:

> Now, – at the age of 37, – my ideal of love is a powerful, strongly built man, of my own age or rather younger – preferably of the working class. Though having solid sense and character, he need not be specially intellectual. If endowed in the latter way, he must not be too glib or refined. Anything effeminate in a man, or anything of the cheap intellectual style, repels me very decisively.[21]

It is these links between masculinity and homosexuality which were problematised after Oscar Wilde's trials for gross indecency in 1895. This is discussed in greater depth in Chapter 6, but it is worth acknowledging here that Ellis is reasserting links between art and masculinity and between homosexuality and masculinity, links that the Wilde trials had tried to pathologise. Ellis in his own way is attempting recuperation here, one which is underlined by scientific rather than provisionally legal or moral considerations. That Ellis is trying to recuperate what Nordau had sought to demonise in *Degeneration* is also evidenced by his celebration of Nietzsche, Zola and Huysmans in *Affirmations* (1898).[22] However, it must also be acknowledged that Ellis is often inconsistent in his account of the relationship between sexuality and gender. His case history of the 'masculine' homosexual, for example, while arguing the case that there existed a discrepancy between appearance and desire, also implies that the gender script is coherent and a priori agreed upon. In his discussion of female 'inverts' he argues that 'in the inverted woman the masculine traits are part of an organic instinct which she by no means always wishes to accentuate' (*Sexual Inversion*, p. 54). On a specific case history he comments that the female subject 'is feminine' in appearance except that 'the feminine angle of arm is lost' (p.56). So Ellis does tend to reinscribe gender distinctions in his discussion of identity because he, on occasion, leans towards corroborating an essentialist link between sex and gender.

The relationship between biology and gender is problematised in Ellis because of this inconsistent approach to the relationship between sex and gender. However even when this link is asserted there still persists the general suggestion that the gender script can only be problematically ascribed to sex, because it is applied to biology at some points and to social behaviour at others, and therefore identity (specifically sexual and gender identity) is represented as unstable. Ellis attempts to explain this in scientific terms but the problematic application of gender indicates just how far the prevailing masculine scripts had been imbricated with a model of crisis that even a very different commentator such as Smiles had attempted to respond to earlier in the century.

The issue of 'sexual inversion' is central to the sexological analysis of gender identity. Edward Carpenter in *The Intermediate Sex* (1908) discussed the presence of 'Urnings' whose sexual orientation was at odds with their gender attributions. Carpenter notes of the homosexual man that:

> Formerly it was assumed as a matter of course, that the type was merely the result of disease and degeneration; but now with the examination of the actual facts it appears that, on the contrary, many are fine, healthy specimens of their sex, muscular and well-developed in body, of powerful brain, high standard of conduct, and with nothing abnormal or morbid of any kind observable in their physical structure or constitution.[23]

However for Carpenter there is an additional complication because even the presence of a homosexual disposition does not mean that sexuality is the primary issue. Often the manifestation of this desire appears at a purely emotional level, rather than through sexual acts (p. 49). However Carpenter, like Ellis, tends to make links between gender and sex at certain stages of his argument when he identifies a continuum along which sex and gender is developed. He notes, for example, of extremely 'effeminate' men that he may 'take pleasure in dressing in women's clothes' and notes that 'his figure not unfrequently [betrays] a tendency towards the feminine, large at the hips, supple, not muscular, the face wanting in hair, the voice inclining to be high-pitched' (p. 50). Biological signs are thus read through the available gender scripts although, paradoxically, such scripts are used to indicate the presence of an instability in sexual identity (here conceived as sexual orientation). The problem that sexologists focus on is the link between sexual desire and physical appearance. There is a conflict between a putative science of signs (the marks of gender) and an essentialist discourse (biology) which appears to be at odds with the provisionality of gender constructions. For Ellis this paradox is to be found in the image of the masculine homosexual. However, Ellis also acknowledges that debates about masculinity have to be seen in relation to a debate about femininity. For him the investment made in masculinity is predicated on the denial of a maternalism that is specifically associated with women. Men therefore represent Art over Nature, and this implicitly (unconsciously) reworks Smiles's claim about the need to cultivate a certain theatricality in performing the role of the gentleman. In Kingsley as well it was the allegedly insistent demands of nature that needed to be resisted. With the sexologists it is nature itself, at least in its guise as a form of supposedly natural desire, which needs to be re-examined. It is in the sexological debates about sex (biology) that we see the debate about gender taking place. The instabilities in certain kinds of gender performance, such as in the masculine homosexual for example, are displaced on to the body and then read back as signs which indicate the presence of a biological chimera that compromises what was, conservatively, understood as constituting the 'natural'. Otto Weininger's *Sex and Character* (1903) relocates many of these aporias, but is also a useful summation of the sexologists' ambitions to map the place at which masculinity and maleness become divorced.

Weininger

Weininger's thesis makes a range of anti-Semitic and misogynistic claims about racial and sexual superiority (for Weininger women are lower beings, more animalistic than men, and Jews are honorary women). Nevertheless it was a book widely discussed in sexological circles, although dismissed by some commentators as part of an anti-feminist backlash against the suffragette movement at the time.[24]

The links between gender and biology in *Sex and Character* are confusing because Weininger, like other sexologists, uses the terms interchangeably. He argues that, 'The doctrine of the existence of different degrees of masculinity and femininity may be treated, in the first place, on purely anatomical lines. Not only the anatomical form, but the anatomical position of male and female characters must be discussed'.[25] This suggests the existence of a biological chimera, (typical to sexological constructions of identity) which Weininger anecdotally notes the presence of when he claims that 'I know several men who have the upper part of the thigh of a female with a nominally male under part, and some with the right hip of a male and the left of a female' (p. 17). As discussed in the following chapter, it is this type of thinking which also influenced Frederick Treves's account of Joseph Merrick (aka 'The Elephant Man') in his *Reminiscences*. Weininger's image of a biological hybridity is a consequence of his insistence that same sex attraction is marked in this physical way. Men who possess the physical attributes of women can be associated with homosexuality. Weininger therefore appears to move the debate beyond Ellis's observation that an attachment to models of masculinity can function to disguise sexual orientation. For Weininger there is no 'psycho-sexual hermaphroditism' (p. 45). However Weininger is not quite the essentialist that this might suggest. Instead he regards the subject as naturally constructed out of a range of sexual (male and female) characteristics. It is a construction which also accounts for the presence of alleged extremes:

> The fact is that every human being varies or oscillates between the maleness and the femaleness of his constitution. In some cases these oscillations are abnormally large, in others cases so small as to escape observation, but they are always present, and when they are great they may even reveal themselves in the outward aspect of the body. (p. 54)

This is the condition of supposedly 'normal' sexual identity because 'In my view all actual organisms have both homo-sexuality and hetero-sexuality' (p. 48).

The slippages in this model of identity relocate the idea of gender. It is not biology that manifests these kinds of prevarications, a case made in very different ways by Lankester and Wells, but gender. Men become like women for Weininger when they embrace femininity, but in doing so they are not actually reconstructed as women, because women are associated with their bodies in ways that men are not. In this he shares a claim with Ellis when he argues that 'man possesses sexual organs; her sexual organs possess woman' (p. 92). Men are therefore not related to their bodies (or do not relate themselves to their bodies) in the same way as women, and this means that men are in control of their bodies whereas women are not: 'The male lives consciously, the female lives unconsciously. This is certainly the necessary conclusion for the extreme cases' (p. 102).[26] It is in the middle of this continuum that a curious admixture of male and female is to be found. However, Weininger's discussion of sex is really about gender. Masculinity becomes divorced from the male body because it can also be discerned in women. What it means to be masculine is therefore freighted with the very mobility that Weininger would prefer to link to the body.

Ultimately these sexological accounts of the body evidence an anxiety of interpretation. Matching the signs of behaviour to biological referents finally fails, but in this failure a new version of subjectivity becomes developed. The subject is now granted a peculiar form of freedom in which they are neither biological nor social. They are both male and female, masculine and feminine, both social and natural. This is the conclusion which a degenerationist such as Nordau sought to pathologise, and Lombroso to criminalize. It is a debate about masculinity and 'nature' that takes on a strange Gothic colouring as it comes to evidence anxieties about what it means to be human. The importance and function of masculinity is potentially erased in these arguments and it is in the Gothic that this debate about a precarious sense of masculine authority is given a particular inflection.

The Gothic: Dracula

Theories of degeneration and sexological accounts of desire constitute two traditions of thought that became Gothicised during the period. Both of these traditions, when read through a British context, appear to share an interest in the theatrical dimensions of masculinity. For Smiles this theatricality is an essential means of entry into a more civilised world, whereas for Ellis it confuses the distinction between biology and desire. Smiles celebrates, indeed encourages, this artificiality, whereas for Ellis it poses a problem for interpretation. However, it is also the case that degeneration and sexology are concerned with how what is 'natural' needs either renegotiation (sexology) or reconstruction (degeneration). Either way the idea that the ideologically self-evident signs of masculinity can no longer determine the male subject informs a certain type of Gothic writing at this time, and this becomes the place in which these debates about 'nature' are given an alternative focus. In turn these Gothic narratives Gothicise such theories, and as discussed in Chapter 2 on Merrick, the link between medical abnormality and Gothic monstrosity reveals just how far a form of Gothic imagining permeates the science of the time.

Kelly Hurley has explored this new '"gothicity" of a range of scientific discourses' (*The Gothic Body*, p. 5) and argues that 'Degeneration … is a "gothic" discourse, and as such is a crucial imaginative and narrative source for the *fin-de-siècle* Gothic' (p. 45). Hurley also claims that the Gothic reflected an ambivalence caused by 'nostalgia for the "fully human" subject whose undoing it accomplishes so resolutely, and yet aroused by the prospect of a monstrous becoming' (p. 4). This is an ambivalence that is central to the form, not just to the period.[27] The great ur-text of this Gothic degeneration is Bram Stoker's *Dracula*.

Daniel Pick in *Faces of Degeneration* writes of *Dracula* that, 'The ambiguities of representation in the novel are in part bound up with contradictions of connotation in the wider discourse of degeneration' (p. 167). This is because while the novel attributes degeneration to an invasive, non-British source (the Count), it also represents degeneration as a blood disease, symbolically transmitted through vampirism, which suggests that degeneration becomes a 'remorseless morbid accumulation' (p. 168). Therefore the vampire hunters are themselves pathologised through contact with the Count. That Stoker has this idea of contagion in mind is also illustrated by how the novel arranges a series of convergences between seemingly opposed characters. Van Helsing, for example, with his claims on leadership and associations with different knowledges (legal, historical and medical) seems like a modern version of the Count. Indeed Van Helsing notes of Dracula that, 'he was in life a most wonderful man. Soldier, statesman, and alchemist – which latter was the highest development of the science-knowledge of his time. He had a mighty brain, a learning beyond compare'.[28] In addition vampirism seems to provide an awakening rather than merely functioning like a disease, and Lucy Westenra's blood transfusions make the vampire hunters behave like vampires (replacing her, and perhaps the Count's blood, with their own). Ostensibly, the vampire represents an old feudal order that needs to be consigned to the past in order to enable the bourgeoisie to assert its political, economic and cultural standing. However, if there exist these subtle shadings between vampirism and the bourgeoisie, then it also suggests the continuing presence of pathology. Pick also notes that the novel articulates a contemporary anti-Semitic view in the associations between the Count, eastern Europe and disease, which tapped into a popular anxiety of 'a perceived "alien invasion" of Jews from the East who, in the view of many alarmists were "feeding off" and "poisoning" the blood of the Londoner' (p. 173). However, degeneracy is not just the marker of fears of racial decline, they are also associated with the ideas of a potentially pathologised masculinity that we have explored throughout this chapter.

One of the significant characteristics of the Count is his association with degeneracy. Mina Harker notes this when she tells Van Helsing that 'The Count is a criminal and of criminal type. Nordau and Lombroso would so classify him' (p. 342). Mina's conclusion is partially based on an earlier description of the Count recorded by Jonathan Harker in his journal, where he notes of Dracula:

> His face was a strong – a very strong – aquiline, with high bridge of the thin nose and peculiarly arched nostrils; with lofty domed forehead … His eyebrows were very massive, almost meeting over the nose, and with bushy hair that seemed to curl in its own profusion. The mouth, so far as I could see it under the heavy moustache, was fixed and rather cruel-looking, with peculiarly sharp white teeth; these protruded over the lips … For the rest, his ears were pale and at the tops extremely pointed; the chin was broad and strong, and the cheeks firm though thin. (pp. 17–18)

Pick notes that this suggests images of the born criminal, and Leonard Wolf identifies the description as only a slight reworking of Lombroso's portrait of the archetypical criminal.[29] The irredeemable criminality of the Count suggests that there is no cure for the effects of this disease (except the 'release' promised through staking). The Count therefore appears to be Other to the group, but because they too mirror his behaviour (despite their apparent probity, for example, they bribe officials and are guilty of breaking and entering) they are themselves pathologised. The links between pathologisation and masculinity are perhaps most clearly developed through the representation of Jonathan Harker.

Harker is represented as possessing a sexual and physical (and indeed intellectual) passivity which, given Stoker's conservative views, associates him with femininity. What Harker learns from his encounter with Dracula is that he needs to transform himself (in a moment of Smilesean self-help) into a man of action. It is not just that Harker appears powerless at Castle Dracula; it is also the case that he is powerless *because* he is a bourgeois professional. The middle-class male professional might, so the novel suggests, regress when confronted by the supposedly elemental forces of vampirism. The middle-class male is therefore, as he is in Smiles and Kingsley, potentially corruptible, although in this instance he is also both masculine and feminine. However, the Count gives the unstable male subject, which had so taxed the sexologists, an object lesson in masculinity. Harker's representation as a feminine man is one that is contrasted with the more masculine, and paradoxically pathologised Count. Harker's gender instability aligns him with sexological debates while the Count's Lombrosian characteristics associate him with degeneration. Two types of science are Gothicised here, both of which debate what it means to be 'human'. According to Hurley the Gothic does not create this tension because, 'The rupture of classificatory systems holding "the human" in place, so visible in the *fin-de-siècle* Gothic, did not originate with the genre. Within the culture in general such systems were subject to massive stress, no longer able to do their proper work of separating anomalous from monstrous realities' (p. 27). The problem is that norms have become eroded and consequently what is meant by masculinity is open to negotiation, a view that Stoker is ostensibly trying to rectify. However, Stoker repeats the kind of paradox to be found in the 'classificatory systems' of the time, namely that what is meant by an essential 'human' nature is confused, although it is employed as if it were a coherently formulated subjectivity. To this end the Count is a 'Gothic' horror of diseased vampirism, but he is also a projection of bourgeois anxieties concerning *their* potential for decline and degeneration and as such the Other becomes assimilated rather than destroyed.

That these debates have a medical air to them is indicated by their medical associations within the novel, as William Hughes notes, '*Dracula* is a novel preoccupied with pathology rather than health, and in particular with morbid and abnormal states whose boundaries become increasingly nebulous as the narrative progresses'.[30] The scientific practice referred to in the novel is, on another level, also used to contain some of the transgressive Gothic elements associated with vampirism and the supernatural. Hughes, for example, reads the novel as exploiting available medical notions of pathology in order to construct a coherent model of 'truth', a model seemingly compromised by the presence of strange, vampiric forces. However, one unresolved paradox is that medicine is also associated with a Gothic system of pathologies. This process in the novel, in keeping with theories of degeneration and sexology, appears in the link between masculinity and pathology.

For the emasculated Harker, Count Dracula is an implied role model of manliness, but to become like him is to play the degenerate. This is a paradox which the novel never resolves although it is one that can be understood as a consequence of the link that the novel makes between masculinity and class. What is at issue is the role of a specifically bourgeois masculinity; the question is how can Harker be a respectable lawyer and a man of action? The answer is, of course, that he cannot but this question, which is implicit in the novel, directs the focus on what could revitalise a specifically bourgeois model of masculinity. It was an idea developed earlier by Stevenson in *Dr Jekyll and Mr Hyde*.

Jekyll and Hyde

Oscar Wilde, who in 'The Decay of Lying' commented that 'the transformation of Dr Jekyll reads dangerously like an experiment out of *The Lancet*', noted the medical ambiance of Stevenson's novella.[31] *The Strange Case of Dr Jekyll and Mr Hyde* is dominated by the representation of aging bourgeois professionals, doctors and lawyers. If in *Dracula* Stoker suggests that this is the group most in need of revitalisation, Stevenson represents the bourgeois male in a state of terminal decline. This mood of alienated decline is emphasised in the opening of the novella, 'Mr Utterson the lawyer was a man of rugged countenance, that was never lighted by a smile; cold, scanty and embarrassed in discourse; backward in sentiment; lean, long, dusty, dreary, and yet somehow loveable' (p. 29). How exactly Utterson is meant to be loveable is unclear. Certainly the opening pages construct him as a lifeless, soulless character, whose inability to enjoy life is emphasised in the stilted relationship between him and 'his distant kinsman' (p. 29), Richard Enfield. This distance is as much cultural as biological because of Enfield's credentials as a 'well-known man about town' (p. 29). The relationship:

> ... was a nut to crack for many ... It was reported by those who encountered them in their Sunday walks, that they said nothing, looked singularly dull, and would hail with obvious relief the appearance of a friend. For all that, the two men put the greatest store by these excursions, counted them the chief jewel of each week, and not only set aside occasions of pleasure, but even resisted the calls of business, that they might enjoy them uninterrupted. (pp. 29–30)

It is this meeting of opposites which foreshadows the discussion of Hyde and the speculation on the kind of relationship which he might have with the respectable Dr Jekyll. This initial focus on incompatible worlds is one that emphasises the fundamentally alienated lives of bourgeois professionals such as Utterson, Lanyon and Jekyll.

Hyde at one level seems to correspond with a degenerationist argument concerning the possibility of decline. Fred Botting has noted how *Jekyll and Hyde* develops ideas drawn from Darwin, Lombroso and Nordau.[32] The novella frequently represents Hyde in simian terms, as possessing an 'ape-like fury' (p. 47), as a 'thing like a monkey' (p. 68) who has 'ape-like tricks' (p. 96) and an 'ape-like spite' (p. 97). Many critics, including Botting and Punter, have discussed the idea that this represents an anxiety about a potential reversion to an atavistic state.[33] However, the tensions between Jekyll and Hyde also suggest that the bourgeois professional has already become moribund. Jekyll and Utterson are hollowed out by their allegiance to a Smilesean notion of decency, one which suggests their alienation from each other and from a biological identity. The adherence to cultural identity advocated by Smiles and Kingsley is no longer possible. The theatricality associated with the performance of the bourgeois gentleman is ostensibly threatened by the feral qualities of Hyde, but an alternative case can be made that it is the demands of the performance that creates the possibility of this horror. David Punter notes that, 'Jekyll's view seems to be that the split in his being has derived much less from the presence within his psyche of an uncontrollable, passionate self than from the force with which that self has been repressed according to the dictates of social convention' (*Literature of Terror*, Vol. 2, pp. 2–3). This might seem to suggest that the novel anticipates Freudian ideas about repression. However, the real source of horror is the fact that Utterson and Jekyll have become effectively non-human. Their allegiance to a particular class-bound notion of respectability has effectively dehumanised them to the point that it is they who function as the Gothic horrors in the text. Stevenson also emphasises this through the fragmentary nature of the narrative which is told from different points of view, including third person narration. This kind of restless narrative mobility echoes the instability of the self, but also the very emptiness of that self. The novella, unlike *Dracula*, does not head towards a moment of closure, because its culminating moment rests on the claim that when Utterson sees the body of Hyde he 'knew that he was looking on the body of a self-destroyer' (p. 70), but at that point we cannot be sure if Hyde has killed Jekyll or Jekyll has killed Hyde. Additionally 'Henry Jekyll's Full Statement of the Case' which concludes the novella is equally unclear. It appears as though Jekyll is narrating but he slips into describing Jekyll in the third person, 'Jekyll was now my city of refuge' (pp. 91–2), which suggests that it is Hyde who has taken control of the narrative. The closing lines of the novella refer to the possibility that Hyde kills Jekyll, 'I lay down the pen, and proceed to seal up my confession, I bring the life of that unhappy Henry Jekyll to an end' (p. 97), even though the ostensible voice is that of an apparently suicidal Jekyll.

   If Jekyll represents the end of a certain kind of middle-class masculinity, Hyde represents the possibility of an alternative life of activity, energy and growth. Hyde's threat is pathologised as an absence within a bourgeois culture that perceives deformity but cannot account for it. Enfield's failed description of Hyde indicates a failure of interpretative strategies, one which misapplies a medical language and so indicates just how far contemporary science is implicated in constructions of pathology: 'He must be deformed somewhere; he gives a strong feeling of deformity, although I couldn't specify the point. He's an extraordinary-looking man, and yet I really can name nothing out of the way ... And it's not want of memory; for I declare I can see him this moment' (p. 34). Hyde provokes feelings of degeneracy without really manifesting them. Hyde repeatedly fulfils an unconscious dimension in the text as he becomes a product of degenerate, male, bourgeois imaginings. Utterson dreams of Hyde before he meets him and feels that he needs to recognise Hyde, only to find that 'the figure had no face by which he might know it; even in his dreams it had no face, or one that baffled him and melted before his eyes' (pp. 37–8). When Utterson meets Hyde he is struck by a senseless feeling of revulsion, a 'hitherto unknown disgust, loathing and fear' (p. 40), that cannot be accounted for despite Utterson's best attempts: 'There must be something else ... There *is* something more, if I could find a name for it. God bless me, the man seems hardly human!' (p. 40). This can be linked to science, and the claim that Jekyll makes concerning the moral indifference of the potion that effects the transformation, 'The drug had no discriminating action; it was neither diabolical nor divine' (p. 85). Botting notes of this:

> Scientific theories disclose the instability of the dualities that frame cultural identity. The proximity and reversibility of good and evil cannot be restricted to a case of individual pathology ... the ambivalence, the moral indifference, of Jekyll's drug undermines classifications that separate normal individuals from deviant ones. (p. 140)

As in sexological accounts of the subject, identity becomes unstable, mobile, refracted and ultimately undetermined; along the way masculinity becomes pathologised as the signs of gender become detached from a body which can no longer be read. All that is left in its place is a reading of a perception (like Enfield's and Utterson's) that relocates the idea that the degenerate really does reside within the apparently 'normal' self.

Accounts of masculinity in theories of degeneration and sexological accounts of character emphasise the theatrical nature of masculinity. They also indicate how precarious that theatricality was. The apparent sexual instabilities that define the male subject in sexology are in reality debates about gender performance and just how far that performance deviates from sexual orientation. While theories of degeneration pathologise certain contraventions of ideal masculine types, sexologists register such transgressions in a more neutral, putatively scientific language. This is to acknowledge that the political aspects of theories of degeneration are more overt than that of the sexologists (although Weininger's anti-Semitic comments and views on the Women's movement are an exception).

The debate about masculinity also has clear links to the idea of the nation. In Smiles, Kingsley and Lankester the idea of biological regression suggests the potential for national decline. Nation is not such an explicit concern in sexology, but as Somerville has suggested, there are covert links made to ideas of race. Punter, amongst others, has noted how Gothic narratives such as *Dracula* and *Jekyll and Hyde* indicate the presence of an anxiety about colonial decline.[34] In Chapter 2 on Treves's *Reminiscences* these links between the Gothic (his account of Merrick), gender (Treves's narrative construction of the inner life of a female hysteric) and the colonial (his account of a stay in India, during which he experienced a particularly Gothic nightmare of racial assault) are explored.

This language of pathologisation also becomes articulated through Gothic literature of the time. This is an important link because it reveals how certain scientific discourses became Gothicised. Chapter 3 shows how *Jekyll and Hyde* influenced reporting of the Whitechapel killings in 1888. Such an influence reveals the extent to which the Gothic participated in a cultural narrative that helped to demonise the male bourgeois professional. The gothicisation of medicine, and the medicalisation of the Gothic, is therefore the principal subject of the following two chapters.

Notes

1 Kelly Hurley, *The Gothic Body: Sexuality, Materialism, and Degeneration at the Fin de Siècle* (Cambridge: Cambridge University Press, 1996) p. 9. All subsequent references are to this edition, and are given in the text.

2 Robert Louis Stevenson, *The Strange Case of Dr Jekyll and Mr Hyde* (1886) in *The Strange Case of Dr Jekyll and Mr Hyde and Other Stories*, ed. Jenni Calder (Harmondsworth: Penguin, 1984) p. 81. All subsequent references are to this edition, and are given in the text.

3 Daniel Pick, *Faces of Degeneration: A European Disorder, c.1848–c.1918* (Cambridge: Cambridge University Press [1989] 1994). All subsequent references are to this edition, and are given in the text.

4 This is not to deny that there are certain national differences, see Pick, *Degeneration*, p. 225. Lombroso began writing in the 1870s and published widely over the next 30 years.

5 Max Nordau, *Degeneration* (Lincoln, NE and London: University of Nebraska Press [1895] 1968) p. 19.

6 Egmont Hake, *Regeneration: A Reply to Max Nordau* (London: Archibald Constable, 1895). Also quoted in Sally Ledger and Roger Luckhurst (eds), *The Fin de Siècle: A Reader in Cultural History c.1880-1900* (Oxford: Oxford University Press, 2000) p. 18. All subsequent references are to this latter edition, and are given in the text.

7 Hake's interest in empire is also evidenced by his role as editor of the last journals of General Gordon in 1885. See Ledger and Luckhurst, *The Fin de Siècle*, p. 23.

8 William James, review of *Degeneration* in *Psychological Review*, 2 (May 1895) 289–90, 290. George Bernard Shaw, *The Sanity of Art: An Exposure of the Current Nonsense about Artists Being Degenerate* (London: New Age Press, 1908).

9 Samuel Smiles, *Self-Help: With Illustrations of Conduct and Perseverance* (London: John Murray [1859] 1877) p. 224. All subsequent references are to this edition, and are given in the text.

10 Charles Kingsley, 'The Science of Health' (1872) in *Sanitary and Social Lectures and Essays* (London: Macmillan, 1880) pp. 21–48, p. 26. All subsequent references are to this edition, and are given in the text.

11 Charles Kingsley, 'The Tree of Knowledge' (1880) in *Sanitary and Social Lectures and Essays*, pp. 167–86, p. 170. All subsequent references are to this edition, and are given in the text. Another connection to this rewriting of the Fall in terms of degeneration is noted by Jonathan Dollimore who notes that 'Morel based the theory of degeneration on his reading of Genesis, recasting the Fall narrative in pseudo-medical terms' in this recasting 'evil not only erupts from within a divine order ... but also originates with those beings closest to God – Satan and then "Man"', so that 'Original sin is thus more aptly regarded as original perversity', from 'Perversion, Degeneration, and the Death Drive' in Andrew H. Miller and James Eli Adams (eds), *Sexualities in Victorian Britain* (Bloomington, IN and Indianapolis: Indiana University Press, 1996) pp. 96–177, p. 101.

12 Kingsley had touched on this idea of the corrupting propensities of urban living in a lecture he gave in Bristol in 1857 on 'Great Cities and Their Influence for Good and Evil' in *Sanitary and Social Lectures and Essays* (London: Macmillan, 1880) pp. 197–224. In the lecture he claimed that 'the social state of a city depends directly on its moral state' (p. 191), and he contrasted the pleasant sedentary qualities of country living with the rapidity of life in cities. Other commentators developed Kingsley's idea that the city was responsible for creating the possibility of degeneration in the nineteenth century. It was an idea central to Charles Booth's compendious *Life and Labour of the People of London* (1889), which influenced contemporary debates on crime and health. Also, an article by another commentator entitled 'Are We Degenerating Physically?', published in *The Lancet* in December 1888, noted that degeneration: 'is undoubtedly at work among town-bred populations as the consequence of unwholesome occupations, improper [diet], and juvenile vice ... while the optimistic view has most to urge in its favour, it would be wrong to ignore the existence of widespread evils and serious dangers to the public health' (cited in Pick, *Degeneration*, p. 201). However, Kingsley's emphasis is on the effect that this specifically has on men, and he therefore keeps in focus a debate about a debased male presence which echoes Smiles's concern with the necessity of controlling supposedly 'natural' urges for the greater good.

It should be noted that the concern about the effects of urban life is not just to be found in these nascent accounts of degeneration. Some commentators were concerned with the effects of poverty, not only Charles Booth but also Andrew Mearns in *The Bitter Cry of Outcast London* (1883) and William Booth *In Darkest England and the Way Out* (1890), while W.T. Stead's '*The Maiden Tribute of Modern Babylon*' (1885) highlighted the problem of child prostitution. Gustave Le Bon in 'The Mind of Crowds' (1895) anatomised what he saw as a mob mentality that was produced by urban living, whereas the sociologist Georg Simmel in 'The Metropolis and Mental Life' (1903) explored the influence that the city had in constructing a specific metropolitan consciousness. I will discuss this idea of the impact of London on theories of masculinity in depth in Chapter 5 when I examine writings by De Quincey, Dickens, Collins, Doyle and Bram Stoker.

13 Edwin Lankester, *Degeneration: A Chapter in Darwinism* (London: Macmillan, 1880) p. 30. All subsequent references are to this edition, and are given in the text.

14 H.G. Wells, 'Zoological Retrogression' in *Gentleman's Magazine*, 271 (1891), 246–53, 248. All subsequent references are to this edition, and are given in the text.

15 J. Edward Chamberlain, 'Images of Degeneration: Turnings and Trans-formation' in J. Edward Chamberlain and Sander L. Gilman (eds), *Degener-ation: The Dark Side of Progress* (New York: Columbia University Press, 1985) pp. 263–89, p. 267.

16 Ibid.

17 Ania Loomba, *Colonialism/Postcolonialism* (London: Routledge, 1998) p. 152.

18 Siobhan B. Somerville, 'Scientific Racism and the Invention of the Homosexual Body' in Lucy Bland and Laura Doan (eds), *Sexology in Culture: Labelling Bodies and Desires* (Cambridge: Polity, 1998) pp. 60–76, see pp. 69–70. The article was first published in the *Journal of the History of Sexuality* 5, 2 (October 1994), 243–66.

19 See Joseph Bristow, 'Symond's History, Ellis Heredity: *Sexual Inversion*' in Bland and Doan (eds) *Sexology in Culture*, pp. 70-99, p. 80 for an account of how Ellis has been regarded as distancing himself from the degenerationists.

20 Havelock Ellis, *Man and Woman: A Study of Human Secondary Sexual Characteristics* (London: A. & C. Black, 1894) quoted in Lucy Bland and Laura Doan (eds), *Sexology Uncensored: The Documents of Sexual Science* (Cambridge: Polity, 1998), see pp. 23–4. All subsequent references are to this latter edition, and are given in the text.

21 Havelock Ellis, *Studies in the Psychology of Sex*, Vol. II: *Sexual Inversion* (Philadelphia: F.A. Davis [1897] 1915) cited in Bland and Doan (eds), *Sexology Uncensored*, p. 53. All subsequent references are to this latter edition, and are given in the text.

22 In *Affirmations* (London: Constable [1898] 1929) he also discusses the exploits of Casanova, as well as St Francis.

23 Edward Carpenter, *The Intermediate Sex: A Study of Some Transitional Types of Men and Women* (London: Swan Sonnenschein, 1908) cited in Bland and Doan (eds), *Sexology Uncensored*, p. 49. All subsequent references are to this latter edition, and are given in the text.

24 See Judy Greenway, 'It's What You Do With It That Counts: Interpretations of Otto Weininger' in Bland and Doan (eds), *Sexology in Culture*, pp. 27–43, p. 32.

25 Otto Weininger, *Sex and Character* (New York: AMS Press [1903] 1906) pp. 11–12. All subsequent references are to this edition, and are given in the text.

26 Which is obviously a view that contrasts with Kingsley's idea that women are able to transcend their biology whereas men cannot.

27 See David Punter, 'Mutations of terror: theory and the Gothic', *The Literature of Terror* (London and New York: Longman, 1996) Vol. 2, pp. 181–216 for an account of some of the major ambivalences and ambiguities of the Gothic.

28 Bram Stoker, *Dracula* (Oxford: Oxford University Press [1897] 1996), p. 302. All subsequent references are to this edition, and are given in the text.

29 See Pick, *Degeneration*, pp. 171–2. Leonard Wolf, *Annotated Dracula* (London: N. Potter, 1975) p. 300.

30 William Hughes, *Beyond Dracula: Bram Stoker's Fiction and its Cultural Context* (Basingstoke: Macmillan, 2002) p. 141.

31 Oscar Wilde, 'The Decay of Lying' in *The Complete Works of Oscar Wilde*, ed. G.F. Maine (London: Collins, 1992), pp. 909–31, p. 912. Pick, *Degeneration*, also uses the same quotation, p. 165.

32 Fred Botting, *Gothic* (London: Routledge, 1996) p. 137. All subsequent references are to this edition, and are given in the text.

33 Ibid. pp. 135–43. See also Punter, *Literature of Terror*, Vol. 2, pp. 1–6.

34 Punter, *Literature of Terror*, Vol. 2, pp. 3, 22.

2

Pathologising the Gothic: the Elephant Man, the Hysteric, the Indian and the Doctor

D.G. Halstead in his memoirs, *Doctor in The Nineties* (1959) writes that 'The Elephant Man was the product of one of those ghastly genetic mutations which, once in a million times, results in some science-fictional monster instead of a normal human being.'[1]

Sir Wilfred Grenfell notes in his memoirs, *A Labrador Doctor* (1920) that 'A special room in a yard was allotted to him, and several famous people came to see him – among them Queen Alexandra, the Princess of Wales, who afterwards sent him an autographed photograph of herself. He kept it in his room, which was known as the 'elephant house,' and it always suggested beauty and the beast.'[2]

In his memoirs, *The Elephant Man and Other Reminiscences* (1923), Sir Frederick Treves writes of his first meeting with Merrick that

> The thing arose slowly and let the blanket that covered its head and back fall to the ground. There stood revealed the most disgusting specimen of humanity that I have ever seen. In the course of my profession I had come upon lamentable deformities of the face due to injury or disease, as well as mutilations and contortions of the body depending upon like causes; but at no time had I met with such a degraded or perverted version of a human being as this lone figure displayed.[3]

What is surprising about these observations is that they are all made by doctors. That Merrick is not discussed in medical terms, but rather perceived as a monster from science fiction (Halstead), or as a beast (Grenfell) or described in tones of moral outrage (Treves) indicates the limits of a medical language which cannot account for deformity in strictly medical terms, and which instead slips into a more properly Gothic discourse concerning the horrors of monstrosity. What these descriptions also evidence is the need to plot Merrick into literary narratives: science fiction, romance and the Gothic. The reason for this is that the failure of a medical discourse concerning pathology is related to a failure to link Merrick to wider discourses concerning health, especially those discourses which read pathology as the indicator of social degeneracy. Before discussing this it is helpful to sketch in some biographical details drawn from Merrick's own brief autobiographical document.[4]

Merrick was born in 1862 in Leicester. He states that he went to school until his mother died when he was aged twelve. His father subsequently married the landlady of their lodgings who treated Merrick cruelly and forced him to find work, which he did, rolling cigars in a cigar factory until he was aged fifteen when the progression of his deformities meant that he could no longer continue. He gained a peddler's licence which enabled him to sell, but he found that people, scared by his deformities, would not buy from him and despite some assistance from an uncle, he fell into poverty and entered Leicester Union Workhouse in 1879. He stayed in the Workhouse intermittently until 1884 when he approached Sam Torr, proprietor of the Gaiety Palace of Varieties, and began his career as a sideshow exhibit. He was subsequently exhibited in London by another showman, Tom Norman, and it was while being exhibited in a shop near the London Hospital in 1884 that he was first encountered by Frederick Treves. Treves subsequently displayed Merrick at the Pathological Society of London, and wrote up his observations in a paper entitled 'A Case of Congenital Deformity' for the journal *Transactions of the Pathological Society of London*, which was published in March 1885.[5]

In many ways Merrick would seem to conform to theories of degeneracy mapped out in the period by a range of scientists and social commentators such as Lankester and Kingsley (ideas also developed by Nordau and Lombroso). Degeneration to some degree provided a catch-all explanation for a variety of social ills including urban decay, the economic and political decline of the nation, and a perceived decline in sexual morality. By the 1880s the idea that urban conditions were creating the possibility of degeneracy became linked to wider medical and political concerns related to the social and physical health of the nation. To this end an analysis of degeneracy opens up all kinds of questions about cause and effect relating to how the health, particularly of the urban poor, could be improved. In 1888, for example, at the height of the Ripper murders in the Whitechapel area, discussed at length in Chapter 3, it was the barbaric condition of the East End slums which was perceived as having created the context in which the murders could occur.[6] That this link between environment and health collapses in the case of Merrick is perhaps surprising given that Merrick's life of poverty and institutional care illustrates all of the elements which had been linked to a perceived decline in the mental, moral and physical health of the nation. That Merrick cannot quite be made to fit this model can be seen in Treves's account of Merrick's deformities in his paper on Merrick from 1885. It is one in which the idea of cause and effect breaks down, a breakdown which leads to Merrick's reconstruction as a truly Gothic subject.

In his paper Treves argued that Merrick's deformities were composed from a series of minor pathologies which had escalated in a grand manner. However this medical reading of Merrick is purely descriptive. Treves merely itemises the presence of a range of deformities but can find no explanation for their presence. It is a display of deformity but to no purpose other than to display that deformity: no medical knowledge is produced. The problem with Merrick is that he is, medically speaking, overdetermined. He is unique. His biological make up cannot be explained through an analysis of heredity – he comes from nowhere and goes nowhere. If a medical language fails then another type of description takes its place and in Treves's *Reminiscences* the language is one of moral outrage, monstrosity and public display. Merrick might not signify anything for medicine but he is forced into meaning in other ways.

So, the question arises, what does Merrick demonstrate if not a medical notion of pathology? One answer to this lies in the illustration which accompanied Treves's journal article (see Figure 1). It is important to note that Merrick's body was subject to deformity in all areas except two; one was his left arm, and the other was his genitals, which in the illustration are concealed beneath a loincloth. Remembering that this is a medical journal, and that he has been seen anyway at a meeting of the London Pathological Society, one wonders why there is a need for such coyness unless it is to hide the norm and pathologise the Other. Merrick crosses the street, displayed as a freak on one side and as a medical curiosity on the other but in cultural terms he has not really gone that far. So why the problem with Merrick's sexuality? If he comes from nowhere biologically (theoretically) speaking and goes nowhere, then sexuality should hardly be an issue. But what horrifies Treves in the *Reminiscences* is the possibility that Merrick might have sexual urges, and it is this concern which tips Treves's memoirs over into a Gothic idiom which reworks Gothic notions of the monstrous. What is central to this issue of a Gothic narrative is the status and function of aesthetics. It is how Merrick is portrayed which plays an important part in Treves's representation of Merrick and in his initial interpretation of him.

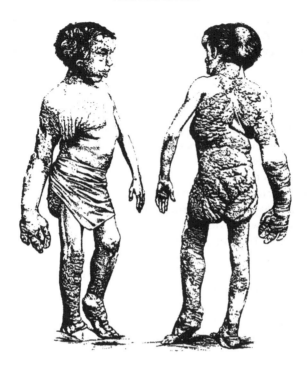

Figure 1	Joseph Merrick (Frederick Treves, 'A Case of Congenital Deformity',
Transactions of the Pathological Society of London, XXXVI (March 1885), 494–8 Plate XX

What we witness is how crucial a role a Gothic aesthetic plays in Treves's emphasis on a language of theatricality. It is a language which exists independently from theories of degeneration (i.e. it is about openly displaying not secretly hiding). The emphasis on issues of representation and Merrick raises, as we shall see, interesting questions about the textual and pictorial reconstructions of Merrick, ones which, for Treves, capture an aspect of Merrick's identity that science overlooks.

We first encounter this issue of representation in Treves's account of his discovery of Merrick. When Treves went to see him being displayed in the shop across the road from the London Hospital, he first had to pass through a curtain on which there was a painting of Merrick. Treves noted in his *Reminiscences* that, 'This very crude production depicted a frightful creature that could only have been possible in a nightmare' (p. 1). He goes on to say that, 'This fact – that it was still human – was the most repellent attribute of the creature' (pp.1–2). Treves also relies on this language of the fantastic when describing his first sighting of Merrick, who was warming himself over a brick heated by a Bunsen burner. He writes of Merrick: 'It might have been a captive in a cavern or a wizard watching for unholy manifestations in the ghostly flame' (p. 3). Merrick is then made to take off his blanket, and what we witness is the disintegration of Treves's language when confronted with what becomes a bizarre chimera. Treves employs a comparative language which refers to Merrick's 'cauliflower-like skin', his 'Thumb [which] had the appearance of a radish', some flesh which hangs from his chest as 'like a dewlap suspended from the neck of a lizard', and in a move which takes us away from the non-human, he describes Merrick's left arm as 'delicately shaped ... covered with fine skin and provided with a beautiful hand which any women might have envied' (p. 5). That Treves sees Merrick as caught up in a field of representation is additionally suggested by his claim that Merrick leads a life of seclusion similar to that 'as the Man with the Iron Mask' (p. 6). Additionally the cloak which Merrick wears in order to disguise his deformities was something which Treves describes in theatrical terms, claiming 'I had only seen such a garment on the stage wrapped about the figure of a Venetian bravo' (pp. 6–7). It is this model of Merrick which in aesthetic, rather than biological terms, conforms to Kelly Hurley's claim that in the period: 'the Gothic represents human bodies as between species: always already in a state of indifferentiation, or undergoing metamorphoses into a bizarre assortment of human/not-human configurations'.[7]

Treves tries to move beyond a purely Gothic language, one which is here prone to dispersal, in order to supplant it with a more coherently deployed model of romance which can contain, through parody, Merrick's threatening sexuality. However, before Treves effects this break with a Gothic idiom he implicitly accounts for his relationship with Merrick in terms which gloss the relationship which the creature has to Victor Frankenstein in Mary Shelley's novel. Firstly, Treves sees Merrick as a composite being, and secondly, Treves sees it as his mission to bring Merrick back to life by introducing him to a world of 'civilised', good, bourgeois values from which Merrick had inevitably been excluded. Treves writes: 'To secure Merrick's recovery and to bring him, as it were, to life once more, it was necessary that he should make the acquaintance of men and women who would treat him as a normal and intelligent young man and not as a monster of deformity' (p. 20). Treves's *Reminiscences*, like Shelley's novel, devotes some space to the consideration of the shaping of character. Treves provides a speculative, synoptic account of Merrick's childhood

which resembles that of the creature's in *Frankenstein*: 'He had had no
boyhood. He had never experienced pleasure. He knew nothing of the joy
of living nor of the fun of things. His sole idea of happiness was to creep
into the dark and hide' (p. 16). Moreover, Treves discovers that Merrick,
like Victor's creature, is unable to distinguish between histories and
fictions.[8] Treves notes, 'He had read a few stories and some elementary
lesson books, but the delight of his life was a romance, especially a love
romance. These tales were very real to him, as real as any narrative in the
Bible [which he also read], so that he would tell them to me as incidents in
the lives of people who had lived' (pp. 14–15). Merrick might confuse
fiction with reality but then Treves, in his search for a language which can
represent Merrick, does this as well. In effect he moves from a Gothic
discourse which was associated with Merrick's early life and his sideshow
career, to one in which romantic fiction governs Merrick's experience of
the world. It is an experience which Treves seems to have been keen to
encourage, and it is this which takes us back to the suppressed Gothic
narrative found in the article of 1885.

In Treves's journal article it was the case that Merrick's genitals were
coyly concealed beneath a loincloth. What was truly monstrous for Treves
was what he found in the painting of Merrick: that the 'fact – that it was
still human – was the most repellent attribute of the creature'. To this end
Treves suppresses the evidence of the norm by focusing on deformity. This
concealed Gothic narrative of monstrosity informs the doctor/patient
scenario here, but Treves again conceals this by mapping on a chaste
narrative of romantic fiction. Treves writes that Merrick possesses 'some
of the tempestuous feelings of a man' (p. 15) and that 'He was amorous.
He would like to have been a lover' (p. 29), although Treves makes sure
that all of this becomes sublimated through romantic fiction. In effect he
uses the romantic narrative in order to keep in check the Gothic narrative.
For Treves this becomes strangely efficacious; Merrick bursts into tears
when introduced to his first female visitor, and thereafter 'He must have
been visited by almost every lady of note in the social world' (p. 22). This
inspires Merrick to indulge in role-play. He asks Treves for a silver-fitted
dressing-bag (containing brushes, a comb, razors, a toothbrush, a shoe-
horn and a cigarette-case) for Christmas. Thus equipped by Treves,
'Merrick the Elephant Man became, in the seclusion of his chamber, the
Piccadilly exquisite, the young spark, the gallant' (pp. 27–8). He continues,
'the bag was an emblem of the real swell and of the knockabout Don Juan
of whom he had read' (p. 28). In effect, in becoming a mock dandy, he is
removed from the terrain of Gothic exclusion (which emphasises his

Otherness) and transposed to a more controllable one of bourgeois inclusion, one in which Merrick's allegedly troublesome desire becomes refigured through parody. This image-making constructs Merrick along the desired chaste lines supported by Treves who goes on to speculate: 'He fell in love – in a humble and devotional way – with, I think, every attractive lady he saw. He, no doubt, pictured himself the hero of many a passionate incident' (p. 29). In making Merrick conform to notions of the society fop he pushes Merrick over into another discourse which feminises him. Earlier he had mentioned how Merrick's left arm was like that of a woman's. He also claims that, 'He showed himself to be a gentle, affectionate and lovable creature, as amiable as a happy woman, free from any trace of cynicism or resentment, without a grievance and without an unkind word for anyone' (p. 17).

Here other loincloths are deployed by Treves. If we move beyond this concealment we can glimpse that the real problem is related to the failure of a scientific, and somewhat Gothic, language of degeneracy. Merrick resists any attempt to coherently define him in these monstrous terms, and to this degree he helps to identify a failure within these scientific claims for certainty. He comes to represent that which science cannot touch, but also identifies how the terms of that science, especially the marginalisation of a sexuality that might reproduce deviancy, are carried over into another, romantic, medium in order to extend its censorious moral vision. In doing so the example of Merrick helps to highlight the fragility of the claims for scientific certainty in the period. Hurley writes, 'classificatory schema are merely functional, artificial rather than natural, and anomalous phenomena are abominable because they throw into relief the *provisionality* of the categories they confound' (*The Gothic Body*, p. 25, Hurley's emphasis). That Treves acknowledges that there were, for him, two different types of Merrick is registered in his closing comments: ones which again take us back to the idea of a Gothic narrative which is supplanted by a romantic one. It is one which Treves organises around a body/soul divide: 'As a specimen of humanity, Merrick was ignoble and repulsive; but the spirit of Merrick if it could be seen in the form of the living, would assume the figure of an upstanding and heroic man, smooth browed and clean of limb, and with eyes that flashed an undaunted courage' (p. 37). This move from monster to romantic lead identifies (through displacement) the provisional nature of categorisation in a scientific discourse which sublimates its practice and its fragility into literary and theatrical terms, ones which only serve to demonstrate its problematic construction of Otherness. It is Treves's attempt to relocate the scientific idea of deviancy into a chaste romantic discourse of non-sexual love which effects the very denial of sexuality that the loincloth represents. The failure of science becomes victoriously concealed beneath an alternative romantic language, the very presence of which only points towards the inability of science to account for the anomalous in scientific terms.

Treves plays these issues out in relation to models of gender. The attempt to sanitise Merrick's desires is constructed through an implicit reconfiguration of Merrick's sexual persona. By turning him into a dandified fop Treves enters into that highly ambiguous domain of gendering which was later to be explored by sexologists such as Havelock Ellis and Edward Carpenter. To some degree these sexologists are drawing on an already available discourse associated with homosexuality. However, these debates of the 1890s evidence some confusion about the function of gender in relation to biological sex. As shown in Chapter 1, for Carpenter, and to a degree Ellis, the confusion arises because it is possible for a masculine man to be homosexual and for a feminine man to be heterosexual. To some degree this is to get ahead of what Treves maps onto Merrick, but Treves's reconstruction of Merrick as a dandy and his hints at a biologically female presence (the 'girlish' left arm) anticipate these debates about the complicating factor of gender. It is this complicating factor which is also evidenced in Treves's move from a male Gothic idiom to a female romantic one. As we have seen, Treves's narrative is full of evasions, especially about sexuality, and consequently the issue of sexuality is partially, because problematically, concealed. The failure of science is thus complicated by the presence of this issue of gender and its relationship to science. Ultimately it seems as though Merrick, paradoxically, represents a 'normal' but pathologised version of male desire.

That Treves is concerned with the failures of science and its links with gender scripts, is an idea pursued elsewhere in his *Reminiscences*. In a chapter entitled 'A Cure for Nerves', Treves takes on the persona of a nervous, neurotic woman, through which he explores both science and the masculine culture of the medical profession. He also extends this into a wider critique of other forms of patriarchy, especially marriage.[9]

Doctoring hysteria

The nameless narrator of 'A Cure for Nerves' explains the nature of her ailment: her apparently uncontrollable fears when confronted with the seemingly mundane aspects of everyday life. She also describes her encounters with various doctors and the lack of sympathy which she receives from them and from her husband. Towards the end of the narrative she is placed in a nursing home where she is forced to undergo a complete bed rest and where she is put on a diet designed to increase her strength. It is while at this nursing home that an operation is conducted on a woman in a room above the narrator. The patient nearly dies through loss of blood, some of which spills onto the floor, seeps through the ceiling, and drops onto the narrator's coverlet (or at least so she imagines, as the narrative is ambiguous on this point). The narrator gains strength from this moment, and sees in the woman a role model of courage and fortitude which she strives to emulate, and so a cure, of some sorts, is effected.

However, the focus of the narrative is on the lack of support which she receives from the medical profession and on the nature of her ailment. It is the feelings associated with her illness which push the narrative over into a Gothic narrative of despair. She, for example, associates her feelings with a series of images concerning incarceration. In trying to explain the nature of her ailment she draws a parallel between herself and (in a moment of gender confusion) the feelings of a condemned man waking on the morning of his execution: 'I know the cold sweat that breaks over the whole body and the sickly clutching about the heart that attend such an awakening, but doubt if any emerging from sleep can be really worse than many I have experienced'.[10] What is of significance here is not just this feeling of Gothic doom, but also how it reworks, through the image of the condemned man, a hostility towards male culture. This is in part provoked by the insensitivity of her husband when confronted by her feelings of discomfort in public places ('It is useless for my husband to nudge me and tell me not to make a fool of myself' p. 75), but also by doctors who suggest that the proper conduct of wifely duties should provide a sufficient corrective. One doctor 'said that what would cure me would be a week at the washing tub' (p. 77).

What this testifies to is the failure of the medical profession to properly investigate the nature of what is perceived to be a specifically female malady. One doctor who had appeared sympathetic, suggested that she visit a doctor abroad and provided her with a letter of introduction. The narrator fails to undertake this journey and subsequently reads the letter, only to find that it contains idle consideration of each other's golfing handicaps and that she is relegated to the postscript where the 'kindly' doctor writes, 'The lady who brings this is Mrs. —. She is a terrible woman, a deplorable neurotic. I need say no more about her, but I hope you won't mind my burdening you with her, for she is the kind of tedious person who bores me to death. However she pays her fees' (p. 78). Her husband, far from sharing in her outrage, sends the letter back to its author 'because he thought the memoranda about the golf handicaps would be interesting for him to keep' (p. 78).

The dismissive way in which the narrator is treated indicates how the masculine discourse of medicine functions as one aspect of patriarchy (alongside marriage and ideas concerning domestic duty). Additionally, medicine is represented as a clubbable, gentlemanly profession, one which is built around the exclusion of women. It is this type of relegation of female experience which Treves is, at least ostensibly, trying to rectify. This experience of marginalisation in turn explains why the narrator imagines herself as incarcerated and obscurely punished for her condition: a symbolic incarceration which is subsequently literalised when she is placed in the care of the nursing home. The narrative is, as was the account of Merrick, edged by a language of Gothic horror which appears to come from the failure of medicine to conduct itself in a scientific fashion; so that the anxiety that confronts the narrator concerns where these feelings of horror originate.

The narrative is ambivalent about where danger lies. The narrator initially regards her fear as a symptom of her disease, but later considers that it is masculinity which is in some way to blame. This idea of a 'dangerous' masculinity, which Treves had seen in the case of Merrick, is here moved from the apparent margins of biological anomaly to the centre of institutionalised masculine culture, as represented both by the medical profession and the duties of the wife. These Gothic images of imprisonment are translated into images of direct male assault when the narrator tries to formulate an image which illustrates her fears about surgery, fears provoked in the nursing home by the thought of what the woman in the room above her has to endure. The narrator writes of these fears that, 'It must be as if a man knelt upon your chest and strangled you by gripping your throat with his hands' (p. 80).

These representations of incarcerated and murderous men are Gothic reworkings of the wider horrors generated by a masculinist culture which depends upon the subjugation of the feminine. The narrative ultimately establishes a debate about who has the greater right to feel fear. It is a debate inaugurated by the arrival of the soon to be operated on woman, in which the narrator realises:

> I now began to learn that there were others who were in worse plight than myself. I, on the one hand, had merely to lie in bed and sleep. They, on the other, came to the home with their lives in their hands to confront an appalling ordeal. I was haunted by indefinite alarms; they had to submit to

the tangible steel of the surgeon's knife ... Compared with me these women were heroines. (pp. 81–2)

This image of female courage enables her to supplant the Gothic narrative which had so far edged her fears, although the reasons for this edging are in part due to the threatening masculine culture to which such fears refer. 'A Cure for Nerves' thus experiments with narrative devices in ways familiar from the account of Merrick. With Merrick a world of male Gothic terrors are displaced by a narrative of chivalry. In Treves's account of the neurotic woman it is a Female Gothic narrative which is more properly developed.[11] This narrative, one focused on female resistance to images of incarceration, is developed through the narrator as she comes to perceive the failings of the masculine world. These associations with failure are also developed in the account of the operation on the woman who has started to become the narrator's role model.

Initially there is optimism with the arrival of 'the great surgeon of the day' (p. 82) and 'I knew when the surgeon and his assistants arrived, for I heard his voice on the stair. It was clear and unconcerned' (p. 84). In contrast to this is the woman who is waiting to undergo the operation. She is seen in terms which echo the narrator's vision of the condemned man used earlier, 'What of the poor soul who was waiting? She also would be looking at the clock. Three minutes more and she would be led in her nightdress into this chamber of horrors' (p. 84). In keeping with the Gothic discourse which defines the woman as a victim, the narrator hears a series of moans as the woman is chloroformed. However, something goes wrong in the operation and one of the doctors is forced to hastily retrieve something from another building in order to staunch the flow of a burst blood vessel. The blood drips onto the floor and the narrator notices in 'expressionless horror' that 'a small patch of red' appears on her own ceiling. This moment is replete with Gothic images of fear and loathing, but it also functions as a baptism of blood. The narrator notes of the patch of blood, 'It became a deeper crimson until at last one awful drop fell upon the white coverlet of my bed. It came down with the weight of lead. The impact went through me like an electric shock' (p. 87). The feelings of revulsion escalate as the narrator becomes immobilised by fear. She recounts that:

> Another drop fell with a thud like a stone. I would have hidden my head under the bedclothes but I dared not stir. As each drop fell on the bed the interval came quicker until there was a scarlet patch on the white quilt that grew and grew and grew. I felt that the evil stain would come through the

coverings, hot and wet, to my clenched hands which were just beneath, but I was unable to move them. My sight was now almost gone. There was nothing but a red haze filling the room. (p. 87)

The narrator loses consciousness and regains a new, empowered sense of herself. She becomes cured because, 'It was absurd to say that I could not walk in the street when that brave woman had walked, smiling, into that place of gags and steel' (p. 88). The narrator has to go through a Gothic narrative in order to effect this. She has to move beyond a medicalised Gothic discourse in order to find a practical example of fortitude, one which stands in opposition to a medical discourse which had, it seems, very nearly bungled the operation. This demonisation of medicine is closely related to these issues about gender. The Gothic plays an important part in this as it captures not only the narrator's sense of her own plight, but also illustrates the failings of medicine.

Treves's account of Merrick and an imaginary female hysteric emphasises the deficiencies in scientific practice. In his account of Merrick it is the case that models of degeneracy could not be mobilised with any meaningful efficacy. The Gothic language of the discourse of degeneration was thus supplanted by a more successful model of containment which could be found in romantic fiction. In 'A Cure for Nerves' there is no explicit reference to a pseudo-scientific language of degeneracy, although there is an obvious parallel between the plight of the narrator and the scientific model of neurotic attribution in the late nineteenth century. What links Treves's two chapters is their reliance on a Gothic language and an exploration of how it is possible to circumvent that language by replacing it with more optimistic and, significantly, non-scientific discourses associated with chivalry. With Merrick the application of this language lampoons his alleged amorous intent, but with the female narrator we can see a development of some aspects of the Female Gothic through images of escape and optimism, images which are based on the refutation of all kinds of masculine experience and institutional structures such as marriage and medicine.

Nightmares of Empire

Treves returns to a Gothic idiom in a chapter entitled 'A Restless Night' which employs a range of Gothic images including a projected attack by rats, a murderous assault by a racial Other, and themes of paranoia and entrapment. All of these images are used to contextualise a particular, and solely imagined, encounter that Treves relates as an account of a dream he

had while on a visit to India. In the chapter Treves recounts a visit to
Rajputana where he meets a doctor from the Indian Medical Service. While
on a journey with this man they stay for one night at a dak bungalow
where the officer tells Treves of an Indian patient he had treated for an eye
which had become infected by a splinter of stone (the patient was a
stonemason). The officer told the Indian that he had to remove the sightless
eye because there was a good chance that he would lose the sight in the
other eye due to the effects of sympathetic ophthalmia. However, the
patient sought a second opinion from 'a magician'[12] which delayed the
removal of the eye for so long that the patient ultimately lost the sight in
his one good eye, for which he blamed the doctor, indeed 'He called upon
every deity in the Indian mythology to pour torments upon this maimer
of men, to blast his home and annihilate his family root and branch' (p.
141). Treves describes the unlikely setting of the bungalow in Gothic terms
referring to his bedroom as 'this particular sepulchre' (p. 141) and the
gloom of the place affects his imagination in such a way that he has a
dream in which he encounters this blind Indian patient.

This description of the bungalow will be returned to in a moment but
it is worth noting that Treves makes no overt reference to any wider
geopolitical context which might reflect on colonialism. However, this sense
of a colonial intervention is implicit in the language of othering that he
uses in his description of the climate, the locale, and finally in his 'encounter'
with the blind Indian who is, to some degree, held responsible for his own
condition. Treves moves beyond science in this instance as he develops a
more 'occult' understanding, and yet the dream has a certain hold over
Treves because it symbolically captures a truth about West/East relations
which the colonial doctor's flippant anecdote about the man's blinding
only partially reveals. Treves notes that 'I fell asleep and then at once
embarked upon a dream, the vividness and reality of which were certainly
remarkable' (p. 146). However, for the dream to take on an aspect of 'reality'
then context is all, and this is revealed through Treves's initial descriptions
which link his sense of place to both Gothic and medical notions of disease
and primitive states.

He writes of the locale of the bungalow that 'So elemental was the
landscape that it might have been a part of the primeval world before the
green things came into being' (p. 137). The place is prehistoric and
monstrous: 'If a saurian had been in sight browsing on this ancient scrub
the monster would have been in keeping' (p. 137). The human inhabitants
are, inevitably, also associated with this 'pre-civilised' past, and he relates
the presence of 'a native village, simple enough to be a settlement of

neolithic men' (pp. 137–8). The bungalow is also described in these primitive terms, but with the additional hint that it also represents the uncleanliness that, for Treves, is 'typical' of Indian communities, as he notes that the bungalow has 'that unclean aromatic odour which clings to Indian dwellings' (p. 138). It is an image which will also be associated with the man in the dream where there is 'the loathsome smell of the unclean native' (p. 149). These images of pre-civilisation are also suggested by the patient's visit to a faith-healer. The doctor also corroborates this native faith in superstition, 'The average sick man, he told me, had more confidence in a dried frog suspended from the neck in a bag than in the whole British Pharmacopoeia' (p. 139). Treves, implicitly, constructs a whole range of oppositions which ultimately rework an opposition between science and superstition. The doctor's narrative merely confirms the efficaciousness of Western scientific practice, a mode of practice which in its associations with the modern world and with progress, contrasts with the images of primitive communities and faiths.

However, this status of science is thrown into some doubt by Treves's uneasy attempt to sleep. The idea that native culture is superstitious and otherworldly is given a particular emphasis through Treves's quasi-Gothic descriptions of the locale. This Gothic element is given a special prominence in the events leading up to the dream, as Treves lies in bed and hears his pitch black room being infested by an invasion of hungry muskrats which have entered his room through an adjoining bathroom that has an exposed drain-hole which links to the outside. Treves's description of this allegedly real event is tinged by an acknowledgement that his imagination contributes to his interpretation of this curious invasion. The darkness puts him into a position of blindness that obliquely refers to the blindness of the Indian, and by relocating this experience the focus becomes placed on the available Gothic possibilities:

> I dislike rats, and especially rats in a bedroom. This prejudice was not made less when I felt that some of them were climbing up on to the bed. I was certain I could hear one crawling over my clothes which lay on the chair by the bedside. I was certain that others were searching about on the dressing-table ... I recalled stories in which men had been attacked by hordes of rats, and I wondered when they would attack me, for, by this time, the whole room seemed to be full of rats. (p. 144)

Treves frightens away the rats by shouting, but they soon return and he hears a strange scraping noise underneath his bed which turns out to be a 'cake of unleavened bread' being dragged away by them, although initially

'I took [it] at first to be a piece of human skull' (p. 146). Treves's overwrought Gothic imagination does not just simply construct imaginary fears, rather he already associates the place with a kind of Gothic ambience which is then redeveloped and exaggerated through these feelings of paranoia. Treves ejects the rats and, by blocking the drain-hole, guarantees their permanent exclusion. However, at this point he has a dream which develops these images of threatened assault by the primitive and vengeful colonial subject. In the dream he imagines the blind Indian emerging from the bathroom, an image which symbolically relates the Indian to the vermin which Treves has just repulsed. Treves realises that this man is the greater horror, as he relates that:

> Out of the dark there crept a middle-aged man, a native, lean and sinewy, without a vestige of clothing on his body. His skin shone in the uncertain light, and it was evident that his body, from head to foot, was smeared with oil. The most noticeable point about the man was that he was blind. His eyelids were closed, but the sockets of the eyes were sunken as are those of a corpse. With his left hand he felt for the wall, while in his right hand he carried a small stone-mason's pick. His face was expressionless. This was the most terrible thing about it, for his face was as the face of the dead. He crept into the room as Death himself might creep into the chamber of the dying. (pp. 147–8)

We know that Treves is occupying a room which was meant to be allocated to the other doctor, suggesting that Treves, through mistaken identity, will feel the force of the Indian's revenge. However, what this scene comes to suggest is that Treves, as a representative of the West, is rendered immobile when confronted with the revengeful East. This image of the Indian as a zombie suggests both his dehumanisation and his demonisation. Treves's participation in a language of colonial othering thus seems to be clear. However, this language of othering is occulted, and the Indian is strangely impassive while playing out his revenge. In other words, the Other is dangerous precisely because of their apparent inhumanity. Aggressor and victim thus swap places, as Treves becomes paralysed by his own Gothic terrors: 'I was mesmerized as would be a rabbit in a corner within a foot of a snake' (p. 150). A crackling noise made by his lamp 'seemed to call me to my senses' (p. 150) and he hides under the bed while the Indian gropes through the covers with his pick ready to strike. Treves makes good his escape by grabbing the Indian's legs and so dragging him to the floor in such a way that the Indian bangs his head and Treves leaves him either dead or unconscious. He later returns and finds the man gone, although there is some blood on the floor where he hit his head. Treves awakens, looks for the blood and is relieved to find that it is not there, although 'It was almost impossible to believe that the events of the latter part of the night, after the departure of the rats, had not been real' (p. 153).

It is these series of oppositions, West/East, science/superstition, blindness/light and dream/reality, that indicate just how unstable such terms are when developed within a colonial and quasi-scientific context. Again it becomes the case that Treves dwells not on the successes of science, but rather on its failings.

What is striking from the first two examples from Treves's memoirs is how medicine becomes related to non-medical discourses because medicine fails as an 'objective' science. Medicine in Treves's *Reminiscences* is tainted by a range of issues concerning gender, sexuality, race and representation. What is important in this is not only the exposure of medicine as the site where a range of ideological forces meet, but also how an aspect of this ideology controls what can and cannot be shown. In 'A Cure for Nerves', a voice is given back to the victim. It is an attempt to let speak that which is rendered silent by a medical discourse which does not want to acknowledge such marginalised voices. Interestingly the Indian, who had earlier been described as garrulous, is now mute. The encounter between this naked man smeared in oil and Treves lying trembling on his bed in both fear and anticipation also, of course, suggests the idea of a sexual assault. Additionally, the doctor had indicated that the Indian did not just wish to attack him, he also wanted 'to blast his home and annihilate his family root and branch' (p. 141). The Indian is also associated with uncleanliness, although any idea of disease is inevitably implicit.

Also at issue is the sense of being unmanned. Treves cowers in the bed awaiting his death, and is only stirred to action by the noise of the crackling candle. A Freudian might be tempted to read the blindness as representing a symbolic castration, one which Treves identifies with (in his own moment of sympathetic ophthalmia) as he lies in the dark with the rats, and therefore the significance of the light (the phallic candle) as a reviving force, becomes relevant. However, the picture is more complex than this. Treves's sense of masculinity is so closely related to the process and status of science (an issue consciously addressed in 'A Cure for Nerves') that his loss of faith in it, no matter how temporary, pushes him into a world of superstition that leaves him as supine and helpless as the narrator in 'A Cure for Nerves'. What is also significant is that Treves's fascination with the possibility of a Gothic idiom raises questions about what part gender construction plays in this process of demonisation. To be demonic here is to be masculine, and yet the demonic suggests a world of superstition that is opposed to science. Treves constructs a language of othering that is related to images of monstrosity which reveals a continuity between the early descriptions of Merrick and the anonymous Indian. Treves demonises that which science cannot account for; finally, if paradoxically, the Gothic provides a masculine mode of representation which compensates for the deficiencies of Treves's scientific practice.

Ultimately, Treves is also trying to find a form of expression which exists beyond the Gothic, and moving beyond the Gothic discourse of the late nineteenth century means to move beyond a masculinist discourse. Treves's memoirs illustrate that masculinity, as a mode of identity through which the world can be interpreted, is available for sublimation into either an extreme instrumentality (science) or into a world of Gothic dangers. These images are either unsettled, as with Merrick or the narrator in 'A Cure for Nerves', or are represented in somewhat compromising terms: Treves's encounter with a naked Indian in his bedroom. It is by making these connections that Treves's memoirs help us to expose the precise way in which the Gothic, and the medical discourse of the time, are inflected by a range of gender and racial issues during the period.

Masculinity and medicine

What is central to Treves's memoirs is the status and function of the body. What Treves would prefer to perceive in biological terms becomes undermined through the inability of science to understand what it is confronted by and, crucially, its inability to create knowledge. The sense that science can only provide an incomplete and so inadequate solution, closely corresponds to an image of an inadequate and incomplete masculinity. This claim might be open to the charge of oversimplification if it were not the case that medicine was, during the period, deployed as a means of gauging moral and sexual health. Foucault has noted that a Victorian science of health, by scrutinising the healthiness of middle-class sexual behaviour, was instrumental in consolidating the economic position of the bourgeoisie. In this instance the claims of medicine differ from those of the sexologists who were much more ambivalent than the medical profession about the relationship between same sex orientation and health. Indeed, it seems as though medicine has more in common with the degenerationists in respect to notions of moral clarity. And yet, as Foucault points out, the Victorian period is also characterised by a sense of failure and an attendant fear of its own surpassing. The reasons for this are related to issues about power.

In *The History of Sexuality* Vol. 1 (1976) Foucault provides a summary of his identification of power structures and their failures. To some degree this is meant to hold true in general terms, but it is also a summation of his history of Victorian sexuality to that point. It is a model of power which reflects on the failures of Treves's own, often distracted, scientific gazing. Foucault claims that 'Power is not something that is acquired, seized, or shared, something that one holds on to or allows to slip away; power is exercised from innumerable points, in the interplay of nonegalitarian and mobile relations.'[13] The problem with power is therefore the problem with identification. Power relations thus reflect, inevitably, a nonegalitarian world but it is the nature of that reflection which is the complicating factor. Treves, for example, places faith in the scientific claims of medicine. Medicine to some degree functions as a means of social control to the extent that it participates in a wider picture of bourgeois regulation (or policing) of sexuality and health. However, Treves's memoirs also reveal a concern with the limitations of science. That is to say that his memoirs are at their most interesting when science fails and a Gothic narrative takes over. This Gothic narrative appears to develop the conservative social philosophy of the now failing medical claims to truth. It is in the Gothic that a language of Otherness is established through the labelling of evil. However, this alternative taxonomy of good/bad for healthy/unhealthy is not rigorously applied. Instead the instabilities in the labelling reveal that Treves cannot maintain a coherent discourse of Otherness because of the failings of science and the provisional language of Otherness employed in the Gothic. The two languages, the scientific and the fictional become blurred in this shared moment of self-reflection.

However, it is the complicating factor of the Gothic which also directs attention to ideas of Otherness in all the ways that have traditionally characterised the form: class, gender, race and monstrosity (all of which are, of course, inherent in the discourse of medicine in the nineteenth century as well). It is the issue of gender which is the key to Treves's narrative as it contains within it all of the other terms. What is central is the idea of masculinity.

Merrick was a medical curiosity for Treves but by evading medical evaluation it meant that an alternative language of health became deployed. Treves's focus on Merrick's sexuality reveals the links between health and sexuality, especially in those theories which concerned who should be allowed to procreate. Treves cannot explain, let alone cure, Merrick's other pathologies but he can, through fiction, find a means of correcting Merrick's seemingly threatening sexuality. What Treves sees in Merrick is the kind of link between monstrosity and masculinity that was emphasised in theories of degeneration and although Treves makes no overt investment in that language, he is close to exercising some form of eugenic control over the apparently polluted masculinity of Merrick. However, Merrick's masculinity is not the only template for masculinity which is available in Treves's memoirs. The failure of science also represents a failure of a model of masculinity. This link is made apparent in the connections between the male profession of medicine and the Gothic terrors which this provokes in the narrator of 'A Cure for Nerves'. Merrick, however, is a Gothic monster of masculinity, one who is cured through the imposition of an image of the dandy which feminises and civilises any sexual impulses that he may have had.

This narrative move reveals the fragility of Treves's Gothic. Indeed Treves's descriptions of Merrick register an incongruity between his appearance and his self. For Treves, the dandy is a more 'real' version of Merrick than a Gothic monster. It becomes Treves's only way of effecting some sort of cure. Identifying how power works in this example is problematic because power conceals itself through this kind of strategy. Treves's pose of avuncular concern for Merrick diverts attention away from these issues even as they appear to be the obvious signs of a liberal bourgeois ideology. It is in 'A Cure for Nerves' that Treves reflects on the limitations of the medical practice by judging such practice by how it treats the patient. Again it becomes the case that the narrator is not cured by medicine, but by her encounter with an image of fortitude to be found in a woman whose bravery is in part registered by her ability to place her trust in the doctors who so nearly kill her during the operation. Medicine as medicine fails. In its place Treves constructs a power conflict played out along gender lines.

Masculinity and its failings are the subject matter of 'A Cure for Nerves'. It is also a male reading of female resentment towards the profession, one which ultimately dismisses the narrator's 'illness' as imaginary. However, the narrative also focuses on how medicine constitutes a new mode of Gothic. In 'A Restless Night', the model of masculinity is associated with race and with violence. It relies on a language of superstition and the occult which compromises scientific claims to certainty. Treves's Gothic creation, the blind, murderous Indian, appears to him to be more real than a dream. Treves's battle with a colonial Other and the fears and anxieties which the dream articulate reveal the 'real' position of Britain in its colonial relations towards the end of the nineteenth century. Treves might escape, but the dream suggests that the battle is lost.

That Treves cannot maintain a coherent position on science reveals a wider malaise concerning masculinity. Medicine, as both a largely male-controlled profession and as a mode of investigation which incorporates the kind of gender issues referred to in 'A Cure for Nerves', appears to be in crisis, although only so long as the discourse concerning masculinity is itself in crisis.

Treves in the *Reminiscences*, will ultimately revise his views of the Gothic, a revision which is implicit in his dismissal of a faith in supernatural explanations:

> Belief in the supernatural and the miraculous has a fascination for many minds, and especially for minds of not too stable an order. Such persons seem to prefer a transcendental explanation to one that is commonplace. Apparitions are not apt to appear to those who are healthy both in body and mind. Dreams, it will be admitted by all, are more often due to indigestion than to a supernatural or a spiritual agency. (p. 164)

And so the excesses of the Gothic imagination are explained away. However, elsewhere in the *Reminiscences* it is medicine which is itself prone to becoming Gothic.

The relationship which medicine has to social concerns about health is increasingly questioned in the period. This is especially the case when the middle-class standing of the medical profession was questioned. Such concerns include issues relating to masculinity, as the status of the 'good' bourgeois professional becomes an object of scrutiny at the *fin de siècle*. The idea that the urban poor required strategic health regulation from above already contained within it the kind of class dynamic which arguably contributed to poverty in the first place. Foucault's idea that medicine was an essentially bourgeois science, and thus one which protected bourgeois interests, is relevant here. However, Foucault also claims that power relations are not this simple. The contradictions inherent in specific constructions of empowerment, whether relating to class or models of masculinity, become replicated in the wider society in such a way that resistance to power also becomes possible as those contradictions are responded to at different levels within society. Foucault argues that:

> Power comes from below; that is, there is no binary and all-encompassing opposition between rulers and ruled at the root of power relations … no such duality extending from the top down and reacting on more and more limited groups to the very depth of the social body. One must suppose rather that the manifold relationships of force that take shape and come into play in the machinery of production, in families, limited groups, and institutions,

are the basis for wide-ranging effects of cleavage that run through the social body as a whole. (*History of Sexuality* Vol. 1, p. 94)

Foucault also argues that 'Where there is power, there is resistance to, and yet, or rather consequently, this resistance is never in a position of exteriority in relation to power ... These points of resistance are present everywhere in the power network' (p. 95). What Foucault suggests here is the failure of ideology, at least ideology conceived of in Marxist terms. That crisis is therefore evidenced by resistance is revealed not only through unstable relations between classes, but also within classes. Treves's memoirs reflect this as they dwell on the inadequacies of a scientific discourse which participates in a wider discourse relating to the failures of masculinity. Implicit to Treves's memoirs is the idea that medicine creates the problems of mental, physical and moral health that it is supposed to cure, and this is why he relates medicine to the popular literary form of the Gothic. The demonisation of science and the demonisation of a model of masculinity with which it is associated becomes especially relevant during this period.

Three years after Treves first encountered Merrick (and two years before Merrick's death in 1890) the process of demonising medicine, the professional classes and masculinity were played out in a range of popular mediums (especially in the press) reflecting on the 'Jack the Ripper' murders between 31 August and 9 November 1888, which took place around the area of the London Hospital where Treves worked and where Merrick resided. Masculinity, its associations with pathology and how this relates to accounts of the murders is the subject of Chapter 3.

Notes

1 D.G. Halstead, *Doctor in The Nineties* (London: Christopher Johnson, 1959) p. 37

2 Wilfred Grenfell, *A Labrador Doctor: The Autobiography of Sir Wilfred Grenfell*, (London: Hodder and Stoughton, [1920] 1931) p. 60.

3 Frederick Treves, 'The Elephant Man' in *The Elephant Man and Other Reminiscences*, (London: Cassell, 1923) pp. 1–37, p. 3. All subsequent references are to this edition, and are given in the text. Frederick Treves was a well-known Victorian surgeon who became renowned for his pioneering work on appendicitis. He was Surgeon-in-Ordinary to Queen Victoria and was knighted in 1901 for his services to the Royal family. These services included removing the appendix of Edward VII the day before his scheduled coronation in June 1902. See Michael Howell and Peter Ford, *The True History of the Elephant Man* (Harmondsworth: Penguin, 1980) pp. 163–7, for an

account of Treves's professional career.

  4 Joseph Merrick, 'The Autobiography of Joseph Carey Merrick', reproduced in Howell and Ford, *The True History*, pp. 182–4.

  5 Frederick Treves, 'A Case of Congenital Deformity', in *Transactions of the Pathological Society of London*, xxxvi (March 1885), 494–8.

  6 For an account of this see Judith R. Walkowitz, *City of Dreadful Delight: Narratives of Sexual Danger in Late-Victorian London* (London: Virago, 1992) pp. 192–200.

  7 Kelly Hurley, *The Gothic Body: Sexuality, Materialism, and Degeneration at the Fin de Siècle*, (Cambridge: Cambridge University Press, 1996) p. 10. All subsequent references are to this edition, and are given in the text.

  8 Mary Shelley, *Frankenstein: or The Modern Prometheus*, (Harmondsworth: Penguin, 1985) p. 175. The creature, for example, understands *Paradise Lost* as if it were a true history.

  9 There are, incidently, striking similarities between this narrative and Charlotte Perkins Gilman's *The Yellow Wallpaper* (London: Virago [1892] 1990).

 10 Frederick Treves, 'A Cure for Nerves', *Reminiscences*, pp. 69–89, p.72. All subsequent references are to this edition, and are given in the text.

 11 The Female Gothic was a term originally coined by Ellen Moers in *Literary Women* (Women's Press: London, 1978). See also Juliann Fleenor (ed.), *The Female Gothic* (Montreal: Eden Press, 1983); Kate Ferguson Ellis, *The Contested Castle: Gothic Novels and the Subversion of Domestic Ideology* (Urbana and Chicago, IL: University of Illinois Press, 1989); Robert Miles (ed.), 'Female Gothic Writing', special issue of *Women's Writing: The Elizabethan to Victorian period, Triangle*, 1:2, 1994.

 12 Frederick Treves, 'A Restless Night', *Reminiscences*, pp. 135–54, p. 140. All subsequent references are to this edition, and are given in the text.

 13 Michel Foucault, *The History of Sexuality: An Introduction*, Vol. 1, trans. Robert Hurley (Harmondsworth: Penguin [1976] 1984) p. 94. All subsequent references are to this edition, and are given in the text.

3

The Whitechapel Murders: journalism, Gothic London and the medical gaze

London lies today under the spell of a great terror. A nameless reprobate – half-beast, half-man – is at large, who is daily gratifying his murderous instincts on the most miserable and defenceless of classes of the community. There can be no shadow of a doubt that ... the Whitechapel murderer, who has now four, if not five, victims to his knife, is one man, and that man a murderous maniac ... The ghoul-like creature, who stalks through the streets of London, stalking down his victim like a Pawnee Indian, is simply drunk with blood and will have more.

(*The Star*, 8 September 1888)[1]

The rowdy hobbledehoy is developing more and more rapidly into the savage of the slums. He in turn is becoming more and more akin to the monster – half-man, half-brute – who is now prowling round Whitechapel like the 'were-wolf' of Gothic fable. But where is this process of hideous evolution to stop? Are the resources of civilisation powerless against it?

(*Daily Chronicle*, 10 September 1888)[2]

The murder of five prostitutes working in the East End of London between 31 August and 9 November 1888 attracted, as is well documented, considerable attention from the media, social commentators, the public and politicians. The fact that the murderer acquired an almost myth-like status early on in the media discussion of the killings tends to obscure the reality of the murders, so that any discussion of them has to acknowledge both the complex web of social views which informed this process of mythologisation, and make some attempt at disentangling the specific concerns which they articulate. Judith R. Walkowitz's superlative analysis of 'Ripper narratives' in *City of Dreadful Delight* (1992) attempts just such an analysis of the often incompatible narratives (which included anti-Semitism, hostility to the medical profession, anti-vivisectionism, the claims of radical feminism, support for class agitation, and anti-Americanism) which contributed to speculation on the murderer's identity.[3]

In the previous chapter we saw how Frederick Treves, at both conscious and unconscious levels, associates the medical profession with pathologisation. There the failure of medicine represented both an epistemological failure *and* a failure of masculinity (or at least a professional middle-class version of it). One covert anxiety was that Merrick was too human, and that this proximity between normality and abnormality had the effect of destabilising the norm (and indeed the 'abnormal'). Merrick thus represented the presence of a deformed, but still 'normal' model of masculinity, and in this way 'norms' also become deformed. It is a process which was, as we shall see, reasserted by the role played by the medical profession at the time of the Whitechapel killings, and by a Gothic discourse which paralleled this process of deformation.

What was at issue was the nature of cultural visibility and it is important to note that there was a tendency for the victims to disappear in press speculation at the time of the murders, because the newspapers largely (although not exclusively) dwelt on the likely identity of the killer.[4] There has been some doubt about how many women were killed by the Whitechapel murderer, although the five definite victims were Mary Ann Nichols, Annie Chapman, Elizabeth Stride, Catherine Eddowes and Mary Jane Kelly.

Mary Ann Nichols was forty-three years old and had drifted into prostitution after the breakdown of her marriage in 1880. She was murdered in Buck's Row on 31 August. Annie Chapman was a forty-seven year old widow who worked selling matches and occasionally flowers, an income she supplemented by periodically working as a prostitute; she was murdered in Hanbury Street on 8 September. Elizabeth Stride and Catherine Eddowes were both murdered on 30 September. Elizabeth Stride was born in Sweden of Swedish parents, although she moved to London in 1866 when she was twenty-three. By the time of her murder she was forty-five years old, widowed, and had been working as a prostitute for some time; she was murdered in Berner Street. Catherine Eddowes was forty-six years old when she was murdered, she had just returned to London with her partner, John Kelly (whom she had lived with for seven years) from hop-picking in Kent. There is no conclusive evidence that she ever worked as a prostitute, although much speculation that she did. She was the only victim murdered in Mitre Square in the City of London (rather than the metropolitan area). The final victim was Mary Jane Kelly, who was a twenty-five year old widow murdered in Miller's Court, Dorset Street, on 9 November; she had worked as a prostitute since 1884. This chapter will discuss the inquest reports and the autopsies of Chapman and Stride, as well as the inquest and autopsy of Martha Tabram who the police believed at the time to be an early victim of the Whitechapel murderer. Martha Tabram was murdered on 7 August in George Yard, she was thirty-nine years old and had worked as prostitute for some time.

Before examining the way that the inquests discussed the victims and their likely killer, it is worth exploring how the press used elements of the Gothic in their coverage of the murders. Such reportage constructed London as a Gothic place, inhabited by Gothic villains who preyed on prostitutes. The press created, as we shall see, a Gothic ambience at the time which influenced the reporting of the inquests.

In relation to masculinity, two class-bound versions which the press discussed are initially referred to here: the doctor and the working-class 'Jack'. Media speculation that the murderer was an insane doctor became popular after publication of some details of how the victims had been murdered, details which suggested that the killer possessed a certain surgical expertise. After the first two murders, the 'Jack the Ripper' letters were sent to the Central News Agency and contributed to further, alternative speculation about the identity of the murderer. These two, very different versions of masculinity illustrate how widespread (from top to bottom) the fears were about culturally locating the murderer, as well as implicitly pathologising different masculine scripts. They also illustrate the presence of certain class tensions associated with London during the period.[5] However although the figure of 'Jack' in the account of class is touched on here, the principal focus in this chapter is on the figure of the doctor and how, and why, the medical profession became demonised at the time.

Gothic journalism

Concerns about the relationship between the wealth of the West End and the poverty of the East End were popularised by W.T. Stead in *The Pall Mall Gazette* and by journalists working on *Reynolds's Newspaper* (among others). Such journalism attempted to explain the Whitechapel murders as a consequence of class inequalities and typically represented the affluent West preying on the economically deprived East by using Gothic images to represent both the horrors of the East and the alleged sexual and financial corruption of the West. The more sensationalist press also used such images which, in an arguably cruder way, helped to develop a mode of male voyeurism that was central to most media debates (whether tabloid or broadsheet) relating to the murderer's identity.

The two quotations at the beginning of this chapter give some sense of how complicated such a Gothic view was. *The Star* makes reference to a 'half-beast, half-man' who was ghoulishly, vampirically, drinking the blood of his victims. The killer is figured as a largely supernatural figure, racially Othered and beyond redemption. This sensationalist language runs together the unreal (the ghoul) with the real (a more prosaic xenophobia concerning Indians), and this bringing together of the fantastic with social and racial prejudice develops one anxiety of the time: the image of the city overrun with dangerous foreigners. The quote from *The Daily Chronicle* is similar in its tone and treatment of the 'half-man, half-brute', but provides an alternative point of origin for the emergence of this strange 'monster'. Here the murderer has been generated out of their natural habitat of the slum. Significantly the *Chronicle* suggests, via a popular version of pseudo-Darwinian ideas, that this Gothic monstrosity was the product of misdeveloped evolutionary forces. Importantly an additional horror is credited here: the creature is not confined to place 'where is this process of hideous evolution to stop?'[6] An anxiety which was specific to media speculation was that the fashionable, wealthy West End could itself become infected by the poverty-stricken, degenerate East End and the main concern is therefore 'Are the resources of civilisation powerless against it?' However the issue of mobility is perhaps more metaphoric than this and suggests that the affluent middle class, who by attribution are representatives of the 'resources of civilisation', may themselves degenerate. The lure of the jungle becomes greater than that of money, culture and social respectability. This metaphor for the self-generated monstrous decline of civilisation might appear to be overstating the case, but it indicates how important a role figuration played in accounts of the murder and how such figuration incorporated anxieties which were, paradoxically, both genuinely held and 'fantastical'.

That the Gothic provides the literary provenance for much of this reportage is clear. The Gothic had influenced the reporting of particularly gruesome murders earlier in the nineteenth century, and the term 'horripilation' was coined to designate such journalism.[7] The anxieties concerning physical and racial hybridity which characterises at least one version of the monstrous killer facilitates the development in the sensationalist press of certain, already Gothicised notions of degeneracy which were explored in Chapter 1. The Gothic becomes both a literary device through which speculation concerning the identity of the murderer was organised, and a means through which a political vision relating to race, sex, and class, became expressed. However, it is also relevant for the purpose of this inquiry to break down the Gothic into two distinct modes which highlight the role that gender plays in Gothic formations: the Male Gothic and the Female Gothic.

The Male Gothic, with its literary roots in the Gothic of the 1790s, as in Matthew Lewis's *The Monk* (1796), was characterised by its representation of male violence, female persecution, and semi-pornographic scenes. Ann Radcliffe in 'On the Supernatural in Poetry' (1826) discussed the relationship between the Male Gothic and the Female Gothic (although these were not her terms) as one between Horror (associated with direct showing) and Terror (characterised by subtle gesture and implication).[8] This is not solely a matter of a preferred aesthetic; they suggest quite different political views. The Female Gothic is a form of writing which, in its focus on anxieties relating to women's experience of domestic tyranny and response to patriarchal plots, examines the limits of patriarchal experience and the possibility of female empowerment. Also, Radcliffe's use of Terror enables her to construct an often complex debate about the imagination and sublimity which makes explicit the kind of covert patriarchal politics to be found in Idealist philosophical debate at the time.[9] In contrast, Lewis's reliance on Horror is indicated by his evocation of semi-pornographic visual images, and it is the Male Gothic's voyeurism which dominated the newspaper reportage during the murders. The fascination with the killer, with their acts of violence and strange sexual proclivities, overshadows other, more measured debates concerning the victims and the social and economic world that they inhabited. In its most basic media constructions we can observe the fantastical Male Gothic world of the killer, and the alternative Female Gothic world of the victims, which is shadowy, not properly understood, and subject to epistemic concealment. Walkowitz notes how such press speculation actively worked towards the suppression of any Female Gothic elements by reconfiguring such elements as part of a Male Gothic fantasy:

> At the local level, working-class women participated in informal storytelling, providing information that others used to process clues. A similar reprocessing occurred in relation to feminist and antivivisectionist representations of prostitution and of the sexual dangers of medicine. Media coverage of the murders took up the themes and narratives of female reformers and reworked them into a male-directed fantasy, closer in tone and perspective to the literature of urban exploration and the male Gothic than to female political melodrama. (*City of Dreadful Delight*, p. 192)

In this way the bodies of the dead prostitutes were interesting to the press only to the extent that they generated a figurative transcription of the killer's identity. Although some press reports also dwelt on the tragic lives of the victims, these tended to be contrasted with the more mysterious, and therefore more intriguing, world of the killer.

L. Perry Curtis, Jr. has argued that, 'Fleet Street habitually reduced the complex and often disputed facts of felonious crimes to a few morally charged "truths" that continually reinscribed the boundary between normative and deviant behaviour'.[10] In other words the Gothic was used in order to illustrate the presence of cultural norms. However, it is worth emphasising that such a celebration of the 'norm' was related to the idea of normative masculine gender scripts. There is a knotted paradox in this because the Male Gothic is both 'normative', in the sense that it provides expression to dominant patriarchal values, and 'pathological' because such values shade into violent sexual and physical acts. This means that the norm becomes (truly) pathologised, and in part this is indicated by the reliance on Gothic plots which tend to suggest the cultural normalisation of male pathology. This is, of course, a paradoxical and ambivalent position. However, David Punter has argued, with considerable persuasion, that the Gothic is founded on political and moral ambivalence (a form which, like the sensationalist newspaper reports, is fascinated by that which it is ostensibly appalled by). Such ambivalence is rooted in a notion of class, as Punter states, 'The central contradiction ... from which all the others flow, is this: that Gothic can at one and the same time be categorised as a middle class and as an anti-middle-class literature'.[11] A claim about class which, as we shall see, intersects with notions of masculinity.

Media speculation effectively demonised two kinds of masculinity, that of the urban working classes (Jack), and that of the bourgeois professional (a demonic doctor).[12] These fears were generated out of pre-existing anxieties relating to class tensions at the time, and from the idea of a bifurcated London (both civilised and barbaric). The newspapers often exploited literary narratives that apparently confirmed the presence of a Gothic London. R.L. Stevenson's *The Strange Case of Doctor Jekyll and Mr Hyde* (1886) became *the* Gothic narrative that explicitly influenced the reportage of the murders. Before discussing Stevenson's novella it is necessary to politically map what kind of London was configured at the time.

Gothic London: civilisation and its discontents

Andrew Mearns's *The Bitter Cry of Outcast London: An Inquiry into the Condition of the Abject Poor* (1883) represents London in terms of moral monstrosity.[13] The horror was that civilisation and barbarism had acquired an unhealthy proximity in which, 'concealed by the thinnest crust of civilisation and decency, is a vast mass of moral corruption, of heart-breaking misery and absolute godlessness'.[14] For Mearns this represents a failure of the Christian mission to properly morally educate (or redeem) the urban poor for whom 'Incest is common' and in whom 'no form of vice and sensuality causes surprise or attracts attention' (pp. 29–30). The East End is represented as a world of Gothic ruins consisting of 'rotten and reeking tenements' (p. 29). Mearns advocates state intervention as the only viable means of transforming, both physically and morally, the East End. What is important in Mearns's account is the suggested presence of a terrifying urban jungle that threatens the forces of civilisation. The implied threat is that this kind of moral pollution could spread to other, ostensibly more respectable, parts of the city; the necessity of controlling the East is therefore in the interests of the West. Mearns's treatise is couched in a language of moral despair although he acknowledged that the financial difficulties of the area also played a role in forcing people into criminal activity. Nevertheless he emphasises the divided nature of the city and failed to properly address the relationship between the wealth of the West End and the poverty of the East End, an issue which W.T. Stead famously addressed in his 'The Maiden Tribute of Modern Babylon' (1885).

For Stead the two parts of the city were more financially intimate with each other than Mearns suggested. Specifically Stead sexualises the relationship between the two parts of the city by focusing on the trade in underage prostitutes, a trade situated in the East but predominately catering for clients in the West. For Stead the trade had become possible because it followed the dictates of an unregulated market economy. Child prostitution formed a black market economy that horrifically doubled (echoed) the 'normal' amoral objectification of the market place. Indeed, he went so far as to suggest that it was this amorality which produced, not merely marketed, 'vice': 'The more freely we permit to adults absolute liberty to dispose of their persons in accordance with the principles of private contract and free trade, the more stringent must be our precautions against the innumerable crimes which spring from vice, as vice itself springs from the impure imaginings of the heart of man.'[15] Money and immorality were thus closely linked by Stead and so implicated the West in the spread of both economic and moral corruption. Stead rather proved his point about how class interests were being met by being sent to prison, with three months hard labour, for procuring a child prostitute, although this was in the honourable interests of writing his article.[16] However, although Stead is writing out of a radical tradition there are certain textual locutions which align his piece with more fantastical narratives. Walkowitz notes, 'Stead may have positioned himself publicly in relation to the populist traditions of political melodrama, but in fact he kept shifting genres … moving from costume drama to detective fiction, constituting himself corresponding as a modern-day Theseus or as a more up-to-date scientific investigator' (*City of Dreadful Delight*, p. 94). Stead's controlling conceit of the mythic Minotaur devouring the Athenian youths sent to Crete as a tribute for their defeat of Athens, is an uneasy one. Stead often images himself as their saviour, but in his procurement of the prostitute, Lily, he seems to become the Minotaur (no matter how honourable his journalistic intent). For Walkowitz, this final attempt by Stead to authenticate his argument puts him in the awkward position of a faux client and although this was not in the interests of sensationalist journalism, nevertheless a male voyeurism was instituted in the process, 'Disequilibrium and excess shaped Stead's account of the double life and took its toll on the investigator. For he seems to have gone over the edge in his attempt to authenticate and document criminal vice' (p. 101). For Walkowitz, Stead's narrative has 'eerie features' which illustrate this unease. This also helps to develop the notion of ambivalence touched on earlier because it is central to the Gothic and to newspaper accounts of the Whitechapel murders. Stead becomes, at some implicit level, the thing that he detests and the idea that he, Stead, has 'gone over the edge' associates male narratives with pathology. While none of this might have been the conscious intent of Stead, nevertheless the voyeuristic elements in his narrative helped to support a market which catered for a male fascination with the pornographic aspects of sex crimes; his report had 'for a mere one penny … put into circulation lurid images and narratives that were usually restricted to readers of three-guinea volumes' (p. 124). For Walkowitz such male pornography allied Stead with the Male Gothic and indicated his need to project repressed desires while simultaneously attempting to contain or conceal them through an assertion of a restorative rationality and a sense of injustice. Such a notion of repression is familiar from the *fin de siècle* Gothic and is implicit in Stead's interest in the supernatural as evidenced by his editorship, between 1893 and 1897, of the occult magazine *Borderland*. As we shall see, this Gothic ambience permeates the reportage of the murders.

This notion of ambivalence is central to four related issues which came to bear during the Whitechapel murders: desire, masculinity, medicine and class. Stead's narrative indicates a covert ambivalence about desire but he also makes an association between sex and trade that he would return to during the murders. Prostitution and its proximity to notions of West End 'respectability' is the central link here. If for Mearns the poor were largely responsible for their moral depravity, for Stead it was the wealthy middle classes who were really depraved. The idea of a double life, or a conflicted life, complicated such moral clarity and it is not coincidental that the *fin de siècle* Gothic revels in figures of the double to be found in Stevenson's *Jekyll and Hyde*, Wilde's *The Picture of Dorian Gray* (1891) and Stoker's *Dracula* (1897). Such doubling was also reflected in media speculation concerning the very different class attributes of the murderer, a bourgeois doctor or the cockney Jack, which played on Stevenson's class tensions in *Jekyll and Hyde*. However, what is also a key area in these narratives about doubles is the cultural, social, and seemingly psychic space of London. As suggested, the West End becomes related to the East End through financial exploitation or through immoral influence. The city also, at a metaphoric level, became personified as a monstrous Gothic being whose double life appeared to be beyond rational control. That models of masculinity became implicated in this 'horror' (the 'good' bourgeois, the working class 'Jack') received an added emphasis given that accounts of the relationship between West End and East End frequently exploited the language of Empire. As we saw in Chapter 1, commentators such as Hake, Kingsley and Lankester made, at different levels of explicitness, associations between images of nation and formulations of masculinity in their respective writings on degeneration. These links between masculinity and Empire are also evident in accounts of London at the time.

William Booth in *In Darkest England and the Way Out* (1890) makes direct reference to H.M. Stanley's *Darkest Africa* which was published in the same year. Images of the urban jungle and its dangers were popular at the time, but Booth suggests that Stanley's identification of two types of pygmies to be found in Africa, 'one a very degraded specimen ... nearly approaching the baboon' the other 'handsome, with frank open innocent features' reflects, in a deliberately evoked class-bound way, London and its social tensions.[17] For Booth, as for Mearns, the greatest anxiety is caused by the proximity of civilisation and barbarism, 'May we not find a parallel at our own doors, and discover within a stone's throw of our cathedrals and palaces similar horrors to those which Stanley has found existing in the great Equatorial forest?' (p. 46). However, Booth develops the idea that economic corruption has played a significant part in creating the conditions under which such barbarism could flourish. Revealingly, he indicates this by developing Stead's concern about prostitution and its causes and so focuses on the role that masculinity *and* class play in creating corruption: 'A young penniless girl, if she be pretty, is often hunted from pillar to post by her employers, confronted always by the alternative – Starve or Sin. And when once the poor girl has consented to buy the right to earn her living by the sacrifice of her virtue, then she is treated as a slave and an outcast by the very men who have ruined her' (p. 47). The proximity of the West to the East is an economic one, but also a sexual one.

The fascination that the West had with the East was thus conditioned by a form of male voyeurism, one which transformed the East into a spectacle of depravity that simultaneously attracted and repelled. This assertion of a male voyeurism is also clear in the sensationalist newspaper reports of the Whitechapel murders which attempted to give an identity to the killer, but left the victims voiceless and passive, because as Booth states, for the prostitute 'Her word becomes unbelievable' (p. 47). Ultimately, what can and cannot be said was related to issues of visibility and invisibility that implicated a male gaze in the construction of its own 'horrors'.[18]

That London was seen as a Gothic site in which fears relating to race, desire and class were debated has links to this ambivalent expression of male authority. Such authority emphasises control, difference and ownership, however the suggested horrors of the time also imply a challenge to that authority and it was for this reason that *Jekyll and Hyde* became a key Gothic narrative.

Jekyll and Hyde

In Chapter 1 *Jekyll and Hyde* was discussed in relation to theories of degeneration. The novella, at one level, evidences an anxiety that the middle-class professional male could, under certain circumstances, degenerate to a more atavistic state. To that extent the story relocates the tensions between civilisation and barbarism that are familiar both from models of degeneration and accounts of London. True horror, as in Mearns, Stead and William Booth's versions of London, is to be found lurking within. For this reason the novella was taken up during the murders as one of the main narrative forms through which the horrors of the murders could be sensationally exploited and explained.

On 1 September, the *Globe* stated that 'One can almost imagine that Whitechapel is haunted by a demon of the type of Hyde, who goes about killing for the mere sake of slaughter.'[19] It was an image developed in Stead's *Pall Mall Gazette* a week later when the reporter, in an attempt to describe the apparently lawless East End, claimed that 'There certainly seems to be a tolerably realistic impersonification of Mr. Hyde at large in Whitechapel.'[20] As Walkowitz and Curtis note, the *Gazette* exploited Stevenson's novella in order to suggest the double life of the city in which the West preyed upon the East.[21] Stead seems to have been particularly keen in his reworking of some of the ideas from 'Maiden Tribute', to propose that a real life version of the respectable Dr Jekyll, in the guise of Hyde, was preying upon working-class prostitutes, and this became a popular means of representing class conflict during the crisis.[22]

This blurring between literature and reality, or between the metaphorical and the literal, was made graphically clear in the treatment of the American actor, Richard Mansfield, who was appearing in a stage production of *Jekyll and Hyde* which opened in the West End in August 1888. Mansfield's performance was notable for two reasons: he played both Jekyll and Hyde (effecting a particularly gruesome transformation from one to the other via lighting effects and the strategic use of make-up), and he portrayed Hyde as a sexual sadist (which is quite different to Stevenson's Hyde).[23] The play thus emphasised that Jekyll was both Jekyll and Hyde, rather than that Hyde was somehow a different, and distanced, aspect of Jekyll. The proximity of Good and Evil also gave emphasis to the anxieties to be found in the commentaries of Mearns, Stead and William Booth. This also explains why Mansfield was briefly marked out as a suspect for the murders.

It appears that the play touched on these earlier concerns about the relationship between civilisation and barbarism. The reporter for the *Pall Mall Gazette* interpreted the play as illustrating an uncomfortable truth about the British psyche: 'The critic may curse the morbid and the horrible, but the craving for them is deeply rooted. Scratch John Bull and you find the ancient Briton who revels in blood, who loves to dip deep into a murder, and devours the details of a hanging.'[24] However, the mere fact that audiences were drawn to it also implied that such a national malaise was already lurking within the body politic. The reporter's comments also register the kind of ambivalence that characterises the Gothic, as it is unclear what kind of moral message was promoted by the play, or established by the apparent pleasure derived by the audience. Instead the reviewer simply discovers a moment of self-reflection, in which a play about doubling echoes the morbidity of the nation's psyche.

While superficially the novella is a psychodrama about the relationship between its principal protagonists, its representation of doubling is more complex than it initially appears, and an exploration of how the book constitutes the relationship between the city and the self can enlighten us about why the story had a particular grip on the media imagination at the time of the murders.

Stevenson parallels the relationship between Jekyll and Hyde with a class narrative concerning London. The walk around London with which the novella begins addresses the proximity between wealth and poverty. We are informed of the street that:

> The inhabitants were all doing well, it seemed, and all emulously hoping to do better still, and laying out the surplus of their gains in coquetry; so that the shop fronts stood along the thoroughfare with an air of invitation, like rows of smiling saleswomen ... its freshly painted shutters, well-polished brasses, and general cleanliness and gaiety of note, instantly caught and pleased the eye of the passenger.[25]

However:

> Two doors from one corner, on the left hand going east, the line was broken by the entry of a court; and just at that point, a certain sinister block of building thrust forward its gable on the street ... Tramps slouched into the recess and struck matches on the panels; children kept shop upon the steps; the schoolboy had tried his knife on the mouldings. (p. 30)

This is the backdrop against which Hyde makes his first appearance. The novella's representation of a power struggle between Jekyll and Hyde should therefore not solely be seen as a psychodrama; rather it implies the class tensions between different parts of the city. Also, the novella argues the case, in a way that is familiar from Stead, that the two parts of the city have an intimate connection. As Robert Mighall has noted, Hyde's association with Soho (which is in a somewhat unrespectable part of the West End) implies that the area's 'relation to respectable London is ... a topographical replication of Hyde within Jekyll' so that 'When Jekyll effects his dissociation, he reproduces the imaginary mapping of his internal divisions. Placing the anthropologically "low" body of Hyde, in the lower district of the city'.[26] In addition, Stevenson began writing the novel after his friend, W.E. Henley, had passed on to him instalments from Stead's 'Maiden Tribute'.[27] The novella is ultimately pessimistic about the likelihood of any social resolution between such opposing classes and areas of the city. Jekyll suggests that this might become possible when society itself disappears, a time when 'man will be ultimately known for a mere polity of multifarious, incongruous denizens' (p. 82), although this hardly suggests a Utopia.

The novella develops Stead's idea that conflict is a product of wealth. The divided self appears to be a product of the divisions between wealth and poverty. Hyde's relationship is, as discussed in Chapter 1, one in which he becomes unrepresentable because he is an unspoken aspect of the male bourgeois imagination. However, if we isolate Hyde in purely social terms we can see that this problem of representation in which as Enfield notes 'I can't describe him' (p. 34) is a consequence of social proximity. Hyde is too close to these bourgeois interpreters for them to exercise the necessary independent distance at which an objective representation could be made.

Social proximity, visibility and invisibility, would become key issues for debate at the time of the murders. Hyde is not a sex-killer like the murderer, but the novella in implicating bourgeois professionals in his secretive, and presumably nefarious, activities makes supposedly 'decent' men culpable in the generation of vice; a strand which was developed in some of the reportage cited earlier. Also Hyde is somebody whose identity is, for Jekyll's friends, fundamentally mysterious. For Enfield, Hyde is 'an extraordinary-looking man, and yet I really can name nothing out of the way' (p. 34). He is extraordinary and ordinary at the same time because his pathologies demonise class and gender 'norms', while he, simultaneously, seems to operate within those norms. The problem is that Hyde appears to resemble a gentleman, but does not quite convince that he is one. Hyde tells the crowd that surrounds him after the incident where he trampled the child 'No gentleman but wishes to avoid a scene' (p. 32), as he offers the child's family money in recompense, but then a 'true' gentleman would not have harmed the child in the first place.

However, as discussed in Chapter 1, the role of the gentleman was progressively undermined in the period. Although media speculation on the identity of the murderer emphasised class relations, such relations were also regarded, as witnessed by Stead and William Booth, in sexual terms. The pathologisation of men thus became a central, if covert, issue.

We have seen how *Jekyll and Hyde* provided a way of reading the murders which addressed class tensions. Masculinity also became implicated in the killings in part because of an additional emphasis in the novella on male, bourgeois, professionals. As we saw in Chapter 1, such figures as Jekyll, Lanyon and Utterson lead lives that had been hollowed out of all moral and social significance and consequently they are represented as alienated Gothic figures. Class is therefore linked to gender, and this link is re-emphasised in media speculation that a 'mad' doctor was responsible

for the killings. It might seem as though Jekyll functions as the model of a
'mad' doctor here, however the provenance for these anxieties is more
complex because it brings together more than one narrative. Accounts of
the victims' autopsies, for example, also initially suggested this idea of a
deranged doctor as a possible culprit.

Dr George Phillips who carried out the autopsy on Annie Chapman
claimed that the murder weapon could have been of the type 'used for
post-mortem purposes' and that the killer evinced 'some anatomical
knowledge'.[28] *The Times* reported the coroner's belief that there was a
purpose behind the incisions, although why the murderer removed the
uterus was not clear. The lack of motivation was an obvious obstacle to
the investigation. The coroner (Wynne E. Baxter) informed the jury that,
'they were confronted with a murder of no ordinary character, committed
not from jealousy, revenge, or robbery, but from motives less adequate
than many which still disgraced our civilization'.[29]

The idea that a 'mad' doctor was responsible for the murders began to
be widely discussed in the press and this, alongside some of the suggestions
made at the inquest, meant that the police took this seriously. D.G. Halstead
whose views on Merrick were touched on in Chapter 2, trained as a doctor
at the London Hospital in the Whitechapel Road and noted of this period
that: 'Suspicion immediately turned upon my colleagues and myself, and
I often had the feeling, especially when I was walking home late at night,
that the inhabitants were shunning me and that the plain-clothes men
were following my movements'.[30] Chief Inspector Donald Swanson, who
was in charge of the Whitechapel investigation, wrote to the Home Office
on 19 October and stated that 'Enquiries were ... made to trace three
insane medical students who had attended London Hospital, two traced,
one gone abroad'.[31] They were ultimately excluded from the enquiry, but
the notion that an insane doctor was the culprit was considered throughout
the police investigation.

In December 1888 one Dr Robert Stephenson (who was later entertained
as a likely candidate for the killer) wrote to the Home Office concerning
the behaviour of a Dr Morgan Davies, who was treating Stephenson as a
patient at the London Hospital.[32] Stephenson recounted that after a
discussion about the murders, Davies enacted a scene to illustrate how he
thought they had been committed. For Stephenson, the frenetic display
suggested the mental instability of Davies and a first hand knowledge of
the murders: 'He took a knife "buggered" an imaginary woman, cut her
throat from behind; then, when she was apparently laid prostrate, ripped
& slashed her in all directions in a perfect state of frenzy'.[33] This strange,

seemingly insane re-enactment also resonates with a wider view of the medical profession at the time, a view which continued long after the murders had stopped. In October 1889, for example, an anonymous letter was sent to the Home Office relating to 'a Dr. in practice' who was 'rather strange in his manners' and who was additionally suspicious because 'The last letter purporting to be written by Jack the R – was found ... within [a quarter] hours walking distance of Dr's lodgings'.[34] Although Swanson dismissed the letter as 'the product of an excited imagination', it does illustrate the extent to which the public regarded the medical profession with suspicion.[35] A suspicion which can be confirmed by a reading of the autopsy reports.

The politics of the autopsy

When looking at the autopsy reports on the victims we are to some significant degree moving beyond the kind of imaginative speculation to be found in the press. Elisabeth Bronfen has noted in *Over Her Dead Body: Death, Femininity and the Aesthetic* (1992):

> It seems as necessary to stress the fundamental difference between real violence done to the physical body and any 'imagined' one ... [because] it is necessary to explore the way in which these two registers come to be conflated and confused. Not because the latter can then be absolved of any responsibility towards the material of its depiction but because to collapse the two levels on which signification works might also mean not doing justice to the uniquely horrible violence that occurs when a body is used quite literally as the site for an inscription by another.[36]

The accounts of the autopsies bridge these two worlds of the real and the imaginary. They are both accounts of real deaths and textual performances which encode, other, hidden 'realities' relating to the politics of the medical profession in general, and a peculiarly pathologised, strangely directed, male gaze in particular.

The autopsies indicate that what was at issue was not just the way in which the victims died, but how healthy they were at the time of death. That is to say that there was an additional narrative which was looking for signs of disease; typically venereal disease, alcoholism, malnutrition and general indicators of social deprivation which could, at least theoretically, render the victim complicit with their fate.

Martha Tabram, who may or may not have been the Whitechapel killer's first victim,[37] was described by Dr Timothy Killeen in his report to the inquest in these terms:

Her age was about 36, and the body was very well nourished ... The left
lung was penetrated in five places, and the right lung penetrated in two
places. The heart, which was rather fatty, was penetrated in one place, and
that would be sufficient to cause death. The liver was healthy, but was
penetrated in five places, the spleen, which was perfectly healthy, was
penetrated in six places.[38]

The emphasis is on Tabram's relative health at the time of her death, but
this search for pathology reveals how an alternative narrative 'read' the
signs of injury alongside the signs of health. Nothing incriminating can
be learnt about Tabram from the state of her body, she is neither syphilitic
nor alcoholic and so eludes any attempt to 'read' her body as pathologised.

The autopsy report on Annie Chapman contains the seemingly
irrelevant comment that 'The front teeth were perfect, so far as the first
molar, top and bottom, and very fine teeth they were'.[39] Later Dr Phillips
notes:

The deceased was far advanced in disease of the lungs and membranes of
the brain ... The stomach contained a little food, but there was not any
signs of fluid. There was no appearance of the deceased having taken alcohol,
but there were signs of great deprivation, and he should say she had been
badly fed. He was convinced she had not taken any strong alcohol for some
hours before her death.[40]

This part of the autopsy brings together a range of issues relating to the
moral and social standing of the victim. The signs of deprivation and
malnutrition suggest Chapman's social context, although ultimately this
passage represents a search for agency. Chapman's status as a 'genuine'
victim is being evaluated in these claims about social context
(malnutrition) and personal responsibility (the failed search for signs of
alcohol abuse). The implicit question raised here is, to what extent was
Chapman responsible for her death?

Alongside this search for visible signs of disease exists an alternative
narrative concerning the identity of the killer which implicates the medical
profession, because the cuts on Chapman's body appear to have been
inflicted by someone who possessed anatomical knowledge. Dr Phillips
was reluctant to give further details about how Chapman's body had been
mutilated. Baxter cleared the courtroom of women and children and
Phillips, according to the journalist from *The Times*, 'proceeded to give
medical and surgical evidence, totally unfit for publication'.[41] That medicine
and the press agreed that there existed a line beyond which disclosures
could not be made indicates a shared cultural notion concerning 'taste'.

However, it also served to conceal what came to be seen as important 'clues' about the likely occupation, and so identity, of the killer.

Narratives of social deprivation had already, as we have seen, been widely discussed in accounts of London by social commentators and journalists. Such discussion, as in Phillips's search for the signs of alcoholism, had also nodded towards this debate about the moral status of the subjects living in the East End. Such narratives about London helped to make the dangerous, seemingly irrational, urban spaces explicable (at least in social terms) whereas the murders suggested the continuing presence of the irrational and the inexplicable (the murderer's actions being difficult to account for in terms of social context). And yet the murders had a proximity to medicine which was in its own way as troubling as the proximity of the West to the East. The hidden narrative at the Chapman inquest related to how the mutilation of the body after death resembled an autopsy. Dr Phillips informed the now partially emptied court room that: 'The abdomen had been entirely laid open: the intestines, severed from the mesenteric attachments, had been lifted out of the body and placed on the shoulder of the corpse; whilst from the pelvis, the uterus and its appendages with the upper portion of the vagina and the posterior two-thirds of the bladder, had been entirely removed.'[42] For Phillips, 'Obviously the work was that of an expert – of one, at least, who had such knowledge of anatomical or pathological examinations as to be enabled to secure the pelvic organs with one sweep of the knife'.[43] Indeed, in response to questions from the coroner, Phillips evinced some grudging admiration by indicating that it would have taken him around fifteen minutes to effect such an operation, and that if he had done it in a proper manner 'as would fall to the duties of a surgeon it probably would have taken … the best part of an hour' (p. 350).[44] The killer had done this in a matter of minutes.

The question was whether this apparently pathologised autopsy indicated the signs of madness or implied something that was central, but concealed within, models of the 'norm'. *The Lancet* came down on the side of normalisation when it suggested that, 'It is most unusual for a lunatic to plan any complicated crime of this kind. Neither, as a rule, does a lunatic take precautions to escape from the consequences of his act; which *data* are most conspicuous in these now celebrated cases'.[45] The murderer's behaviour was atypical and so suggested sanity. Also, this normalisation of the pathological is relevant to how the autopsies examined what looked like earlier autopsies, rather than murders. In this way there is an unusual moment of self-reflection in which the medical profession confronts a version of its 'normal' processes, although processes which are pathologised because they cause death rather than explain it. Nevertheless it was an encounter that challenged the distinction between 'normal' and 'pathological'. Sander L. Gilman in a commentary on the German expressionist Gottfried Benn's fictionalised account of an autopsy notes how, 'The physician's eye is always cast to examine and find the source of pathology ... hidden within the woman's body', but that this search becomes reflected back on to the Doctor who is rendered pathological in the process (in the cutting up of dead women).[46] Gilman's argument largely addresses the representation of 'Jack', but she also discusses this in relation to medicine and acknowledges the existence of a relationship in which 'Jack' actually represents a form of doctoring:

> Killing and dismembering, searching after the cause of corruption and disease. The paradigm for the relationship between Jack and the prostitutes can be taken from the popular medical discourse of the period: *Similia similibus curantur*, 'like cures like,' the motto of C.F.S. Hahnemann, the founder of homeopathic medicine. The scourge of the streets, the carrier of disease, can be eliminated only by one who is equally corrupt and diseased. (p. 268)

In this way 'Jack' is really a synonym for 'doctor'. Although a coroner such as Baxter expressed considerable sympathy for the plight of the victims, D.G. Halstead referred to them as diseased purveyors of syphilis and claimed that, 'It must have been ... an almost moral urge to purify the East End of these plague-bearing harpies' (p. 56). Halstead's reference to the second victim (Mary Ann Nichols) also dwelt, cruelly, on her alleged immorality, 'The victim was a slut of a woman who had been heard of in the Lambeth workhouse, and had stolen £3 from her employer when working as a servant' (*Doctor in the Nineties*, pp. 46–7).

As we saw in the previous chapter, there were anxieties relating to the conduct of the medical profession expressed within the profession itself. The proximity of the killer's actions to 'normal' medical procedure also suggests this pathologisation of medicine, a view which was quickly developed in the press and which contributed to a widespread cultural distrust of doctors at the time.

Jekyll and Hyde and Hyde's apparent abnormality is relevant to this process of pathologisation because it suggests the presence of an abnormality, a pathology, which is observed but which cannot be accounted for, precisely because it implies (as would the autopsies) that pathology is inherent to specific notions of the 'norm'. This is implicit in the demonisation of medicine, but also reflects on the idea of criminal responsibility. The murders are not ordinary crimes because there is no demonstrable motivation for them (notwithstanding considerable press speculation about this), and paradoxically this suggests that 'abnormalities' in the guise of clues are not produced. The killer cannot be identified because, like Hyde, he becomes a kind of everyman and therefore, as suggested in *The Lancet*, normalised. What is truly horrific is that he represents a kind of male collective unconscious, which would also explain why so many different, frequently incompatible suspects were entertained at various times. The point is that the killer does not appear as a special, specifically and clearly motivated figure.

Crime and symptoms

One strange paradox was that the killer's extraordinariness emerged from his ordinariness. The lack of the usual motivations for his crimes distanced him from the typical criminal and thus rendered the crimes extraordinary. A report by Robert Anderson, who took charge of the Whitechapel investigation from 6 October 1888 until the file closed in 1892, to the Home Office, dated 23 October 1888, noted: 'That a crime of this kind should have been committed without any clue being supplied by the criminal is unusual, but that five successive murders should have been committed without our having the slightest clue of any kind is extraordinary, if not unique in the annals of crime.'[47]

The signs of crime and the symptoms of disease were conflated at this time. To return to *Jekyll and Hyde* for a moment we can see that the novella links Hyde with criminality *and* disease, although it is not clear what Hyde's crimes are. Hyde is not a sexually sadistic criminal but the associations made between sex crime and Hyde in the press (the West End gentleman preying on East End prostitutes) emphasised a link between pathology and sexual criminality. However, the demonisation of doctors (as in media speculation and in *Jekyll and Hyde*) means that the 'norm', or a bourgeois professional middle-class construction of it, also becomes pathologised. Hyde, like the Whitechapel murderer, eludes attempts to interpret him because his pathologies are developed from within (in ways also suggested by Stead). Pathologies therefore produced symptoms which, within the context of the murder investigation, were then read as 'clues' about identity.

Crime also represents the presence of social disease, one which can only be made present through signs of explicable agency. An example of this is to be found in a domestic murder that took place in Whitechapel only a few hours before the murders of Elizabeth Stride and Catherine Eddowes.

The Times carried a report on 1 October detailing how John Brown murdered his wife and then gave himself up to the police at Rochester Row, telling them that he had killed her 'in consequence of [her] unfaithfulness'. *The Times* also noted that 'the Police went to the house, where the woman was found lying dead on the floor with her throat cut. Several wounds had been inflicted in the shape of stabs and cuts'. Brown's actions were explicable because there was a suggestion of motivation, even though it appears as though he was suffering from some mental disturbance at the time; whereas two hours later the murder of Elizabeth Stride by the Whitechapel killer remained a mystery because of the lack of motivation.[48] There were therefore normalised murders, which are made sense of by the domestic context in which they occurred, and other murders which failed to produce evidence. Agency is the key issue here, as Baxter had commented at the Chapman inquest 'There were no meaningless cuts', even though what they signified was unclear. Attention therefore turned to the bodies of the victims, as if they could generate the necessary clues.[49]

At this point narratives about London and degeneration become relevant, but the search for pathology was not just a search for signs of social depravity. There was always the implication that the victims were themselves responsible, at least potentially, for their plights. For this reason, as we have seen, a medical gaze subjected the bodies to an analysis of how healthy they were. We saw this in the Tabram and Chapman autopsy reports, and it appears again in Stride's which includes the claim that 'the brain was fairly normal'.[50] It is this pursuit for the signs of mental instability which suggests that the supposed mental instability of the killer is transferred to one of his victims; and yet, as the Brown murder indicated, mental instability did not in itself generate mysterious murders. Brown's apparently insensible, and manifestly misogynistic act could be rationalised (although not legitimated), but this merely indicates just how misogynistic such rationalisations could become.

As we have seen, the medical profession was seemingly confronted, at least as various authors of the autopsy reports saw it, with an image of themselves. The suggested medical knowledge combined with the idea that they were essentially producing autopsies about autopsies, placed the medical gaze in a strange narcissistic moment in which everything is familiar but unfamiliar at the same time. This constitutes a moment of self-reflection which can be usefully explored through Freud's idea of the 'uncanny', because it provides an insight into the construction of the cultural anxieties which such an encounter generates. It also helps to reposition the debate about the 'normal' and the pathological which illuminates the dilemmas faced by medicine at the time.

Freud, the uncanny and medicine

Freud's 'uncanny' has a special place in the analysis of the Gothic. The eighteenth-century Gothic exploited Burke's notion of Terror (Radcliffe) or developed some of those elements into a version of Horror (Lewis). This kind of Male Gothic 'horripiliation' certainly conditioned a form of male voyeurism in sensationalist newspaper reports on the murders. However, Burke's early attempt at accounting for a psychology of Terror through notions of the sublime became historically replaced by Freud's account of fear in 'The Uncanny'.[51] Freud's notion of the double is clearly relevant here, and as suggested earlier it is central to *Jekyll and Hyde*, Wilde's *Dorian Gray*, and slightly more obliquely to Stoker's *Dracula*. So far *Jekyll and Hyde* has largely been examined in social rather than psychoanalytical terms as this enables us to reconsider the relationship between the text and its reconstruction of the social context of London. At this juncture it is helpful to examine how the autopsy reports can be read through Freud's idea of the uncanny because it clarifies their cultural context (rather than sheds light on the psychology of their respective authors). In spirit this is a line of enquiry indebted to Peter Stallybrass and Allon White, who in *The Politics and Poetics of Transgression* (1986) explored how the body of the urban subject was, in the nineteenth century, read in terms of the body politic of the city. In this way noble thoughts corresponded to the presence of urban civilisation whereas low bodily functions or urges corresponded to the slums and sewers of an outcast London.[52] In other words the prevailing models of urban subjectivity were formed through metaphors of the city, meaning that a psychoanalytical account of such subject formation also tells us something about the city (which also goes some way in explaining why *Jekyll and Hyde* became one of the dominant means of accounting for the murders in social *and* psychological terms).

For Freud the terms of the uncanny, *unheimlich* and *heimlich*, or uncanny and homely, slide into each other in an (uncanny) way; so that the everyday, the homely, also becomes the site of secrets, specifically defining family secrets which condition the self in certain Oedipal ways. The issue of secrecy and visibility is as central to this process as it is to the autopsies which are also trying to explain that 'which is obscure, inaccessible to knowledge'.[53] For Freud the double emerges as our conscience by 'exercising a censorship within the mind' and so represents the emergence of a moral sensibility

(p. 357). However, at some stage in the development of the ego the double starts to take on a more sinister aspect as it goes through a transformation in which 'From having been an assurance of immortality, it becomes the uncanny harbinger of death' (p. 357). This model of psychological development becomes relevant to our enquiry at the point where Freud associates such a feeling of uncanniness with the dead: 'Many people experience the feeling in the highest degree in relation to dead and dead bodies' (p. 364). Such an encounter inevitably creates feelings of anxiety.

In the autopsy reports there is a literalised encounter with the dead, the sense of uncanniness that these bodies generate for the medical profession is in part related to how they appear to have been subjected to a particularly brutal (but in their own way 'skilled') autopsy. In this way the 'normal' and the pathological become conflated. However, this conflation is also subject to a particular diversion which displaces the pathological from the medical context back to the victim. The search for the signs of disease indicate this, while the failure to confirm their presence suggests that culpability is to be found elsewhere. The problem is that this 'elsewhere', the murderer, mimics normalised medical procedure and so indicates that such procedure is *already* pathological.

For Freud the self, in moments of uncanniness, is confronted with an unnerving, pathological experience, which is nevertheless commonplace (commonplace to the degree that it is a shared experience and so can be generalised). The pathological in this instance really does become the psychopathology of everyday life. In the autopsies the attempt to displace this on to the victim fails because the victim cannot generate an alternative narrative which directly involves them in the murder, and thus they cannot be held morally responsible for it. And yet, as in the uncanny, there is always the sense that knowledge is immanent, that understanding is only a moment away. This is apparent in the claims about how the wounds suggest deliberation, agency and purpose, and so the presence of the killer is manifested through a series of symptoms or 'clues'. However, such 'clues' merely echo the supposedly normal medical procedure of the autopsy and as such they are familiar, but paradoxically unreadable because they do not identify a specific 'abnormal' culprit. Any knowledge which is produced is a secondary one which relates to medicine. Instead of the murderer becoming pathologised, it is medicine which becomes pathologised. The search for a 'mad' doctor in 'sane' places (such as the areas in and around the London Hospital) suggests this. The search is for the enemy within, not for an outsider. In this way the sense of *Unheimlich* (uncanny) and *heimlich* (the home) become conflated in a way which

Freud saw as one of the central characteristics of the phenomenon. Medicine is on the side of benevolent order (a caring profession, the 'home') but also associated with secrecy. This is illustrated by the partial clearing of the courtroom at the Chapman inquest, but also in a wider, less specific sense that the murderer was hidden, disguised, by the medical profession, which develops the sinister aspect of *Heimlich*: 'Concealed, kept from sight, so that others do not get to know about it, withheld from others' (p. 344).

The suggestion here is not that one should read the murders in psychological terms, indeed to do so would be to depoliticise the notion of derangement and take it out of its cultural context; rather it is the case that the notion of the uncanny enables us to unravel some of the complexities of that cultural context. This is principally because, as we have seen, displacement and transference characterise the way in which the murders were discussed in the press (as in their evocation of *Jekyll and Hyde*, for example) and the search for 'clues' of either criminality or moral pathology (which were displaced on to the victims). This process of displacement and projection also reflects the epistemic inability to generate 'truth' and consequently implicates medicine and the police in this failure. By extension, it also implicates a pathologised 'normalised' masculine gaze which was held responsible for the murders *and* for the failure to solve them.

The suggestion here is that the medical profession was confronted by its pathologised Other, in a way in which the 'otherness' of the cuts on the victims' bodies becomes familiar to the degree that they represent apparently 'normal' medical procedure. However, a sense of 'otherness', which is linked to this pathologisation (indeed, it indicates the presence of the pathological), is transferred onto the victims' bodies by this search for 'disease'. The murderer of Elizabeth Stride, for example, may indeed have been insane, although in a strictly misogynistic way, but this, as indicated earlier, is transformed into an exploration of *her* brain.

At the Stride inquest Dr Phillips reiterated his view that the murderer possessed some surgical skills, claiming that 'there appears to have been knowledge where to cut the throat'. He also made an implicit comment about the moral heath of Stride when, in response to a question, he indicated that there 'was no trace' of alcohol in her stomach.[54] The story was different with Catherine Eddowes (who was murdered shortly after Stride) because she had been arrested for drunkenness on the evening of 29 August and released by the Police at 1.00a.m. on 30 August. The Corporation of London records contain the inquest report of 4 October and the account of the autopsy made by Dr Frederick Brown, who was the surgeon of the City of London Police. Despite Eddowes's apparent reputation for drunkenness, Brown failed to find signs of pathology which reflected this, noting that the 'liver itself was healthy' and that 'the other organs were healthy'. He also looked for signs of sexual activity but notes that 'there were no indications of connexion'.[55] Brown intimated that the removal of the uterus and a kidney suggested some anatomical skill, although not necessarily a strictly medical one. He remarked, 'It required a great deal of ['medical' – deleted] knowledge to have removed the kidney and to know where it was placed, such a knowledge might be possessed by some one in the habit of cutting up animals'.[56] Aldergate slaughterhouse was in the area, although Brown's suggestion that the murderer could have been a slaughterman does not necessarily exclude the idea that they were a doctor. Indeed in the original report the word 'medical' had been deleted. The comparative health of the victim appears to prompt this new diversion. This is not to suggest that this was deliberate or consciously strategic (after all Brown may have been right), but rather that the failure to mention that it *could* have involved medical knowledge implicates the profession through omission.

In exploring these autopsies it is clear that there is an account of both the reality of the terrible crimes and a narrative process that operates alongside this, one which works within models of the pathological. It is in this adjacent narrative of pathology that complexities emerge. The victims' bodies do not generate 'clues' as to the identity of the killer, but in some instances (such as Chapman's) they do indicate the presence of social disease, although they do not produce the signs of moral pathology.

This is another way of saying that the autopsies were as much cultural as medical procedures, opening up the lives of the victims to a controlling male gaze which could generate the kind of knowledge on which a moral evaluation could be made. It is a process in which the identities of the victims actually become peculiarly obscured because they are rendered in terms of their suspect, latent pathology, one which tells us just how far such a medicalised, masculine gaze had itself become pathologised in its search for confirmation of the signs of depravity. As in Stead's notion of the commodification of young women in prostitution, the victims are ultimately reduced to a series of objects, things, and internal organs. Catherine Eddowes succinctly captured this sense of depersonalisation; when requested to give her name during her arrest for drunkenness (and shortly before she was murdered) she replied 'Nothing': an erasure of identity that was reaffirmed by the autopsy.[57]

We have seen how an examination of the pathologisation of the medical profession implicates a particular model of middle-class masculinity. This specific male gaze articulates an anxiety about authority, one which was referenced through images of a threatened medical profession. Such a process works at a covert level and the issue of concealment and visibility in some way glosses this. The autopsies also indicate a search for disease, especially for the signs of venereal disease. However, as we shall see in Chapter 4, medical discussion of syphilis also replicated this anxiety about the pathologised middle-class male, even as medical textbooks on the disease attempted to conceal it.

Notes

1 Cited in L. Perry Curtis, Jr., *Jack the Ripper and the London Press* (New Haven, CT: Yale University Press, 2001) pp. 122–3. All subsequent references are to this edition, and are given in the text.
2 Cited in Curtis, p. 128.
3 Judith R. Walkowitz, *City of Dreadful Delight: Narratives of Sexual Danger in Late-Victorian London* (London: Virago [1992] (1998) pp. 191–228. All subsequent references are to this edition, and are given in the text.
4 Although, of course, there were differences in how this was discussed in the Tabloid (or Yellow Sheet) press and the broadsheets.
5 Christopher Frayling in 'The House that Jack Built: Some Stereotypes of the Rapist in the History of Popular Culture' in Sylvana Tomaselli and Roy Porter (eds), *Rape* (Oxford: Blackwell, 1986) pp. 174–214, argues that there were three main media inspired culprits: the decadent degenerate aristocrat, the doctor, and the foreigner (as well as other figures associated with socialist ideas). However, my focus is principally on the figure of the doctor, because as Frayling acknowledges, 'The 'mad doctor' thesis represented the most accessible "explanation" at the time' (p. 198). Also the dynamic between Jekyll and Hyde, and between the 'mad doctor' thesis and 'Jack', helps to focus ideas about class. Somewhere between the two figures lies the actual eyewitness descriptions of the murderer which socially place him as 'shabby genteel' or as looking like a 'clerk' (see Frayling, pp. 178 and 179).
6 It could also be argued that this refers to the process of evolution rather than a specific threat concerning territory. However, given the anxieties relating to West and East End parts of the city during the period, I feel that a journalist writing at this time would have a clear sense of the importance of territorial issues, and consequently that the use of 'where' is significant. However, as I also suggest, it does have a metaphorical sense in relation to class.
7 Curtis, *Jack the Ripper*, p. 75.
8 Robert Miles, *Ann Radcliffe: The Great Enchantress* (Manchester: Manchester University Press, 1995) p. 47.
9 I have in mind here how her heroines, such as Ellena Rosalba in *The Italian*

(1797) for example, exert their supremacy over Burke's troubling and troubled masculine sublime.

10 Curtis, *Jack the Ripper*, p. 54.

11 David Punter, *The Literature of Terror* (London and New York: Longman, 1996) Vol. 2, p. 203.

12 There is also a case to be made that the figure of the aristocratic Dandy, or West End swell, was also demonised; although this relocates images of class tensions, such tensions were also referenced through the figure of the doctor. Also, although concerns about a degenerate aristocratic might seem to relate to my later discussion of Wilde in Chapter 7, it was the case that more evidence, and consequently, more media focus, was placed on the medical profession. See Frayling, 'The House that Jack Built', pp. 192–6 for a discussion of the Dandy.

13 There were of course earlier commentators on London including Chadwick, Mayhew and Dickens.

14 Andrew Mearns, *The Bitter Cry of Outcast London: An Inquiry into the Condition of the Abject Poor* (1883), from Sally Ledger and Roger Luckhurst (eds), *The Fin de Siècle: A Reader in Cultural History c. 1880–1900* (Oxford: Oxford University Press, 2000) p. 27. All subsequent references are to this edition, and are given in the text.

15 W.T. Stead, 'The Maiden Tribute of Modern Babylon' (1885), from Ledger and Luckhurst (eds), *The Fin de Siècle*, p. 35. All subsequent references are to this edition, and are given in the text.

16 He did not consummate the liaison.

17 William Booth, *In Darkest England and the Way Out* (1890), from Ledger and Luckhurst (eds), *The Fin de Siècle*, p. 45. All subsequent references are to this edition, and are given in the text.

18 This is not to say that the prostitute's body only articulates a male narrative, but that these male narratives represent 'her' in certain, invariably mute, ways.

19 Quoted in Curtis, *Jack the Ripper*, pp. 118–19.

20 Ibid., p. 126.

21 See Walkowitz, *City of Dreadful Delight*, pp. 206–7 and Curtis, *Jack the Ripper*, p. 126.

22 *Jekyll and Hyde* was not the only Gothic narrative that was used to dramatise the presence of class conflict; the Sunday newspaper *Reynolds's Newspaper*, for example, (founded in 1850 by the Gothic novelist George W.M. Reynolds) carried a poem on 23 September entitled 'The East End of Horror' which included the lines: 'And so, 'mid the brooding darkness, stalks murder with baleful mien / Rich man, stay from your folly, gaze on your Frankenstein!' (Curtis, *Jack the Ripper*, p. 138). Which also addresses the notion of class conflict. Nevertheless *Jekyll and Hyde* was *the* Gothic narrative most typically referred to in a process that conflated reality with fiction.

23 See Walkowitz, *City of Dreadful Delight*, p. 206, and Christopher Frayling's

re-enactment of the transformation in his episode on *Jekyll and Hyde* in his *Birth of Horror* series (BBC, 1996, episode 2).

24 Curtis, *Jack the Ripper*, p. 301, n. 57.

25 R.L. Stevenson, *The Strange Case of Dr Jekyll and Mr Hyde* in *The Strange Case of Dr Jekyll and Mr Hyde and Other Stories*, ed. Jenni Calder (Harmondsworth: Penguin, 1984) p. 30. All subsequent references are to this edition, and are given in the text.

26 Robert Mighall, *A Geography of Victorian Gothic Fiction: Mapping History's Nightmares* (Oxford: Oxford University Press, 1999) p. 151.

27 Walkowitz, *City of Dreadful Delight*, p. 131.

28 *The Times*, 14 September 1888, p. 4, from Stewart P. Evans and Keith Skinner (eds), *The Ultimate Jack the Ripper Sourcebook: An Illustrated Encyclopedia* (London: Constable, 2001) p. 98.

29 *The Times*, 26 September 1888, from Evans and Skinner (eds), *Ultimate Jack the Ripper*, p. 120.

30 D.G. Halstead, *Doctor in The Nineties*, (London: Christopher Johnson, 1959) p. 51. All subsequent references are to this edition, and are given in the text.

31 Quoted in Paul Begg, Martin Fido and Keith Skinner (eds), *The Jack the Ripper A–Z* (London: Headline, 1996) p. 383.

32 See Begg et al (eds), *Jack the Ripper A–Z*, pp. 428–30, for an account of Stephenson's colourful life which included associations with the occult and the theosophical society.

33 Letter sent 26 December 1888, from Evans and Skinner (eds), *Ultimate Jack the Ripper*, p. 670. There were also doubts about Stephenson's reliability as a witness because of his alcoholism.

34 In Evans and Skinner (eds), *Ultimate Jack the Ripper*, pp. 600 and 601.

35 Ibid, p. 601.

36 Elisabeth Bronfen, *Over Her Dead Body: Death, Femininity and the Aesthetic* (Manchester: Manchester University Press, 1992) pp. 59–60.

37 Tabram was certainly regarded by the police as a victim of the Whitechapel murderer, although more recent 'Ripperologists' such as Begg, Fido and Skinner tend to discount her on the basis that the manner of her death contrasts with some of the later victims.

38 *The Times*, 10 August 1888, from Evans and Skinner (eds), *Ultimate Jack the Ripper*, p. 9.

39 *The Times*, 14 September 1888, p. 4, from Evans and Skinner (eds), *Ultimate Jack the Ripper*, p. 96.

40 Ibid, p. 98.

41 *The Times*, 20 September 1888, p. 3, from Evans and Skinner (eds), *Ultimate Jack the Ripper*, p. 109.

42 Quoted in Begg et al. (eds), *Jack the Ripper A–Z*, p. 350.

43 Ibid.

44 Ibid.

45 Quoted in *The Times*, 14 September 1888, p. 4, from Evans and Skinner (eds),

Ultimate Jack the Ripper, p. 100.

46 Sander L. Gilman, '"Who Kills Whores?" "I Do," Says Jack: Race and Gender in Victorian London' in Sarah Webster Goodwin and Elisabeth Bronfen (eds), *Death and Representation* (Baltimore, PA and London: Johns Hopkins University Press, 1993) pp. 263–84, p. 267. All subsequent references are to this edition, and are given in the text.

47 Quoted in Evans and Skinner (eds), *Ultimate Jack the Ripper*, p. 149.

48 *The Times*, 1 October 1888, from Evans and Skinner (eds), *Ultimate Jack the Ripper*, p. 134. The following day *The Times* discussed Brown's recent release from a convalescent home, see Evans and Skinner (eds), *Ultimate Jack the Ripper*, p. 135.

49 *The Times*, 27 December 1888, from Evans and Skinner (eds), *Ultimate Jack the Ripper*, p. 118.

50 *The Times*, 4 October 1888, p. 10, from Evans and Skinner (eds), *Ultimate Jack the Ripper*, p. 177.

51 This is a history which I explored in *Gothic Radicalism: Literature, Philosophy and Psychoanalysis in the Nineteenth Century* (Basingstoke: Macmillan, 2000).

52 Peter Stallybrass and Allon White, *The Politics and Poetics of Transgression* (London: Methuen, 1986) see pp. 144–5.

53 Sigmund Freud, The 'Uncanny' in *Art and Literature: Jensen's Gradiva, Leonardo Da Vinci and other works*, in Vol. 14 Penguin Freud Library, trans. James Strachey, Albert Dickson (ed.), (Harmondsworth: Penguin, 1985) pp. 335–76, p. 346. All subsequent references are to this edition, and are given in the text.

54 *The Times*, 6 October 1888, p. 6, from Evans and Skinner (eds), *Ultimate Jack the Ripper*, pp. 182, 183.

55 From Evans and Skinner (eds), *Ultimate Jack the Ripper*, p. 231.

56 Ibid.

57 Quoted in Begg et al. (eds), *Jack the Ripper A–Z*, p. 123.

4

Reading syphilis: the politics of disease

Syphilis was a disease and a metaphor for disease at the *fin de siècle*, both a medical problem and a trope for social and cultural degeneration. In other words, there was the reality of the disease and a cultural fear of it. That this anxiety was fundamentally cultural is illustrated by how, at the end of the nineteenth century, it was the behaviour of the middle-class client, rather than the working-class prostitute, which concerned the medical profession and social reformists alike. This shift in apportioning responsibility for the spread of the disease was clearly linked to contemporary debates about the importance of marriage and discussions about the future of the bourgeois family. What was unusual was that this attack on the syphilitic male was enacted in medical circles *and* in a radical, feminist, literary culture (although as we shall see in rather different ways). The 'New Woman' novels such as Sarah Grand's *The Heavenly Twins* (1893) and Emma Brooke's *A Superfluous Woman* (1894), address the relationship between syphilis, marriage and class.[1] It was a theme that Grand returned to in *The Beth Book* (1897) which also associated the medical profession with degeneracy.[2] Infamously at the time, Ibsen focused on hereditary syphilis and male responsibility for its transmission in *Ghosts* (1881).

These literary expressions of an anxiety about syphilis illustrate the extent to which the disease was culturally debated at the time. That these debates also infiltrated a medical context is evidenced by how medical textbooks on syphilis during the period addressed the role of the predominately middle-class client in the spread of the disease. A close reading of Sir Jonathan Hutchinson's *Syphilis* (1887) and Alfred Cooper's *Syphilis* (1895) illustrates how the medical profession came to terms with this new idea of the pathologised male subject. Such books indirectly developed this link between men and disease, and in many ways attempted to suppress this link while, paradoxically, they were constructing it. These textbooks can almost be read as if they were literary texts and their use of language and metaphor function in much the same way as we saw that Merrick's loincloth did in his illustration in the *Transactions of the Pathological Society of London*, and with the same result: such attempted discretion only reveals what is really hidden. Both texts also construct a certain way of 'reading' syphilis which is dependent on negotiating the way around the complex semiotics (symptoms) of the disease in order to construct certain, and in some cases quite different, interpretations of a narrative about syphilis which implicates men in its spread. This specifically male reading strategy is helpfully illuminated by an exploration of how Nordau reads (and misreads) the signs of syphilis in *Ghosts*. Nordau's account of Ibsen will be discussed after outlining some of the changes in the perception of the disease during the nineteenth century.

Syphilis in the nineteenth century

Mary Spongberg has explored how changes in attitude towards prostitution from the eighteenth century to the end of the nineteenth century were developed in medical contexts, and how this relates to the prevailing models of gender. She notes, for example, that, 'From the 1830s onwards the female body came to be medicalized, not merely as a sexed body but as a diseased body – a space where disease could and did fester'.[3] This medicalisation of the pathologised, sexed and gendered, disease-ridden body, was an unstable one given that the notion of gender was, as we saw in Chapter 1, contested at the time. Although this contestation appeared to challenge what was understood as 'feminine', such debate also critically reflected on the 'masculine' (an idea which is particularly relevant given that the medical profession at the time was largely a male, middle class, profession). Spongberg comments: 'debates about venereal disease in the nineteenth century marked more than the struggle between men and women over the definitions of femininity and female sexuality and control over women's bodies; they did nothing less than subvert (perhaps inadvertently) the idea of masculinity and femininity as "natural"' (p. 14). For Spongberg this was an inevitable consequence of a bifurcated model of femininity, one which designated some women (prostitutes) as unnatural and degenerate, and other women (predominantly middle-class wives and mothers) as respectable. This bifurcation looked suspiciously like a masculine ploy to assign certain gender ascriptions to particular 'types' of women. In reality however, as we shall see, such a ploy constructed a seemingly divided male subject (a by now familiar Jekyll and Hyde figure) who appeared to be unable to control his desires.

This attempt to pathologise the prostitute was one aspect of a particularly coercive form of control, one that was built on conceptions of proper and improper versions of femininity. It was also a form of control which was made manifest in specific expressions of institutionalised male power. Josephine Butler, for example, who campaigned against the Contagious Diseases Acts, quoted from a Chatham prostitute in 'The Garrison Towns of Kent' (1870):

> It is *men, only men,* from the first to the last that we have to do with! To please a man I did wrong at first, then I was flung about from man to man. Men police lay hands on us. By men we are examined, handled, doctored. In the hospital it is a man again who makes prayer and reads the Bible for us. We are had up before magistrates who are men, and we never get out of the hands of men till we die! [4]

Such prostitutes had their activities circumscribed by the Contagious Diseases Acts of 1864, 1868 and 1869, which had been specifically passed in order to control the spread of the disease from prostitutes to soldiers. However, the Acts also included wider powers that could enable the police to detain any woman who was alleged to be a prostitute and enforce a medical examination of her. As Paul McHugh notes: 'The Acts were based on the premises that women but not men were responsible for the spread of venereal disease, and that while men would be degraded if subjected to physical examination, the women who satisfied male sexual urges were already so degraded that further indignities scarcely mattered.'[5] After the repeal of the Acts it was largely the male client who became held responsible for the spread of the disease.

Josephine Butler led the movement that eventually resulted in the repeal of the Acts in 1886 (up until 1869 opposition to the Acts had been led by Florence Nightingale). The way that this opposition to the Acts was expressed indicates how literary tropes came to influence the tenor of political arguments. Judith R. Walkowitz claims that Butler's 'propaganda against the Acts faithfully adhered to the gender and class expectations of traditional stage melodrama'.[6] Butler used melodrama in her speeches and articles in order to characterise the working-class prostitutes as victims and their clients as villains. Walkowitz notes 'the melodramatic representation of power and virtue was entirely compatible with the democratic, antiaristocratic, and antistatist traditions of popular radicalism' (p. 87). Such a use of a fictional form had a direct consequence for the way that the medical profession was perceived. Walkowitz again writes: 'The instrumental rape of registered women [registered as prostitutes] not only epitomised the villainous conspiracy of men, but it rendered that conspiracy even more sinister and perverse. In the name of medical science, it legitimated a cruel and irrational sexual violation, one that inflicted pain and sexual mutilation on women' (p. 92). Butler, in a letter to Joseph Edmondson in 1872 (a fellow repealer working in Halifax), was quite explicit about this alleged sexual element of medical interventions: 'If these doctors could be forced to keep their hateful hands off us, there would be an end to laws which protect vice, and to many other evils; for this indecent outrage is surrounded and connected on every side with fraud and lustful purpose'.[7] The use of melodrama in the cause of repeal was not just an eccentric quirk of Butler's. In Chapter 3 we saw how *Jekyll and Hyde* was influential in directing discussion of the Whitechapel murders. In addition, as we saw in Chapter 2, Treves also used fictional devices in order to illustrate what were, at some level, medical case histories. This relationship between narrative and science also had, as we shall see, a central place in medical accounts of syphilis during the period.

The association that Butler makes between medicine and the Acts argues the case that the medical profession institutionalised certain forms of sexual abuse. However, the picture is perhaps more ambivalent than she suggests. There were male doctors who queried the effectiveness of the Acts and as we saw with Treves's *Reminiscences* and his account of the female hysteric, there was ambivalence about how doctors exercised their power over women.[8] Feminist attacks on the profession, such as Butler's, sought to pathologise doctors (as diseased sexual predators they seemed to become a metaphorical representation of the prostitute's client, or at least seemed so in Butler's eyes). That the medical profession responded to the repeal of the Acts is illustrated by how accounts of syphilis tended to shift their focus on to the behaviour of the client, and away from the prostitute. We will see however, that this shift was not necessarily a radical one and that such a refocus was often coyly and reluctantly expressed. The pathologisation of the male client posed a problem for medicine even while such a redirection became a cultural imperative.

These changes in medical opinion on syphilis were related to the questioning of dominant masculine scripts during the period. This questioning was not just evidenced in the 'New Woman' novels, but was also central to Butler's efforts to repeal the Acts. The idea of a bifurcated male subject, one who because of his frequenting of prostitutes placed his family at risk, increasingly became a subject for debate. This was especially the case in discussions of congenital syphilis. Spongberg notes that investigations of congenital syphilis towards the end of the nineteenth century led 'Some doctors ... to believe that it was possible for men to pass on syphilis to their children without infecting their mother. Such an idea challenged the connection between femininity and disease and implicated men in the spread of syphilis' (*Feminizing Venereal Disease*, p. 143). Such discussions of congenital syphilis also tended to imply that degeneracy was latent in the male body because as Spongberg notes, 'The idea of paternal infection created a model of degeneracy that presumed that some acquired pathology in the father was the direct cause of the stigma of degeneracy in the next generation' (p. 152). In other words the debate about syphilis became transferred to the family.

This concern with sexual health, specifically of the middle-class family, illustrates the claim made by Foucault that the period was characterised by the emergence of a *scientia sexualis*. This science of sexuality gauged the physical, and the implied moral, health of the subject by categorising their sexual behaviour through a series of putatively scientific models which identified (or constructed as deviant) 'aberrant' sexual practices (such as homosexuality and masturbation, for example). What was needed was a particular kind of scientific practice which could police the boundaries between 'normal' and 'abnormal'. Foucault claims that in this science, 'Sex was not something one simply judged; it was a thing one administered. It was in the nature of a public potential; it called for management procedures; it had to be taken charge of by analytical discourses'.[9] Although Foucault's argument does not always address the role of gender, it is nevertheless relevant to an understanding of how the medical profession made an intervention in the treatment of syphilis. At the end of the nineteenth century this was not just a treatment of the physical effects of the disease, it was also an assessment which had direct social effects. By the end of the century, for example, doctors would frequently adjudicate on when (or whether) a man who had contracted the disease should defer marrying and so delay starting a family. In this way, in the instance of syphilis, medicine policed the boundaries between family health and sexual disease; this localised policing also had a relationship to the wider body politic because, as Foucault notes, 'strange pleasures it [a science of sex] warned, would eventually result in nothing short of death: that of individuals, generations, the species itself' (p. 54).[10]

The idea that in the case of congenital (or hereditary) syphilis it was the man who was responsible for the child's acquisition of the disease led, in some circles, to the conclusion that the disease was transmitted through semen. Additionally, Spongberg argues that some radical commentators of the time 'claimed that not only syphilis but a multitude of other skin diseases were caused by sperm being deposited in the pregnant woman's womb' (*Feminizing Venereal Disease*, p. 155).

Spongberg notes that during the 1890s the medical profession sought to discriminate between those who had innocently contracted the disease (women and children) and those who were responsible for its transmission (men).[11] However the medical profession was perhaps rather more reluctant to come to this conclusion than she suggests. In this chapter there will be an in depth discussion of how medical textbooks on syphilis, published after the repeal of the Acts, subtly pathologise the middle-class male as they, paradoxically, attempt to discreetly conceal this pathologisation. Such textbooks used a range of narrative devices in order to enact this concealment and this process indicates just how far these textbooks supported a political vision that was at odds with what was increasingly regarded as a purely medical issue. One could claim that such texts struggled to tell the scientific 'facts' about the role of the middle class male client because this conflicted with the bourgeois male ethos of the medical profession. These male readings of the disease are helpfully culturally contextualised by an examination of Nordau's account of Ibsen's *Ghosts* in *Degeneration* (1892).

Ghosts

At one level *Ghosts* is a play about hereditary syphilis. It is also a play about secrets within marriage. The widowed Mrs Alving, who was married to the ostensibly respectable Chamberlain Alving, has concealed from the local community that her husband had led a sexually dissolute life. Ibsen appears to mock bourgeois notions of respectability and expressions of social concern (Mrs Alving intends to finance an orphanage, to be dedicated to the memory of her husband) because these are compromised by the presence of seemingly sordid sexual misdemeanours. Marriage does not provide a corrective to such proclivities, as Mrs Alving tells Pastor Manders (who is in charge of the building and administration of the orphanage), 'After nineteen years of married life, he was as dissolute – in his desires, at any rate – as he was when you married us'.[12] Alving's behaviour cannot be dismissed as 'youthful indiscretions' (p. 49) as Manders would like. Due to the breakdown of the marriage contract public standards of morality (in the play rather loosely defined as respectability) start to unravel. Oswald, the Alvings' son, who is an artist staying with his mother over the winter, shocks Manders by mentioning that he has friends who are unmarried couples with children. Manders regards these as 'irregular unions' (p. 43), but Oswald is adamant that such couples have made a commitment to each other and their children which is not necessarily found in marriage. Oswald tells the Pastor that the only occasions in which he has discovered 'immorality in artistic circles' (p. 44) is when, 'one or two of your model husbands and fathers have come abroad to have a little look around on their own account, and have done the artists the honour of calling on them in their horrible lodgings. Then we learned a thing or two; these gentleman could tell us about places and things we'd never dreamed of' (p. 44). The Pastor does not want to believe that such hypocrisy could be possible, despite Mrs Alving's assertion that if there is hypocrisy here then it is his own refusal to acknowledge what he has always known, 'You know perfectly well the sort of life my husband was leading in those days, and the excesses he was guilty of' (p. 46). Manders would prefer to think of them as 'rumours' rather than facts (p. 46).

The closing scene of the play centres on Oswald's admission to his mother that he is suffering from a fatal disease, which is clearly meant to be syphilis even though this baffles Oswald because 'I've never led a dissolute life at all – not in any way' (p. 73). A doctor had told him that he had inherited the disease, pronouncing that 'The sins of the fathers are visited on the children' (p. 74), however because Oswald believes that his father was respectable he thinks that he has, somehow, caught the disease himself. For Oswald, 'If only it had been something I'd inherited – something I wasn't to blame for ... But this! It's so shameful to have thrown away my health and happiness – everything in the world – so thoughtlessly, so recklessly ... my future – my life itself!' (p. 75). At the end of the play Oswald has made a suggested alliance with the housekeeper, Regina; however, Mrs Alving knows that Regina was born as a result of a liaison between her husband and the former housekeeper, Johanna. In order to stop this alliance before it becomes incestuous, Mrs Alving informs them of her husband's dissolute past. Oswald's physical decline is rapid and at the end of the play it appears as though he kills himself with a drug overdose. The final horror for Mrs Alving has been realised. Earlier she had indicated to Manders that her husband's money would be used to finance the orphanage (which at the end of Act Two burns down, symbolising the destruction of Alving's reputation) and that Oswald will only inherit her money because she did not want him 'to inherit anything whatever from his father' (p. 52).

The play became infamous because of its representation of syphilis, suggestions of sexual immorality, its critique of moribund Christian beliefs

(as figured in Pastor Manders), and its apparent celebration of a more
'honest' (morally consistent) life that could be led outside the constraints
of some loosely defined notion of bourgeois propriety.

The play therefore seems to be about degeneration and how it could
develop through families, a concern which was central to much medical
writing on disease. Also, the suggestion that men are responsible for the
transmission of the disease, *and* its victims (Oswald is infected not Regina)
suggests a curious double pathologisation of men. However, although
Nordau would list 'Ibsenisms' in his pantheon of degenerate influences, it
was not because the play explored disease. Rather, Nordau's celebration of
marriage, and somewhat coy analysis of disease, suggests a desire to reaffirm
the importance of the social contract that marriage implies. His reading
of *Ghosts* constitutes a particular male strategy of attempting to conceal
the role that men might play in the spread of the disease. This is a reading
strategy which was echoed in medical writing at the time which also sought
to marginalise the disease in the interests, paradoxically, of promoting the
importance of the family.

Nordau's Ibsen: denying syphilis

Nordau's critique of Ibsen is focused on the mind rather than the body.
That Ibsen was suffering from mental degeneracy was, according to
Nordau, indicated by how his alleged egomania was characterised by a
degenerative interest in mysticism. Such a mystical vision of human
relations celebrates the individual and so undoes the bonds that keep
society together. Mrs Alving's interest in alternative moral codes, for
example, compromises the social bond that is implied by marriage.

Nordau argues that for all of Ibsen's alleged realism and hard-hitting
social commentary, his vision was essentially mystical. He claims that 'this
"modern," this "realist," with his exact "scientific" observation, is in reality
a mystic and an egomaniacal anarchist'.[13] Ibsen's mystical theology is
indicated by his interest in original sin (the sexually dissolute Alving),
confession (the revelation of Alving's past) and self-sacrifice (Mrs Alving's
attempts at concealing the past, and Oswald who at the end becomes a
kind of martyr). Ibsen's use of symbolism, such as the burning down of
the orphanage, also indicates the presence of a degenerate mind because
it reveals an interest in symbols (signs, portents) rather than reality. Nordau
relates such mysticism and symbolism to 'the symbolism of the insane',
which occurs because 'their brain is not yet trained to attention' and so
cannot 'suppress irrational associations' (p. 396). What is disturbing, at

least for Nordau, is that the play does not represent the reality of disease but rather uses it in order to make a symbolic point about decay. This failure to represent the reality of disease indicates the presence of a diseased imagination. In effect, one disease is traded for another and this is not simply a replacement, rather it is as though Nordau evokes one disease *in order to suppress* the presence of another: syphilis. Nordau argues that, 'From all that is said in the piece the disease inherited by Oswald from his father can only be diagnosed either as syphilis *hereditaria tarda*, or *dementia paralytica*. The first of these diseases is out of the question, for Oswald is depicted as a model of manly strength and health' (pp. 353–4). This is despite the play's emphasis on Oswald's tiredness and admission of poor physical and mental health. Nordau seems aware that he cannot simply deny that Oswald's disease is meant to be syphilitic and he returns to it later in order to suggest that Ibsen is merely using the disease to support one of his strange, degenerate, mystical visions concerning the idea of sin and punishment. Nordau summarises Ibsen's representation of the disease as symbolising 'a chastisement for the sins of [Oswald's] father, and for the moral weakness of his mother in marrying for self-interest a man she did not love' (p. 382). Nordau's principal objection is the link between syphilis and immoral sexual activity, that, 'Oswald's state is the consequence of a complaint which may be contracted without any depravity whatsoever. It is a silly antiquated idea of the bigoted members of societies for the suppression of immorality that a contagious disease is the consequence and punishment of licentiousness. Doctors know better than that' (p. 382). The threat of syphilis is played down because it does not necessarily reflect on the moral failings of the male subject. Indeed the syphilitic subject can, for Nordau, be regarded as a victim. Nordau claims of doctors that, 'They know hundreds – nay, thousands – of cases where a young man is infected for his whole life, for no other act than one which, with the views now prevailing, is looked upon as venial' (p. 382). He also claims that, 'Even holy matrimony is no protection against such a misfortune, to say nothing of the cases where doctors, nurses, etc., have contracted the malady in the discharge of their duties, and without carnal transgression' (p. 382). Syphilis becomes completely hollowed out, stripped of all significance other than as it exists as a mark of how Ibsen, falsely, suggests a link between disease and dissolute male behaviour.

Nordau's principal criticism of Ibsen rests on the notion that Ibsen's mystical, and therefore false, interpretation of the 'real' world suggests the presence of a potentially dangerous disease. Nordau's view of Ibsen up to this point in *Degeneration* had centred on Ibsen's supposed mental failings.

These are greater than any moral failings which Ibsen might allege become written on the body through the transmission of syphilis. Nevertheless Nordau needs to relate this idea of an abstracted mental aberration to a model of society in order to show how such an aberration has social effects. Nordau therefore seeks to get back to a version of the body which only becomes diseased because of mental failings rather than moral ones. In this model he develops a theory that relates the physical body to the wider body politic:

> We know that man, like every other complex and highly-developed living being, is a society or state, of simpler, and of simplest, living beings, of cells and cell-systems, or organs, all having their own functions and wants. In the course of the development of life on earth they must have become associated, and have undergone changes, in order to be able to perform higher functions than are possible in the simple cell and primitive agglomeration of cells. The highest function of life yet known to us is clear consciousness; the most elevated content of consciousness is knowledge; and the most obvious and immediate aim of knowledge is constantly to procure better conditions of life for the organism, hence to preserve its existence as long as possible, and to fill it with the greatest possible number of pleasurable sensations. In order that the collective organism may be able to perform its task, its constituent parts are bound to submit to a severe hierarchical order. Anarchy in its interior is disease, and leads rapidly to death. (p. 409)

This organic, healthy, society is threatened by the presence of the anarchic aspects of Ibsen's egomania because it puts the individual before the social contract. The mental 'aberration' suggested by this egomania becomes, in this account of the body politic, a physical disease. Nordau thus relocates Ibsen's conception of syphilis (his own version of middle-class degeneration), but in the interests of a conservative politics.

Implicit to Nordau's critique of Ibsen is a coy reference to marital sex, a reference that is captured in the image of a social consciousness which seeks out 'the greatest possible number of pleasurable sensations', in what is a socially sanctioned version of pleasure. That Nordau has marriage in mind is clear from his later discussion of how marriage provides a social blessing to pleasure because it enables society to reproduce, and so perpetuate, itself. Ultimately, Nordau's strategy is to question the significance of syphilis in order to celebrate some vaguely defined notion of family values (one which *Ghosts* seems to violate).

Nordau's account of marriage develops an Hegelian master and slave dialectic, one which achieves its quite literal synthesis in marriage. Ibsen's perversity is that he champions the possibility that women, such as Mrs Alving, can find an alternative, and meaningful life, outside of marriage. Nordau claims that such women are 'hysterical, nymphomaniacal, perverted in maternal instinct', they are 'not fit for marriage'; indeed, for Nordau, they reveal the presence of a form of atavism that evokes Ferraro's model of the degenerate prostitute.[14] The distinction between pure and impure women was, as we saw earlier, one of the central contradictions in debates about prostitution and syphilis at the time. Nordau's solution is to suggest that such markers of degeneration transcend class distinctions and so an apparently respectable woman, such as Mrs Alving, could be associated with disease and degeneration (in a move which would transfer images of syphilis from her husband and her son to herself).

Nordau develops this master and slave dialectic through the relationship between masochism and sadism. It is unnatural, so Nordau claims, for the man to occupy the position of masochist which is dismissed as a 'perversion' in a man (p. 414). For Nordau both Sacher-Masoch and Ibsen had falsely given credibility to the idea of an empowered, independently minded, female subject who manipulates men. This suggested relationship 'is the inversion of the healthy and natural relation between the sexes' (p. 414). It suggests an anarchic attitude towards the necessary hierarchies of the body politic. For Nordau, Ibsen provides a false model of female emancipation because it is both at the expense of men's 'natural' dominance, and because for women to question such hierarchies qualifies as a perversion.[15]

Nordau's ultimate claim is that women do not find their champion in Ibsen because, 'Ibsen is not their friend. No one is who, as long as the present order of society exists, attacks the institution of marriage' (p. 414). The link between marriage and the individual becomes the key link between the individual and society. It is a link which also has a central role in medical writing on syphilis which similarly sought to minimise the significance of the disease in order to champion the importance of the family. It is marriage which, for Nordau, provides some security against promiscuity, even though such a view revises his earlier claim about the spread of syphilis that 'Even holy matrimony is no protection against such a misfortune'. He writes, 'Marriage is a high advance from the free copulation of savages. To abandon it and return to primitive promiscuity would be the most profound atavism of degeneracy. Marriage, moreover, was not instituted for the man, but for the woman and the child. It is a protective social institution for the benefit of the weaker part' (p. 415).

Nordau's reading of Ibsen constructs a version of pathology that is highly relevant to medical readings of syphilis. Nordau claims that syphilis is merely used by Ibsen as a metaphor for middle-class decline. However, this is a false model of degeneracy because the disease is not per se inimical to the family. Also, according to Nordau, the disease can be contracted through a variety of innocent, non-sexualised contacts and therefore cannot be associated with fundamental moral failings. It is not syphilis which threatens the family but rather the way that a fear of the disease, as in *Ghosts*, challenges the idea of marriage because it is used to question the conventional adherence to social values that marriage implies. For Nordau, to question this link is to undo one of the most basic social contracts upon which the body politic is founded. The displacement of the disease on to Ibsen represents an attempt to conceal, through relocation, how the disease could itself undo some of the central moral tenets of such a body politic.

Nordau's account of syphilis is developed through a series of evasions, projections and prevarications which also govern Hutchinson's *Syphilis*, which was one of the key medical textbooks on the subject during the period. However, this concealment never quite works, and this is clear in both medical textbooks and Nordau's idea that marriage is to the benefit of the woman and child. The real danger is not irrational, pathologised, atavistic, promiscuous women, but 'natural' man: 'Man has not yet conquered and humanised his polygamous animal instincts to the same extent as woman. It would for the most part be quite agreeable to him to exchange the woman he possesses for a new one' (p. 415). Which suggests (given his earlier views on how some women exhibited a potential for atavism) that Nordau has a somewhat flexible notion about what constitutes 'natural'.

What is important about Nordau's account of syphilis is that it represents a particular way of reading the disease. This way of reading is in many ways (implicitly) hostile to the idea of a radical critique of the disease which, like Butler's, works towards the pathologisation of men. However, the slippages in this reading strategy acknowledge that this pathologisation has taken place and that men are associated with disease. It is a way of reading that is also echoed in how medical textbooks interpret the disease.

Hutchinson's Syphilis: *interpreting the signs*

Sir Jonathan Hutchinson's *Syphilis* was published in March 1887 and was first reprinted in October of that year. In all there were eight reprints until 1904, and a second edition was published in 1909. The book is dedicated to Alfred Fournier who in 1880 had published *Syphilis and Marriage*, and explores the development of the disease, its possible treatments (Hutchinson was a great champion of mercury) and discusses certain encounters with predominately male patients.

Hutchinson saw syphilis as amplifying what was an inherent tendency within the male subject to manifest disease. This threatened immanence of disease echoes those contemporary theories of degeneracy which saw disease as a lurking presence in both the physical body and the body politic.[16] Hutchinson argues that 'the syphilitic poison may be regarded as bringing to light latent peculiarities of structure'.[17] The disease becomes difficult to identify because it appears to mimic other ailments, or as he puts it (the emphasis is Hutchinson's) '*Syphilis, whilst it can produce no originals, may imitate all known forms of skin disease*' (p. 104). An additional problem is that other, non-syphilitic diseases resemble the disease, creating a 'syphilitic counterfeit' which needs to be discriminated from the real thing (p. 342). The basic problem that Hutchinson has with the disease is one of interpretation. Taken as a purely physical disease, the doctor is forced to acknowledge that before treatment can commence it is necessary to determine both the reality of the disease and its specific manifestation. Another problem is caused by a number of factors, which although not in themselves related to the disease, nevertheless have an effect upon it. Smoking, for example, is identified by Hutchinson as the principal cause of the spread of the disease to the mouth and throat. Warm clothing can also be responsible for the spread of the disease to the skin. Hutchinson cites an incident where he tried to console one of his male patients by commenting on their improved, if not cured, condition. The patient replied, 'Yes ... you may say so; but see the difference from what I was. If I smoke I get sores in my mouth, and I used to be able to smoke all day; if I work my brain I get headache, which I never did before; and now I have got this rash from, as you say, my vest and the hot weather. I had none of these things before I had syphilis' (p. 116). Throughout *Syphilis* there are a series of portraits of middle-class male subjects who are represented as subtly worn out by the effects of the disease. These images of the fatigued male subject (here tired both physically and mentally) suggest alienation. That Hutchinson implicitly develops this idea of alienation is underlined by the male subject's estrangement from the world and its comforts and pleasures. Smoking and warm clothing are only one such source; Hutchinson also notes that syphilitic sores can appear on the hands if a walking-stick or an umbrella is used (p. 117). He even suggests that modes of transportation could also be the source of some danger, citing a patient who claimed to have contracted the disease after being bitten by a flea during a journey on an omnibus (p. 35). In one of the more unusual incidents, one of his patients catches the disease after a bicycle accident: 'In the accident he had been knocked down, and his clothing punctured at various places by one of his own wheels' (p. 53). This created the opening for the disease which was subsequently contracted, so Hutchinson speculates, after the patient dried himself on a bath towel which had previously been used by someone with syphilis.

The recurring narrative is that men contract the disease in a way which suggests, as does Nordau, that they are innocent victims (on bicycle trips and bus rides), or else to be pitied because the world has become curiously hostile to them (clothes, cigarettes, umbrellas and walking-sticks). It is almost as if the world is conspiring against men, and as a consequence *Syphilis* maintains a tone of suppressed paranoia concerning the prevalence of the disease and the likelihood of contracting it.

Although Hutchinson dedicated his book to Fournier, the function of the doctor to vet their patients for fitness to marry is allocated a surprisingly small space in his book. The section 'On Syphilis and Marriage' appears in the appendix and occupies just over two pages in a book of some 570 pages. However, this seeming relegation of the issue does not quite make it disappear as it provides a largely unspoken context for his discussion of hereditary syphilis, which occupies much of the book. Nevertheless, although brief and appendicised, Hutchinson's view of the doctor in this matter articulates a range of class concerns relating to the potential acquisition and consequent spread of the disease. He notes that:

> It is to be remembered that although, in fear of syphilis a surgeon may forbid marriage, he cannot enforce continence. In most cases the risk – often an imaginary one, or at most infinitesimally small – is simply shifted from a wife to a concubine, from one of the richer classes, it may be, to one of the poorer. Procreation is not prevented, and children are brought into the world under less advantageous conditions, whilst women are left to live spinsters who might have been happy wives and mothers. (p. 555)

Like Nordau, Hutchinson minimises the risk of contracting or disseminating the disease through sexual contact although elsewhere in *Syphilis* the disease is characterised by its near ubiquity. Indeed, in this section, Hutchinson suggests that the disease has been given undue prominence as there are several other diseases which are more dangerous than syphilis, 'Such diseases as insanity, tuberculosis, and even gout, are far more real dangers to the race than is syphilis', and this is in part because he is concerned that anxiety about the disease could lead to the regulation of marriage which 'would be disastrous to social progress and would greatly reduce the sum of human happiness' (p. 555). Hutchinson questions the doctor's right to exercise moral control over the disease because 'Counsels of perfection are often not trustworthy', and that 'We must not attempt too confidently to control nature, nor must we bring our imperfect knowledge rashly into predominance in practical affairs' (p. 555). As with Nordau's reading of syphilis, it would appear that the major threat to the family is not the spread of the disease, but rather the attempt to control marriage.[18] Indeed Hutchinson advocates that where possible the former presence of the disease should be concealed from the wife. He notes of one former patient who 'died nearly thirty years after his syphilis' that, 'His wife, who had remained throughout in good health, and who knew nothing whatever of the nature of her husband's ailment, regarded her marriage, I believe, as a very happy one' (p. 295).

Hutchinson does not deny that it is the man who is largely responsible for the spread of syphilis; he simply proposes its concealment. He suggests that the reason for this is to protect the wife from any unnecessary upset. In his discussion of inherited syphilis he raises the difficulty that the doctor may encounter when questioning the father of a child with syphilis about the father's sexual history:

> In most cases the surgeon is precluded, either by moral obligations or by motives of kindness from asking any direct questions, or even such as may excite suspicion. If it is the mother of the patient to whom such questions are put, it is very possible that they may be the means of inducing her to suspect that which she had never dreamed of, and which, whether true or otherwise, may poison the happiness of her life. There can be no duty more imperative, in the exercise of our profession, than that of abstaining from needlessly exciting in the minds of our patients suspicions as to conjugal purity. (p. 406)

This process in which men become both pathologised and concealed is typical of this male reading of syphilis, as we saw with Nordau.

Throughout *Syphilis* there is an emphasis given to the idea that the diseased middle-class male should be concealed due to the need to support a wider moral and social code which sanctions marriage and which evidences support for the family. To this degree *Syphilis* might appear to compromise Foucault's claim that a science of health functioned to police behaviour and to expose the presence of allegedly injurious sexual practices. Foucault grounds his claim in the idea that by the end of the nineteenth century the bourgeois family became the unit through which the middle classes could perpetuate their power. However, Hutchinson's textbook tries to strike a balance between wanting to police the causes of syphilis, controlling its spread, and supporting the family.

As discussed earlier in this chapter, the problem, according to Hutchinson, is firstly that the disease apes the symptomology of other diseases and so makes it difficult to detect. An additional problem is that some non-syphilitic diseases appear to mimic classic syphilis. Not only is it difficult to distinguish between 'true' syphilis and 'counterfeit' syphilis, another problem is one of causality. Indeed Hutchinson goes to some lengths to give credence to other, non-sexual modes of infection. The extent of infection raises another problem because Hutchinson claims that certain types of clothing, or even smoking, exacerbate the symptoms of the disease. The implication is that having successfully identified the disease it becomes difficult to gauge its seriousness because of the presence of these additional complications. Finally, Hutchinson even goes so far as to suggest that there exist more dangerous diseases than syphilis.

As represented in *Syphilis* the disease has a strangely protean form, possessing a discretion matched only by Hutchinson's suggestion for the need to maintain a strategic, diplomatic silence on the means of transmission. It reads, as does Nordau's account of syphilis, like a guarded attempt to place the male subject beyond identifiable reproach. In this way Hutchinson advocates that the medical profession needs to play a role in what he regards as a necessary concealment.

Cooper: sexing disease

Alfred Cooper's *Syphilis* (1895) also develops the view that men should not be specifically identified as the purveyors of the disease because they are also its most frequent victims. Cooper's treatise is marked by a reactionary politics which is partly manifested in his unqualified support for the Contagious Diseases Act, and also by his questioning of a perceived bias which he saw as characterising the disease in earlier medical texts. Cooper claims that, 'There is much difference of opinion with regard to the question of *sex* as influencing the intensity of the disease. It is generally stated that women, as a rule, suffer more severely than men, but our experience leads us to quite the opposite conclusion'.[19] This is because Cooper distinguishes between prostitutes and 'women belonging to the well-to-do classes' (p. 342). The former's disease is exacerbated by their poor living conditions, whereas the middle-class woman is better off than the middle-class male because menstruation has a 'depurative action on the blood and other fluids of the body' and thus has a positive effect 'in diminishing the severity of the disease' (p. 343).

Cooper therefore emphasises the idea that biological differences are instrumental in the development of the disease. Men are identified as the 'natural' victims of the disease. In his chapter on hereditary syphilis he is also sceptical about theories of hereditary transmission which identify men as predominately responsible for its cause. In particular Cooper raises the question of whether a syphilitic child acquires the disease because the mother is syphilitic or because, during pregnancy, the fetus becomes syphilitic due to extra sexual contact. For Cooper it is pregnancy itself which could mask the presence of the disease, 'the symptoms in the mother do not always appear during the first pregnancy or immediately after it. She may remain apparently healthy, or the symptoms may be of a very slight, ill-defined character' (p. 349). The very vagueness of this claim is a consequence of Cooper's lack of hard scientific evidence to support it. Rather, he claims that there does not exist the hard scientific evidence to refute it. Therefore it is a testable, because plausible, hypothesis, based on some ideas about how the disease *might* progress in certain circumstances. Ultimately this enables Cooper to claim that hereditary syphilis has a shared paternity.

Central to Cooper's reading of the disease is an interpretation of symptomology. For Hutchinson the disease posed a problem for interpretation. In Nordau's reading of the disease the signs of syphilis needed to be replaced by the signs of Ibsen's mental pathology. With Cooper the semiotic confusion of these signs enables him to rework a politically conservative agenda that subtly seems to play down the significance of the male subject in the spread of the disease.

Cooper quotes at length a case which had appeared in *The Lancet* on 9 June 1894, in which a Dr J.A. Coutts of the East London Hospital for Children appeared to have discovered a case in which a father and the child were infected but not the mother. However, the mother, some years after the birth of the child, exhibited signs of syphilis which were not discernible at the time. Cooper concludes from this that:

> Whether in these cases the syphilis is so modified that its effects are not made manifest, or when manifested, the resulting lesions are so slight as to escape nature or appear at a very late period, the fact remains that neither direct infection of the ovum by that father, nor infection of the mother by her syphilitic offspring [through wet-nursing], has been proved. (p. 362)

The problem, however, it that it has also not been disproved. The very indeterminacy of the signs of the disease makes it complex and difficult to either identify or interpret and ultimately, as constructed by Cooper, the disease appears to be quite malleable.

That Cooper wants to construct the male subject as the potential victim of the disease is clear in his chapter on 'Syphilis and Insanity', where he claims that the fear of contracting the disease can induce a variety of, largely depressive, mental ailments in the male subject. Specifically, this appears as a mental response to a physical ailment:

> A man may contract syphilis, and become in consequence depressed; this depression may become true melancholia, accompanied by insomnia and a suicidal tendency. Or a man may contract syphilis after marriage, and may be haunted with the fear of infecting his wife and children. In these two instances, the knowledge of the syphilis present acts as the idea around which the melancholic feelings group themselves, the whole being but an exaggeration of the real fact. (p. 414)

Mental states are therefore divorced from physical realities. Cooper, like Hutchinson and Nordau, plays down the significance of the physical disease. As with Nordau, what is more pressing is the presence of the signs of mental ill-health. Cooper addresses this pure form of mental disease in his account of 'true syphilophobia' in which the male subject has a purely imaginary fear that they have contracted the disease.

These associations between mental trauma and the threat, either real or imagined, of transmission are plotted by Cooper as a solely male form of mental illness. It is a model which is close to hysteria in its symptomology as it includes a range of anxieties and conditions including 'Dread', 'Delirium', 'Mania', 'Mental Disorder', and 'Morbid Self-consciousness' (pp. 414–15). The effects of the disease are therefore greater than its purely treatable physical form. It is Cooper's, and indeed Hutchinson's, confidence in the possibility of controlling and treating the disease which explains why these anxieties concerning contracting the disease appear as mental or unreal concerns. Nevertheless, the anxiety is a 'real' ailment in its own right and suggests that if the male subject has good cause not to fear the physical harm that it could inflict, then there must be an alternative explanation for the presence of this anxiety.

What Cooper refers to as the 'Insane Dread of Syphilis' can be understood in class and gender terms as a consequence of certain familial expectations placed on the middle-class male, or at least this is what Cooper states in his chapter on 'The Prevention of Syphilis'. However, an alternative anxiety appears here which is related to visibility, an issue which, as we saw in Chapter 3, played an important role in the Whitechapel murders. In Hutchinson's *Syphilis* and in Nordau's reading of *Ghosts*, syphilis is strategically marginalised and so becomes a discreet presence. Indeed discretion, in a variety of guises, plays a role in how the disease is discussed. Discretion governs the discussion between the doctor and the middle-class male patient. The disease also appears to be discreetly developed as its effects can be explained as exacerbated by non-sexual factors, such as clothing and smoking. In Cooper such discretion is more difficult to maintain. For Cooper, the signs that the disease has been contracted by the male subject can be all too visible, and at that point the mental despair of detection reveals just how much the 'Insane Dread of Syphilis' is associated with infection. Cooper notes:

> If there is much disfigurement, due to the ravages of the disease, delusions may occur that the victim of them is a leper, and is pointed out as such. The patient is first of all morbidly self-conscious of his disfigurement, and is likely to drown his thoughts in drink. This leads to hallucinations and delusions of persecution, and this form of insanity is frequently complicated with homicidal or suicidal mania. (p. 415)

This decline into drunkenness and insanity may be accounted for as a consequence of a 'delusion', but it illustrates just how far an anxiety about detection can affect the subject. It is a delusion, such as in the case of 'syphilophobia', which for Cooper complicates the doctor's adjudication of whether the male subject is healthy enough to marry.[20]

Throughout these accounts of syphilis it is the issue of visibility that is addressed. For Nordau, Ibsen makes visible (in symbolic terms) the idea of male sexual impropriety, whereas, according to Nordau, such impropriety can be regulated by marriage. With Hutchinson such male sexual behaviour is less important than the validation of marriage and the future of the family. Nordau's reading of syphilis and Hutchinson's construction of it work towards the same ends, which is the suppression of the truth in how the disease is contracted in the interests of bourgeois family life. Cooper's contribution to this strategic concealment is more problematic. For him, the signs of syphilitic stigmata are there to be seen, and the male subject understands only too well how this stigmata identifies him with the disease (notwithstanding Cooper's assertion that this is a delusion). For Cooper, this pathologised male subject cannot be properly concealed, despite his argument concerning sexual equality in the transmission of the disease. He claims that, 'A large majority of the young men of the upper and middle classes suffer in youth from some form of venereal disease' (p. 430).[21] However, in keeping with his account of hereditary syphilis, he refuses to isolate the middle-class client from the working-class prostitute.

Hutchinson had suggested that the disease could be caught in a variety of non-sexual encounters, but Cooper is explicit about the chief means of contraction: 'Excluding the hereditary form, syphilis is propagated principally by sexual intercourse' (pp. 430–1). He is equally explicit about the origins of the disease, 'The source of the virus is prostitution, and the questions arise, can the disease be checked at its source?' (p. 431). In this way Cooper attempts a final concealment of the pathologised male subject whose self-consciousness about the disease had earlier been dismissed as a delusion. Cooper shifts the debate onto social policy rather than addressing the role of the married middle-class client. He argues that, 'If things are allowed to take their own course, if as in London at the present day, prostitutes are allowed to ply their calling in any place they may select, without the slightest interference, the result must be that their number will increase, and that the spread of syphilis will be proportionally facilitated' (p. 431). Cooper advocates state intervention in regulating prostitution; the state should 'exercise a careful supervision over an evil which it cannot repress' (p. 431). In effect Cooper proposes resurrecting the old Contagious Diseases Acts in order to control the incidence of the disease in prostitutes. He claims that the repeal of the Acts was a mistake and that, 'It is to be hoped that another Parliament will rectify the mistake, and that another Government may be found willing to assume responsibility even at the risk of incurring unpopularity among a certain influential but ill-informed class of the community' (p. 435). However, despite these overt revisionist calls for a resurrection of some form of regulation, the issue of the pathologised middle-class male does not entirely disappear. He refers to syphilis as 'an epidemic' (p. 438) which has now become an inherent 'feature of English life' (pp. 437–8), in which the true horror is not the alleged ease of access to prostitutes, who 'are now allowed to congregate in all our public places' (p. 431), but rather what this means for the middle-class family. He claims of this 'epidemic' that it 'is one of the most dreadful now existing among mankind', and its chief horror is that it 'communicates itself from the guilty husband to the innocent wife, and even transmits its taint to her offspring' (p. 438).

Cooper's concluding remarks on the 'Prevention of Syphilis' therefore finally make visible what he tried to conceal: the presence of the pathologised middle-class male subject. Cooper's attempt to rework a bifurcated version of femininity, of prostitute and 'respectable' wife, is a reconstruction of an unworkable distinction that had dogged earlier accounts of the disease. It is also these concluding remarks which compromise his earlier claims about shared responsibility for the spread of the disease in the instance of hereditary syphilis, a consequence of putting sex back into a discussion of the disease.

We have seen how accounts of syphilis indicate the presence of cultural anxieties about masculinity and class, and how these anxieties were reproduced in medical textbooks on the disease.[22] What characterises these texts is a particular way of reading the disease, where the symptoms of syphilis function as signs of disease within a bourgeois male culture. The disease is therefore never just, or simply, about 'illness' but has associations with a pathologised male subject who threatens, at least theoretically, to undermine the credibility of the bourgeois family. To follow Foucault, this would be to jeopardise the economic power base of the middle classes, and therefore the policing of 'aberrant' behaviour became a matter of considerable political importance. The unspoken problem as it is represented in medical accounts of syphilis was that such male behaviour appears to be far from aberrant. Indeed the spread of the disease seems to be a consequence of the inability of the male subject to properly commit to some abstract notion of bourgeois family life. The danger here is that one could generalise, and so over-simplify, this paradox. However, the peculiar reading (and subsequent writing) practices evidenced in these accounts of syphilis (including Nordau's) do indicate a desire to both discuss the dangers of apparently normative middle-class male sexual conduct, and an attempt to conceal such conduct. Although Hutchinson and Cooper provide specific examples, they are nevertheless constructing a highly politicised version of the disease and consequently their account of it is just as partial (rather than objectively scientific) as that of Nordau's. The relationship between visibility and invisibility is crucial here. The pathologised male is effectively disguised, even while all the evidence points towards him in what is a complex negotiation between signs and symptoms, interpretations and readings, and ultimately desire and pathology.

The question that such texts nervously raise is, if, in the instance of syphilis, some socially dominant 'norm' becomes pathologised then where is real value (moral, social and cultural) to be found? It is this idea of concealment, disguise, and ultimately of displacement, which will also concern us in Chapter 5 on male readings of London. As we shall see, the labyrinthine dimensions of the city are textually relocated as conceits about a barely concealed narrative concerning a masculine identity politics that is threatened from within because, as in Nordau, Hutchinson and Cooper, it can no longer be unambiguously affirmed.

Notes

1 Sarah Grand, *The Heavenly Twins* (New York: Cassell, 1893) and Emma Brooke, *A Superfluous Woman* (New York: Cassell, 1894). Also see Lesley A. Hall, '"The Great Scourge": Syphilis as a Medical Problem and a Moral Metaphor, 1880–1916', at http://homepages.primex.co.uk/~lesleyah/grtscrge.htm, p. 8.

2 Sarah Grand, *The Beth Book* (London: Heinemann, 1897) Also see Hall, '"The Great Scourge"'. An important additional, later text was Christabel Pankhurst's *The Great Scourge and How to End It* (London: E. Pankhurst, 1913).

3 Mary Spongberg, *Feminizing Venereal Disease: The Body of the Prostitute in Nineteenth-Century Medical Discourse* (Basingstoke, Macmillan: 1997) p. 35. All subsequent references are to this edition, and are given in the text.

4 Josephine Butler, 'The Garrison Towns of Kent', *Shield*, 9 May 1870 cited in Judith R. Walkowitz, *City of Dreadful Delight: Narratives of Sexual Danger in Late-Victorian London* (London, Virago: 1992) p. 92.

5 Paul McHugh, *Prostitution and Victorian Social Reform*, (London, Croom Helm: 1980) p. 17.

6 Judith R. Walkowitz, *City of Dreadful Delight: Narratives of Sexual Danger in Late-Victorian London* (London, Virago: 1992) p. 92. All subsequent references are to this edition, and are given in the text.

7 Josephine Butler to Joseph Edmondson, 28 March 1872 (Fawcett Library), cited in McHugh, *Prostitution*, p. 25.

8 See McHugh, *Prostitution*, pp. 154–5, for an account of pro-repeal support in the medical profession.

9 Michel Foucault, *The History of Sexuality: An Introduction* Vol. 1, trans. Robert Hurley (Harmondsworth: Penguin [1976] 1984) p. 24. All subsequent references are to this edition, and are given in the text.

10 See Walkowitz, *City of Dreadful Delight*, p. 198 for a discussion of the relationship between the Whitechapel killings and the body politic.

11 See Spongberg, *Feminizing Venereal Disease*, p. 155.

12 Henrik Ibsen, *Ghosts and Other Plays* (Harmondsworth: Penguin, 1964), pp. 21–102, p. 49. All subsequent references are to this edition, and are given in the text.

13 Max Nordau, *Degeneration*, (Lincoln, NE and London: University of Nebraska Press [1895] 1993) p. 357. All subsequent references are to this edition, and are given in the text.

14 See Nordau, *Degeneration*, p. 413.

15 There is, of course, a contradiction here in the idea that supposedly 'normal' woman can be perverted by the pernicious influence of Ibsen, as this compromises the alleged existence of the inherent 'natural' propensities upon which these hierarchies are formed.

16 See Daniel Pick, *Faces of Degeneration: A European Disorder, c. 1848–c.1918*, (Cambridge: Cambridge University Press [1989] 1996).

17 Jonathan Hutchinson, *Syphilis*, (Cassell: London [1887] second edition, 1909) p. 345. All subsequent references are to this edition, and are given in the text.

18 Hutchinson believed that a two year remission period was sufficient to guarantee that the subject was free of the disease.

19 Alfred Cooper, *Syphilis*, (London: Churchill, 1895) p. 342. All subsequent references are to this edition, and are given in the text.

20 See Cooper, *Syphilis*, p. 425.

21 Cooper does also acknowledge that working-class men are also subject to the disease, see *Syphilis*, p. 430.

22 There is also another narrative in these books which concerns race. In particular Hutchinson implicitly reveals the presence of an anxiety that the disease could be contracted in a colonial country and then brought back to the centre of Britain, and so the coloniser becomes colonised.

5

Displacing masculinity: Sherlock Holmes, Count Dracula and London

Sherlock Holmes's association with an abstracted, instrumental and superior gaze has suggested to critics the presence of a specifically masculine intellect, one which is contrasted, in the tales, with images of feminine irrationality.[1] Joseph A. Kestner in *Sherlock's Men: Masculinity, Conan Doyle, and Cultural History* (1997) suggests that rationality was 'strongly gendered masculine in the culture, so Holmes's initial appearance [in a scientific laboratory] and early demonstrations of "deduction" signal not only rationality but also masculinity' (p. 43). However (and as Kestner acknowledges), Doyle's tales often challenge the idea of rationality and consequently examine the expectations and limitations associated with dominant masculine scripts. Holmes is, as we shall see, at his most interesting when his claims for rationality become compromised by encounters with seemingly unconventional forms of masculine conduct. Such unconventionality is witnessed by how the tales represent male figures in disguise and how this raises often unresolved questions about the stability of gender scripts. This is in part to endorse Kestner's wider claim that 'The Holmes texts ... often present conflict which remains unresolved, resolutions which remain inconclusive, and masculinity which remains under siege rather than secure'(p. 45). However, although these are important associations we will move beyond simply addressing the link between rationality and masculinity in order to explore an alternative, but related drama, which concerns the status and function of London.

London has often merely been treated as a backdrop to Holmes's mysteries, as the place where crime is committed and solved. In one way this suggests that the social tensions and complexities that exist between competing social classes are responsible for an urban criminality that simply requires solution by the application of the superior (masculine) rationality identified by Kestner. To argue in this way is to overlook the role that London possessed during the period in defining certain gender expectations. An examination of this suggests that the ability to decode urban mysteries is dependent upon a reading of an already gendered space. This is not to claim that London is an exclusively masculine or feminine space, but rather to suggest that it becomes a site within which gender debates are determined by a form of political geography. London is not neutral in Doyle's tales because its complexities, mysteries, and seeming social and political instabilities, suggest that it too generates a discourse about gender that has not been properly accounted for, hitherto, in analyses of the tales. In other words we should move beyond solely reading Holmes's rationality in gender specific terms in order to explore how the city contributed to the debate about masculinity. A concluding reading of *Dracula* will explore how this debate is represented as a struggle for 'mastery' over the city.

At this stage it is important to debunk a myth about Holmes because Doyle's London with its fogs and alleyways only has a place in a strictly populist understanding of the tales. However, very few of the tales are actually set in London, and this chapter will later account for why Holmes is typically sent to investigate crime a day's train journey away from London. This is not to say that Holmes's mentality is anything other than a metropolitan one, but the reasons for this displacement are ones that indicate changes in attitudes towards masculinity in the period because they represent a feminine displacement of a metropolitan, masculine consciousness.

Before discussing Holmes we will examine earlier accounts of London and explore how gender issues have influenced the way that London has been read. This helps to locate the Holmes tales within a certain cultural narrative, spanning the nineteenth century, of male readings of the city. It is these readings which cumulatively indicate how writing on the city is freighted with ideas about gender, so that the city itself becomes figured as a space which possesses often conflicting gender identities. These early and mid-nineteenth century narratives also provide a conceptualisation of the city which underpins Doyle's and Stoker's versions of the city at the *fin de siècle*. To this end I will explore Thomas De Quincey's nightmares of London and his construction of an urban sublimity before briefly exploring Dickens's attempt to impose rationality on such threatened urban discord in *Bleak House* (1853). I will also briefly examine how Collins's *The Woman in White* (1860) stages a debate about gender, identity and the city. All of these narratives about London are gendered textual constructions – albeit ones influenced by a real, extra-textual geography of gender.

This chapter is an exploration of literary, rather than journalistic, accounts of London. This is a somewhat different version of London than that examined in Chapter 3, although there are various similarities with how London was discussed in class and gender terms by journalists and social reformers at the time.

De Quincey's urban nightmares: rationality, opium and cherchez la femme

Thomas De Quincey's account of London in *Confessions of an English Opium Eater* (1821) develops a range of issues relating to how the frightening, indeed Gothic, features of the city can be interpreted. The reason why, in the *Confessions*, London takes on such a Gothic quality is due to De Quincey's inability to rationalise the complex, labyrinthine aspects of the city. He recounts a nightmare in which London is an 'unfathomed abyss' where 'I saw London expanding her visionary gates to receive me, like some dreadful mouth of Acheron'.[2] The nightmare is consequent upon his earlier, waking, anxieties about London on the night preceding his journey to the city, in which:

> now rose London – sole, dark, infinite – brooding over the whole capacities of my heart. Other object – other thought – I could not admit ... More than ever I stood upon the brink of a precipice; and the local circumstances around me deepened and intensified these reflections, impressed upon them solemnity and terror, sometimes even horror. (p. 195)

While in London, the terrors seem to be more prosaic, as due to a lack of money he spent most of his time confronted with starvation, 'I now suffered, for upwards of sixteen weeks, the physical anguish of hunger in various degrees of intensity; but as bitter perhaps, as ever any human being can have suffered who has survived it' (p. 45). It is because De Quincey experiences London in this visceral way that it forms (if somewhat paradoxically) a strange romantic vision, one in which the disorder of the self (his apparent mental and emotional disorientation) is matched by the city's own Gothic complexities. The narrative structure of the book also reflects this with its hesitations, repetitions and revisions. Throughout there is a sense of De Quincey, as both actor and author, searching for some mechanism through which coherent meaning can be made to appear. The text suggests that there exist two possible, mutually incompatible solutions to this problem. One is via an account of how opium use stimulates, although artificially and only temporarily, a quasi-Kantian notion of rationality. In this instance the apparently threatened disorder of the (urban) sublime is supplanted by the consoling presence of a higher level of reason (a version of the supersensible) which suggests that an interpretation, although deferred, can at some future, if unspecified point, be made on rational grounds.[3] The second solution is that by searching for Ann, the prostitute who treated him kindly by giving him food, he can reclaim a version of the city which has a moral sense to it. In both cases the question is one of how to 'master' the city.

De Quincey's discussion of opium use is interesting to the degree that he argues that it stimulates rational thought, even as it alienates the subject from 'reality'. As in De Quincey's horrified (although retrospective) anticipation of London, it is the imagination which plays a central role in determining perception. De Quincey is able to overcome feelings of disorientation (and, momentarily, hunger) through drug use. This anticipates Sherlock Holmes who, when he is not working on a case, uses cocaine for mental stimulation. Also, in both instances the mind is peculiarly abstracted and disembodied. It is a disembodiment which enables De Quincey to transcend a frightening, because predominately visceral, sense of the city. In this romantic context the city provides an example of a Burkean sublime moment as it corresponds to a model of the sublime seemingly without transcendence. For Burke, 'Whatever is fitted in any sort to excite the ideas of pain, and danger, that is to say, whatever is in any sort terrible, or is conversant about terrible objects, or operates in a manner analogous to terror, is a source of the *sublime*' (emphasis Burke's).[4] De Quincey attempts to resolve this through a Kantian faith in the presence of reason. However, De Quincey's account of opium addiction glosses Burke's attempts to define the sublime through a variety of contexts and contrasts. De Quincey initially achieves this by contrasting the effects of wine with opium concluding that 'the main distinction lies in this, that whereas wine disorders the mental faculties, opium, on the contrary (if taken in a proper manner), introduces amongst them the most exquisite order, legislation, and harmony' (p. 73). Here opium is the rational man's drug of choice because it introduces order whereas wine stimulates disorder (as it leads, for De Quincey, to moral laxity and mental confusion). The subject realises their full moral and intellectual potential through opium use, 'The opium-eater ... feels that the diviner part of his nature is paramount; that is, the moral affections are in a state of cloudless serenity; and over all is the great light of the majestic intellect' (p. 75).

This privileging of rationality gives back, at least temporarily, an authority to an otherwise marginalised and alienated masculine self. This new, empowered, version of the self is able to transcend emotion by claiming for itself an intellectual and moral superiority. This is also to acknowledge that De Quincey's feelings of disempowerment in London are enacted in gender terms, which is in part represented through how a figure such as Ann (herself a marginalised and alienated figure) is able to exercise a superior ability to function within the city than De Quincey. He becomes an urban victim who is looked after by Ann and her subsequent disappearance turns the city back into a nightmarish form in which subjects become both literally and figuratively (morally) lost. Ultimately, however, it is a loss which is not compensated for by the artificially stimulated intellect, because De Quincey acknowledges that this model is crucially compromised as it is staged purely within the realms of an abstracted imagination. He notes that while the opium user retains a moral sensibility, 'his intellectual apprehension of what is possible … infinitely outruns his power, not of execution only, but even of power to attempt' (p. 102). Any superiority is therefore solely a theoretical one, and it is this which is associated with another narrative concerning gender which is linked with Ann.

Ann's links with prostitution tie her closely to London and to a narrative of illicit sexual activity. Ann's disappearance compromises De Quincey's claims about the possibility of asserting a rational interpretation of mystery. Her disappearance is an urban irrationality that De Quincey's failure to account for represents, for him, a personal crisis. Ultimately the city defies coherence, but then De Quincey had himself acknowledged that any such coherence is essentially mental rather than real. Ann thus testifies to the presence of another narrative relating to an unfathomable world of urban decay and sexual licence that puts her beyond the intellectual and moral values of the opium induced reverie. The loss of Ann takes on a symbolic dimension which comes to inhabit all kinds of associated images of failure. For Julian Wolfreys: 'The anxiety caused by the loss of Ann is, in itself, merely symptomatic of the larger effect of London on De Quincey. For London is a city of losses, disappearances, obscured identities, dreariness and dream-like states. It is the place of anxiety and anguish, of both body and mind'.[5] In this way Ann becomes the unconscious of the text and represents the failure of a conscious, masculine mode of rational perception (for De Quincey opium use is a male pastime) that should be able to discover her through a reasoned, deductive, mode of enquiry:

The search after the lost features of Ann, which I spoke of as pursued in the crowds of London, was in a more proper sense pursued through many a year in [opium induced] dreams. The general idea of a search and a chase reproduced itself in many shapes. The person, the rank, the age, the scenical position, all varied themselves for ever; but the same leading traits more or less faintly remained of a lost Pariah woman, and of some shadowy malice which withdrew her, or attempted to withdraw her, from restoration and from hope. (p. 139)

The failed pursuit of the lost woman thus conditions the failure of rationality. By becoming part of the opium dream she displaces the rational and replaces it with a more complex notion of identity, the complexity of which is mirrored within 'the labyrinths of London' (p. 64).

If Ann, and the world of sexuality with which she is associated, is the unspoken aspect of the narrative then it suggests that De Quincey's model of rationality is predicated on excluding desire. It is this association which has links with the Sherlock Holmes tales, concerning which Catherine Belsey has argued: 'these stories, whose overt project is total explication, total verisimilitude in the interests of a plea for scientificity, are haunted by shadowy, mysterious and often silent women. Their silence repeatedly conceals their sexuality, investing it with a dark and magical quality which is beyond the reach of scientific knowledge.'⁶ In both De Quincey and the Holmes tales, the mysteries of women become the mysteries of London. It is an issue that Dickens developed in *Bleak House* and Collins in *The Woman in White*.

Urban Gothic: Dickens and Collins

Robert Mighall in *A Geography of Victorian Gothic Fiction* explores how G.W.M. Reynolds's *The Mysteries of London* (1846) reworks an earlier, Radcliffean, form of the Gothic in order to construct a specifically urban version of terror. For Mighall, Reynolds's novel transposes 'the moral and aesthetic meanings of the traditional Gothic landscape ... to specific parts of the metropolis'.⁷ This is not however a simple matter of appropriation and reconstruction, rather Reynolds also 'shows how parts of the modern city surpass what was once considered the pressure of the Radcliffean landscape' (p. 48). This is because there exist unique dimensions to this urban sublime, relating to the complexity (and indeed for Mighall, the aroma) of the city. The claim made for *The Mysteries of London* is that it constitutes one of the first urban reformations of the Gothic tradition. Mighall also notes how this development of the Gothic influenced

Dickens's *Bleak House*, because 'labyrinthine London had already been firmly established as the modern urban equivalent of the Gothic castle or mansion' (p. 70). In this way Dickens's representation of aristocratic decline, as represented by Chesney Wold (the home of Lord and Lady Dedlock), is linked to urban decay due to its associations with images of moral and physical dilapidation, associations which more properly configure the urban Gothic of London.

In *Bleak House* repeated images of labyrinthine complexity stimulate a variety of attempted explanations of the mysteries relating to crime, family, identity and urban decay. Esther Summerson functions as one of the detectives as she ponders on the connections between herself and Chesney Wold (connections which are revealed when Lady Dedlock is exposed as her mother). The narrative structure of the novel also generates complexity by the use of a third-person narrative voice whose pessimism suggests that even if coherent designs can be identified, it is impossible to rectify them (as in, for example, the connections between the pestilential slum Tom All-Alone's and its political mismanagement). Ultimately it is an outsider, Inspector Bucket (an outsider to the family although an insider to the city) who reveals the existence of a coherent chain of events which helps link Esther to Lady Dedlock. This process of interpretation also implies the presence of a submerged narrative relating to gender. As Deborah Epstein Nord comments: 'Lady Dedlock enters the nighttime labyrinth of the city on her own ... risking identification with the homeless women, the women by the river, the women who have drowned themselves in the Thames. Esther, on the other hand, goes in the protective company of Inspector Bucket, holder of secrets, who can traverse the city without danger.'[8] Mighall's analysis is a particular historicist reading of the Gothic, one which marginalises questions of gender. However, as Nord suggests, *Bleak House* constructs its urban mysteries in gender specific terms which contribute to a popular representation of London which dogs Doyle's account of London in the Sherlock Holmes tales.

Alison Milbank has argued (as did Mighall subsequently) that the Radcliffean Gothic underpins much of Gothic writing in the mid-nineteenth century, especially influencing the work of Dickens and Collins. Following the work of Ellen Moers, she argues that Dickens in *Bleak House* relocates Radcliffe's development of a specifically Female Gothic.[9] This is manifested in the central dynamic concerning the gradual revelation of the relationship between Esther and Lady Dedlock. Esther is also associated with a world of domesticity in ways which, familiar from the Female Gothic, question the organisation, function and control of domestic spaces. These formal similarities to the Female Gothic aside, Milbank also argues that the two competing narrative voices, that of Esther's narrative and the third-person narration, correspond to Female and Male Gothic idioms. She notes that Esther in her account of the Dedlocks, 'Asserts the possibility of change and fruitfulness as the representative of a "female" Gothic vision, while the angry thunderings of the third-person narrator … has the fatalism of the "male" Gothic voice' (p. 97). It is the tension between these two voices which means that mystery becomes interpreted in gender terms (or at least as such terms were formulated within certain pre-existing Gothic narratives). The novel debates the respective merits of Esther's optimistic narrative concerning the possibility, and indeed need for, change with the 'male' Gothic voice which dwells on the failure to render the events into a meaningful moral and political vision. Esther thus functions like a detective in that she searches for patterns and explanations, whereas the 'male' Gothic voice merely accepts that matters of influence (such as they can be perceived) are beyond one's power to control. London is thus associated with instability to the degree that it is represented as posing a problem for interpretation. The mysteries of Chancery are reflected in the complex social and economic identities of the characters that become involved in it, and these complexities reflect the social diversity of the city itself.

Esther gains authority by acting upon the world in a way which suggests the importance of her agency in ordering, and so controlling, domestic spaces. As Milbank has noted, the novel also underlines the importance of writing, which suggests that Esther's narrative control, and her ability to self-reflect, usurps and so marginalises the pessimistic male voice in the novel.[10] The problem is to arrange a set of seemingly disparate moments into a coherent narrative. This presence of disorder is, to give one example, glossed in the names of Miss Flite's collection of caged birds, 'Hope, Joy, Youth, Peace, Rest, Life, Dust, Ashes, Waste, Want, Despair, Madness, Death, Cunning, Folly, Words, Wigs, Rags, Sheepskin, Plunder, Precedent, Jargon, Gammon, and Spinach'.[11] These words acquire sense through their relationship to each other, and so emphasise the importance of writing as a creative force which constructs narrative order. The point is to discover the underlying patterns that enable the points of convergence between different types of experience to be seen. Towards the end of the novel Esther recounts how 'poor crazed Miss Flite' (p. 927) tearfully informs her that she has released the birds, a moment of symbolic, if melodramatic, significance given that it is related to Esther's own feelings of release after the discovery of her mother and the idea of escaping from Chancery. The novel is also, of course, a tragedy because of the death of Lady Dedlock, but the focus throughout has been on how the existence of disparate forms of information can be rationalised. This range of information is generated by the urban context, meaning that rationalising such information becomes a means of asserting authority over London itself. This process is underpinned by gender considerations, a process developed in a more overt way by Wilkie Collins in *The Woman in White*.

The mystery in *The Woman in White* has its origin in a specific encounter on a road into London: 'There in the middle of the broad, bright high-road – there, as if it had that moment sprung out of the earth or dropped from the heaven – stood the figure of a solitary Woman, dressed from head to foot in white garments, her face bent in grave inquiry on mine, her hand pointing to the dark cloud over London, as I faced her.'[12] It is this first encounter with Ann Catherick on the way to London that provokes Walter into a mood of reassessment. Ann's appearance and account of herself are, for Walter, a 'fathomless' mystery, that leads him to question 'Was I indeed Walter Hartright?' (p. 50). Identity and its construction are thus signalled from the start as the narrative's principal concern.

The Woman in White is an explicit exploration of how gender is related to analysis. At one level the novel is as much about this link as it is about mystery. The novel self-consciously focuses on the representation of gender. Many critics have noted, for example, that Marian Halcombe is the principal detective for the first part of the novel and that she functions in this way because of certain masculine characteristics relating to her appearance, characteristics which also suggest the presence of a particular temperament. Walter Hartright, the other principal detective, notes of her that, 'She had a large, firm, masculine mouth and jaw; prominent, piercing, resolute brown eyes; and thick, coal-black hair, growing unusually low down on her forehead. Her expression – bright, frank, and intelligent – appeared, while she was silent, to be altogether wanting in those feminine attractions of gentleness and pliability' (pp. 58–9). At this stage in the novel the emphasis is on how Hartright interprets character through a strict adherence to the dominant gender script. The self-conscious irony that the reader is invited to consider is that Marian has authority over Walter because she is both his employer and more masculine than him. Walter, a drawing master who offers his services to wealthy young ladies, becomes transformed into a man of action after a series of adventures in South America embarked on in order to ease his broken heart when Marian has dismissed him because of his attachment to Laura Fairlie, whom he had been employed to instruct. This masculinisation of Walter from drawing master to man of action can be read as Collins's parodic take on masculinity. We are invited to understand the irony where Walter does not. This is also clear in Walter's retrospective account of an early drawing of Laura Fairlie which contrasts with the earlier, narrative portrait of Marian. He notes that the sketch shows 'A fair, delicate girl, in a pretty light dress, trifling with the leaves of a sketch-book, while she looks up from it with truthful, innocent blue eyes' but he then acknowledges that 'that is all the drawing can say'. The drawing is inadequate for Walter because it fails to reflect his feelings for her; it is a 'dim mechanical drawing' (p. 75). And yet the picture is accurate; Laura on a gender level *is* the purely two-dimensional character that is represented in the drawing. Again, it is Walter's conservative assessment of gender which is at fault here, something intimated by his sense that the drawing is a failure because 'At one time it seemed like something wanting, like something wanting in *her*: at another, like something wanting in myself, which hindered me from understanding her as I ought' (p. 76).

The Woman in White is therefore about gender as much as it is about interpretation. In one sense gender *is* the mystery that the novel tries to unravel, as Walter is confronted with a series of characters such as Marian, Mr Fairlie and Fosco, who challenge his faith in the impermeability of dominant gender models.

London and its association with gender narratives run through these accounts of London by De Quincey, Dickens and Collins. This also indicates how a literature about London provides the context within which Doyle's debate about gender takes place.

Sherlock Holmes – rational man

The unifying issue which has brought De Quincey, Dickens and Collins into an alliance is their shared anxiety concerning the erosion of male power. This operates at different levels across the texts, and it is certainly true that *The Woman in White* is much more explicit *about* that concern than De Quincey, but nevertheless the status and function of a rationalising masculine gaze is a central issue. The gradual emergence of a self-conscious scrutiny of gender is charted in these texts and it constitutes a tradition of scrutiny which is developed by Doyle in the Sherlock Holmes stories. Gender is one of the key elements of the Holmes tales and has, as discussed at the beginning of this chapter, conditioned critical examination of the tales. Gender and rationality appear to be linked, as Kestner claims, but Holmes's association with rationality, gender, and the city needs to be culturally contextualised to the period.

Georg Simmel's sociological analyses of modern life, written in the late nineteenth and early twentieth centuries help to illuminate the construction of a masculine metropolitan consciousness which bears relevance to a reading of Holmes. Simmel in 'The Metropolis and Mental Life' (1903) argues the case that the city is a place composed of such complex scenes and emotions that a type of rational mentality is formulated in order to distance the subject from the overwhelming range of stimuli which depletes 'mental energy' by over stimulating the senses.[13] So for Simmel, 'the metropolitan type … creates a protective organ for itself against the profound disruption with which the fluctuations and discontinuities of the external milieu threaten it' (p. 326). The intellect thus becomes the means by which the subject can move beyond this threatened emotional turmoil. In many respects the roots of this can be found in De Quincey's *Confessions* with its paradoxical pursuit of order through the unreality of the opium dream. For Simmel this rational consciousness is the product of a money-based society. He argues that 'Money economy and the domination of the intellect stand in the closest relationship to one another. They have in common a purely matter-of-fact attitude in the treatment of persons and things in which a formal justice is often combined with an unrelenting hardness' (p. 326). The city, because it is *the* place of commerce, therefore becomes the site through which this mentality is generated. Simmel comments that as a consequence in 'the entire course of English history London has never acted as the heart of England but often as its intellect and always as its money bag' (p. 327). This reification conditions all kinds of human conduct and contact. Nevertheless, Simmel argues for the existence of an 'inner nature' which eludes this process of metropolitan commodification (p. 335). Simmel accounts for this peculiarly divided self in historical terms, arguing that the rise of individualism at the end of the eighteenth century was the product of a throwing off of the older ties which had bound subjects to a predominately agrarian, religious and guild culture. This new liberal culture acquired, via romanticism, the additional burden that the subject needed to assert not only their freedom, but also their unique distinction from other subjects. In this way there emerged a tension between a liberal desire for freedom from the political order (which could unite subjects into new economic and political groups) and an emergent model of individualism which fragmented any such possibility for coherent, concerted group-formation. Ultimately, there was a movement from romantic individualism to the creation of economic 'man'. The result of this unresolved tension is that, at the end of the nineteenth century, there emerges a conflict between the needs of a personal, inner psychic life, and an economic culture which, through its tendency to reify, turns individuals into social 'types'. This tension runs through the texts that we have looked at so far. Social identity, especially in the guise of gender, functions as a form of reification in Collins. Elsewhere this strange doubling between inner and outer worlds interrogates the social construction of identity. It is the presence of this double life which runs through so many of the case histories here such as Joseph Merrick's and Oscar Wilde's, and it is also to be found, as we have seen, in the speculations concerning the Jekyll and Hyde identity of the Whitechapel killer. It is an issue which informs the Holmes tales which possess a fascination with exploring the idea that the social self can be counterfeited, and that it is the detective who can see through such disguises and identify the 'real' criminal.

First it is important to note that in the Holmes tales the mystery of identity is associated with the middle classes. Rosemary Jann has noted how working-class figures in the tales have their criminality decoded through a theory of physiognomy. In this way the working-class criminal is allied to theories of degeneracy, whereas criminals from the middle and upper classes are more difficult to decode because they are able to take on a variety of different guises.[14] As Jann notes of the Holmes tales 'it is almost always characters from the higher classes who successfully counterfeit themselves' (p. 695). Jann however also acknowledges that there is an additional gender issue here because women in the tales tend to be associated with working-class irrationality, 'The common thread … seems to be that women in general (like the lower classes) have less control over their emotions' (p. 697). Jann is right to suggest that there is a conservative agenda at work in these tales, but although Doyle's middle and upper-class criminals might evade such crude typologies, nevertheless they are associated with a level of potential criminality which far exceeds that of other groups. For Doyle, the arch criminal is the middle-class, ostensibly respectable male who abuses or otherwise compromises his class responsibilities. Again, as throughout this book, such figures indicate an increasing demonisation of the middle-class male, a demonisation which is made all the more problematic to the degree that the existing theories of degeneracy fail to 'read' the signs of the potentially pathologised middle-class male.

A tale such as 'The Man with the Twisted Lip' from the *Adventures of Sherlock Holmes* (1892) provides a good example of how middle-class respectability becomes challenged by the fabrication of a working-class persona, one which suggests the presence of deviance even as that deviance is, paradoxically, worn as a disguise. For Kestner 'The tale raises questions about the degree to which any Victorian wife knows the true nature of the family paterfamilias' (*Sherlock's Men*, p. 96).

The narrative begins with a search, one which links the tale explicitly to De Quincey's London:

> Isa Whitney, brother of the late Elias Whitney, D.D., Principal of the Theological College of St. George's, was much addicted to opium. The habit grew upon him, as I understand, from some foolish freak when he was at college; for having read De Quincey's description of his dreams and sensations, he had drenched his tobacco with laudanum in an attempt to produce the same effects.[15]

Watson is persuaded by Whitney's wife to search for the missing Whitney, which requires a visit to an opium den in a deprived part of London.[16] The tale never explicitly states the reason why Watson makes this undertaking, but the implication is that the search requires some discretion and so Watson decides to go alone. The location of the den in Upper Swandam Lane is described in terms familiar from the nineteenth-century urban Gothic: 'Upper Swandam Lane is a vile alley lurking behind the high wharves which line the north side of the river to the east of London Bridge. Between a slop-shop and a gin-shop, approached by a steep flight of steps leading down to a black gap like the mouth of a cave, I found the den of which I was in search' (p. 230). What, however, is surprising is that Watson discovers in the den not only Whitney (who is sent home in a cab) but also Holmes. Holmes is working undercover to gather evidence concerning the disappearance of Neville St Clair, described as a businessman with independent means, and believes that a 'sinister cripple' who works in the opium den can provide some crucial evidence (p. 235). The disappearance of St Clair is initially baffling as he is socially and economically secure, and seemingly happily married. Holmes tells Watson that St Clair 'is a man of temperate habits, a good husband, a very affectionate father, and a man who is popular with all who know him' (p. 233). The disappearance of this model of middle-class respectability into an opium den is in keeping with how the tale produces a series of dialectical social tensions which are apparent between the drunkard Whitney and his ecclesiastical brother, between London and the country (the St Clairs live in Kent) and between St Clair and the 'sinister cripple' that Holmes wishes to interview. All this suggests the presence of a social instability which indicates that identity itself is unstable. As in Simmel's claims concerning the tension between an 'inner life' and a world of social typologies, this doubling threatens notions of a coherent model of the self. In particular it indicates that the role of the middle-class male is itself under threat, although at this stage it appears that this threat is externally manifested by some of the more dangerous characters who haunt the opium den.

It transpires, however, that St Clair has disguised himself as the man that Holmes wants to interview. This character (and it is a character in the sense of it being a role) is complete with a twisted lip and scars which serves to associate him with an urban Gothic world. This man is arrested for the murder of St Clair but it is Holmes who removes the make-up and discloses the features of St Clair, the whole scene working towards emphasising the presence of a double life. Watson notes how, 'Gone was the coarse brown tint! Gone, too, was the horrid scar which had seamed it across, and the twisted lip which had given the repulsive sneer to the face! A twitch brought away the tangled red hair, and there, sitting up in his bed, was a pale, sad-faced, refined-looking man' (p. 242). Beneath criminal identity appears respectability. This association between respectability and criminality links the middle-class male to a potential atavism which specifically threatens domesticity, which is emphasised in the image of St. Clair's abandoned and distraught wife. St Clair explains that he took on the guise of a beggar when he got into financial difficulties and had to pay off a writ of £25. In his youth he had been an actor and at one point had worked for a newspaper as a reporter, where he had once pretended to be a beggar in order to write an article. He had then played this role again in order to pay off his debt. It is revealed that St Clair's financial success has come about because he realised that he could make a considerable amount of money in this way, as he tells them 'Well, you can imagine how hard it was to settle down to arduous work at £2 a week when I knew that I could earn as much in a day by smearing my face with a little paint, laying my cap on the ground, and sitting still' (p. 243). The money generated enables him to buy a house in the country and to pretend to his wife that he has an important job in the city. Unfortunately for him his wife, on a visit to London, had caught sight of him at a window in a room above the opium den where he changed into his beggar's clothes. In his rush to disguise himself St. Clair's respectable clothes had been discovered and this was why he (in the guise of a beggar) was subsequently incriminated in his disappearance.

For Kestner the tale represents: 'theories of the deterioration of the middle-class standards and the crisis of masculinity at the end of the nineteenth century … The tale both indicts and camouflages transgressive masculinity. In suggesting that bourgeois marriage rests on such disguise, the narrative stands as one of Doyle's most searing explorations of Victorian male identity' (*Sherlock's Men*, p. 97). This is a grand claim because although the tale does indicate a 'deterioration' in male 'middle-class standards', it only does so by suggesting disempowerment. St Clair learns that the way to economic success is outside of middle-class work patterns. The tale also challenges bourgeois notions of the family and, as Diana Barsham has noted, of the twelve tales which make up the *Adventures* ten concern errant husbands.[17] However, it is also about how that power is displaced. It is the relationship between the country and the city which is important to consider here. Holmes notes in his and Watson's journey from London that 'We have touched on three English counties in our short drive, starting in Middlesex, passing over an angle of Surrey, and ending in Kent' (p. 237). It is this displacement into the country which shifts the focus onto Holmes, an examination of this shift reveals how it functions as a trope for the displacement of masculinity.

Displacing Urban Man

Franco Moretti in his *Atlas of the European Novel 1800–1900* maps (literally) the scenes of crime and Holmes's movements across London in the first two novels *A Study in Scarlet* (1887) and *The Sign of Four* (1890). Moretti notes that most of the criminal activity takes place in the West End rather than in the more crime-ridden East End of the city. Moretti also acknowledges that much of the action of the other tales does not take place in London. However, he dismisses this by supporting the claim of Loïc Ravenel that because of the proximity of the Home Counties to London 'the countryside is for all practical purposes a mere appendix of the urban context' so that for Moretti 'Doyle's favourite counties ... Surrey, Kent, Sussex' are merely 'code words for a weekend in the country'.[18] However, the displacement of this admittedly urban consciousness cannot just be explained by simply suggesting that the Home Counties really function as some kind of outer London. Holmes is also quite explicit about this, telling Watson in 'The Adventure of the Copper Beeches' (while on a journey through Hampshire) that 'It is my belief, Watson, founded upon my experience, that the lowest and vilest alleys in London do not present a more dreadful record of sin than does the smiling and beautiful countryside'.[19] In response to Watson's protestations Holmes responds by saying that in London:

There is no lane so vile that the scream of a tortured child, or the thud of a drunkard's blow, does not beget sympathy and indignation among the neighbours, and then the whole machinery of justice is ever so close that a word of complaint can set it going, and there is but a step between the crime and the dock. But look at these lonely houses, each in its own fields, filled for the most part with poor ignorant folk who know little of the law. Think of the deeds of hellish cruelty, the hidden wickedness which may go on, year in, year out, in such places, and none the wiser. (p. 323)

The country is therefore a place where crime can be more effectively accomplished and this explains why so many of the tales are set in the country. Also although here Holmes is referring to 'poor ignorant folk', elsewhere in the tales the Home Counties' associations with wealth link them to a world of potentially sophisticated middle-class crime. It is therefore in the country that a greater degree of criminal ingenuity is to be found, whereas in the city 'Man, or at least criminal man, has lost all enterprise and originality' (p. 317). Moretti's literal mapping of the narratives is one which overlooks how the tales symbolically represent issues about power, rather than simply duck the issue of East End crime. Holmes is not being perverse when he argues for the existence of a superior, because more sophisticated, criminal activity in the country. It is in the country that Holmes can reassert a model of masculine rationality (although not unproblematically) that was becoming increasingly squeezed out of the city in the nineteenth century. Thus although Holmes exemplifies the existence of Simmel's metropolitan mind, it is not the case that this rationality finds its home in the city. To appreciate this we need to return to Moretti's idea concerning the significance of locale.

Holmes's lodgings in Baker Street means that he resides close to the areas of Paddington, Oxford Street, Bayswater and Edgware. This was an area over which there was considerable gender contestation from the mid-nineteenth century to the 1920s (the Holmes tales which were published between 1887 and 1927 also cover this period). Erika Diane Rappaport has examined how the growth of department stores in the area meant that it became progressively colonised as a space of female leisure. The growth in markets meant to cater for female, middle-class shoppers might well indicate that the market had found a new group to exploit, but nevertheless 'Although shopping was imagined as connected to a woman's domestic responsibilities, it was primarily conceived as a public pleasure'.[20] In this way the link between the private world of the home and the public world of the market place was broken down. Holmes may possess a metropolitan reified consciousness which, for Simmel, reflects the functions of a money-based society, but for Rappaport the same is not true of the woman shopper, who is introduced to the idea that pleasure can exist outside of the home. There has been some disagreement about how far one can plausibly claim that women shoppers were empowered and Judith R. Walkowitz argues that 'Shopping emerged as a newly elaborated female activity in the 1870s, but it reinforced a public role traditionally performed by ladies as decorous indicators of social distance, visible signs of the social system. As consumers, ladies served as status symbols of their husbands' wealth'.[21] However, Walkowitz also argues that the woman shopper challenged prevailing notions of female propriety (the woman on her own out in public) because they confounded dominant notions of decency by being out in public at all, despite their associations with middle-class respectability. All this suggests the complex renegotiation required in order to make sense of this new semantic shift. It is Holmes who, by virtue of location, is caught up in these new problems concerning gender identity.

Holmes's location in this area goes some way in explaining how his own figuring as a metropolitan man comes to be associated with misogyny.[22] The place of Holmes's consulting room in Baker Street can be read as a gesture of defiance against this encroaching female colonisation. As Barsham notes, '221B Baker Street became a magical site at which deformed, anxious and estranged masculinities encountered the corrective resymbolizations of ... manhood' (*Meaning of Masculinity*, p. 1). This is important to note because the area was not simply one associated with female shopping. It was also an area associated with the emergence of women's clubs.[23] Rappaport notes that from the 1870s the area around Baker Street (specifically around the areas of Piccadilly and Berkeley Square) 'became the heart of female clubland' (*Shopping for Pleasure*, p. 9). Also, Holmes's proximity to Langham Place locates him close to the 'center of the mid-Victorian women's movement' (p. 9).

For Rappaport the real issue at the time concerned a masculine anxiety that the distinction between pure and impure women was threatened. These new female shoppers were frequently accosted as prostitutes, and Mark Twain in 1880 noted that 'If a lady unattended walks abroad in the streets ... even at noonday she will be pretty likely to be accosted and insulted – and not by drunken sailors but by men who carry the look and wear of a gentleman'.[24] A comment which identifies the 'respectable' gentleman as the source of corruption. It also confirms how in the nineteenth century there was a progressive cultural shift which displaced the blame for prostitution from the prostitute to the client, an issue discussed in Chapter 4.

The notion that one could not distinguish between 'proper' and improper' women because of a strictly male (mis)perception of the performance of femininity is also obliquely addressed by Doyle. The idea of streetwalkers in disguise is central to 'A Scandal in Bohemia' from the *Adventures*, a tale in which Holmes is outwitted by an actress.

Role play and gender performance

In 'A Scandal in Bohemia' Holmes is approached by the King of Bohemia who, on the eve of announcing his marriage believes he is about to be blackmailed by a former spurned lover, Irene Adler, who intends to reveal their affair by making public a photograph of her and the King taken at the time. Holmes is employed to retrieve the photograph and so save the King's reputation (the King states that he could not have married Adler, an Opera singer, as she was not of the same social rank as him).

The drama relating to the retrieval of the photograph takes place against a backdrop in which everyone is in disguise, where there are fundamental misconceptions (Adler has no intention of blackmailing the King) and a suggested, potential, relationship between Holmes and Adler. Ultimately the tale suggests that Adler is a deeply disturbing presence for Holmes because she confounds his preconception that women are not able to think rationally and so challenges his own claims for the dominance of a superior, masculine, rational gaze. Watson acknowledges at the start that Holmes respects Adler precisely because she did not behave like women in general, 'To Sherlock Holmes she is always *the* woman. I have seldom heard him mention her under any other name. In his eyes she eclipses and predominates the whole of her sex'.[25] And although Watson is at pains to emphasise that Holmes was not in love with her, because he was incapable of love and that 'He never spoke of the softer passions, save with a gibe and a sneer' (p. 162), nevertheless by a subtle process of doubling Holmes is drawn into the narrative in a personal way.

It transpires that Adler has fallen in love with and subsequently marries a lawyer called Godfrey Norton. She only intends to keep the photograph of her and the King in order to protect herself should the King ever think of trying to harm her. In this way the plot unravels as no crime (blackmail) has taken place. If anything it is Holmes and Watson who intend to break the law in conspiring to steal the photograph. Holmes asks Watson:

'You don't mind breaking the law?'
'Not in the least.'

'Nor running a chance of arrest?'
'Not in a good cause.' (p. 170)

Not only are they positioned on the side of illegality, but the 'scandal' in
Bohemia is imaginary in its connection with the King (because there is no
blackmail) but symbolically real in its relationship to Holmes. It is a
connection which also underlines Holmes's social position as outside
prevailing cultural norms, which is re-emphasised in the later suggestions
of illegality. At the start of the tale, Watson, now happily married and
living in contented domesticity, acknowledges that this contrasts with
Holmes, 'who loathed society with his whole Bohemian soul' (p. 161). It is
Holmes's cultural Bohemia which is disturbed by Adler as she challenges
his sense of intellectual superiority.[26]

The tale also constructs implicit parallels between Holmes and Norton;
the latter is described as 'dark, aquiline' (p. 168), which suggests Holmes.
Also, both are first represented in the same attitude, seen through windows,
pacing up and down, Holmes in thought and Norton in discussion with
Adler. When Holmes pursues Norton and Adler he is surprised to find
them in a church, and is then drawn into their wedding ceremony as a
witness. Holmes at this point is in disguise as a stable hand, but the claim
that he is also a would-be (pretend) 'groom' at a symbolic level is also
implied. Watson notes that Holmes looked like 'a drunken-looking groom,
ill-kempt and side-whiskered, with an inflamed face and disreputable
clothes' (p. 167), which in the context of the implied love narrative makes
him look like a failed, manifestly working-class, love rival.

The key issue here is that of performance. Holmes plays a variety of
roles: a groom, and later, in order to gain sympathetic access to Adler's
house 'an amiable and simple-minded Nonconformist clergyman' (p. 170).
Watson notes of Holmes that 'The stage lost a fine actor, even as science
lost an acute reasoner, when he became a specialist in crime' (p. 170).
However, Holmes is not the only actor; the King of Bohemia first meets
Holmes and Watson wearing a mask although soon discards it as Holmes
has already, cunningly, worked out who he is. The King, at another level,
also performs a particular model of masculinity, something which is
foregrounded in Watson's initial description of him when his identity as
the King has yet to be revealed, and so as a result his identity is first of all
defined by his overstated masculine presence. Watson notes that, 'A man
entered who could hardly have been less than six feet six inches in height,
with the chest and limbs of a Hercules...From the lower part of the face
he appeared to be a man of strong character, with a thick, hanging lip, and
a long, straight chin suggestive of resolution pushed to the length of

obstinacy' (p. 164). No wonder that Adler keeps the photograph 'only to safeguard myself, and to preserve a weapon which will always secure me from any steps which he might take in the future' (p. 175). Adler's intent is to control, rather than destroy. Nevertheless the tale is fundamentally concerned with the idea of displacing such male authority figures, and the image of Holmes as a rejected metaphorical suitor also refers to this. Additionally, much of the important action concerns ownership over the street. Holmes, for example, stages a small riot in the street in which, in the guise of the clergyman, he is 'wounded' and taken into Adler's house. Watson then throws a flare through the open window and raises the alarm that a fire has started, an alarm which has been designed to provoke Adler into trying to secure the safety of the photograph and in so doing to reveal its whereabouts to Holmes. This all-male street theatre is one which performs different kinds of class-bound masculinities, including 'loafers', 'guardsmen' and Holmes as the 'clergyman'. However, although Adler is initially duped she ultimately sees through this drama and, as she had been previously warned about Holmes, sees who is responsible for it.

That ownership of the street is related to these notions of masculine authority is emphasised by the final encounter that takes place in the street. Holmes and Watson return to Baker Street in the evening of these events:

> We had reached Baker Street and had stopped at the door. [Holmes] was searching his pockets for the key when someone passing said:
> 'Good-night, Mister Sherlock Holmes.'
> There were several people on the pavement at the time, but the greeting appeared to come from a slim youth in an Ulster who had hurried by.
> 'I've heard that voice before,' said Holmes, staring down the dimly lit street.
> 'Now, I wonder who the deuce that could have been.' (p. 173)

The following day when they return to Adler's house to retrieve the photograph, they find that Adler has disappeared and where the photograph should have been there is a photograph of her and a letter for Holmes. The letter reveals that the youth was Adler in disguise, 'I have trained as an actress myself. Male costume is nothing new to me. I often take advantage of the freedom which it gives' (pp. 174–5). And so Holmes is beaten by a woman in disguise who stalks him in the streets and teases him with her presence. The street is also owned through a parodic male performance, a woman in disguise, which at one level relocates the contemporary anxiety about distinguishing between women in disguise (prostitutes) and the proper woman. At another level Adler becomes a streetwalker who can infiltrate the streets without fear of being molested because the male costume gives her 'the freedom' to do so. In this way the streets become owned through stealth and subversion, as parts of the city (the parts inhabited by Holmes) became progressively redefined as female-owned (economically, culturally, and intellectually) during the period.[27]

Rationality and the country

The Holmes tales contrast the city with the country through the representation of crime. However, the city is never completely outside of the country because the country is the place where predominately urban debates about gender become staged. Nevertheless the tales represent this displacement into the country as if it were a disempowering of the masculine subject. It is in the country that rationality can seemingly be reasserted, but this process is often compromised by images of damaged masculinity which suggest that any such reassertion can only partially succeed. Its failures are ultimately related to the failure of gender.

A reading of the tale 'The Adventure of the Engineer's Thumb', also from the *Adventures*, helpfully illuminates this issue of confounded gender expectations, and their subsequent displacement into the country. Watson describes Victor Hatherley, the principal protagonist, as: 'young, not more than five-and-twenty, I should say, with a strong, masculine face; but he was exceedingly pale and gave me the impression of a man who was suffering from some strong agitation, which it took all his strength of mind to control'.[28] This struggle between masculine appearance and emotional agitation is subsequently underlined in Hatherley's hysterical response when he contemplates the mysterious events that have prompted him to consult Holmes. Watson attempts to quell the hysterical outburst by telling Hatherley to 'Stop it! ... pull yourself together!' Such advice proves 'useless' and Watson notes that Hatherley 'was off in one of those hysterical outbursts which come upon a strong nature when some great crisis is over and gone' (p. 275). One of the principal reasons for this is because Hatherley, unusually in the Holmes tales, requires medical attention as well as professional advice. He removes a handkerchief which was wound round his hand. Watson relates that, 'It gave even my hardened nerves a shudder to look at it. There were four protruding fingers and a horrid red, spongy surface where the thumb should have been. It had been hacked or torn right out from the roots' (p. 275). Kestner has argued that the tale represents a clear castration anxiety. It is an anxiety about disempowerment which is not only associated with Hatherley but also Holmes (who is unable to catch the criminals) and, for Kestner, Watson who is recuperating from a wound inflicted during his time as an army physician in the Afghan war.[29] These three images of damaged masculinity are confronted by a mystery which concerns the identity of the group who had hired Hatherley (an hydraulic engineer) to inspect a hydraulic press. Hatherley was to be well paid for this because of the need for secrecy, but he became suspicious and was attacked during his escape and lost his thumb. The criminal significance of the hydraulic press was that it was used to counterfeit money. The ostensible problem is locating the scene of the crime as Hatherley, after arriving at a small rural station, had been transported in the dark for, he estimates, twelve miles to the house where the hydraulic press was kept.

The tale is therefore about money, secrecy, and identity. It is also about how counterfeiting works at a series of levels relating to the crime and to notions of gender. For Kestner 'This anxiety about the self is reflected in the manifest subject of the tale, counterfeiting, which alludes to the true project of the narrative, to query whether masculinity is a counterfeit' (*Sherlock's Men*, p. 80). According to Kestner this is indicated by how the German villain, using the false name of Colonel Lysander Stark, represents contemporary anxieties concerning a German invasion, a concern which is here associated with fears about a superior German masculinity which castrates the English Hatherley.[30] However, the tale also illustrates a failure on the part of Holmes because the criminals go undetected. While Holmes is able to reconstruct what has happened to Hatherley, and to discover the motivation of Stark and his associates, he is unable to locate them. The gang have disappeared by the time Holmes arrives although he has been able to determine the location of the house by deducing that it was near the station and that the carriage had merely travelled six miles out and then six miles back. This image of a departure which is really a return indicates a fascination with the symbolic representation of proximity.

Location is freighted with ambiguity because the question of where a crime has been committed constitutes the initial mystery. This emphasises how place is bound up with the wider symbolic drama concerning castration, a drama which is also reflected in the displacement of Holmes from Baker Street into what turns out to be an equally threatening, castrating environment. The point is that it is the very displacement which enacts this castration. As we saw in 'A Scandal in Bohemia' Holmes is defeated in the city by a woman dressed as a man, and this effects a displacement of 'accepted' gender performances. Also, on a symbolic level, the issue of disguise points towards an implicit truth, that Holmes, for example, is a pretend 'groom' at Adler's wedding suggests that he is drawn to her in a personal way. However the tale also implies that Adler is more

of a 'man' than either Holmes or the six-foot-six Herculean King of
Bohemia, and as a consequence normative masculine scripts (arguably
parodically developed in the case of the King) are defeated.

In 'The Engineer's Thumb' the ostensible point of the case, the mystery
to be solved, concerns the whereabouts of the gang and the failure to locate
them suggests that Holmes has been beaten. The tale also closes on an
image of the despairing Hatherley, who did not even get paid for his work
on the press. He complains that 'Well ... it has been a pretty business for
me! I have lost my thumb and I have lost a fifty-guinea fee, and what have
I gained!' Holmes's consoling words seem to fall short of providing any
real recompense for the loss of both money and (symbolically) manhood.
He tells Hatherley that what he has gained is 'Experience ... Indirectly it
may be of value, you know; you have only to put it into words to gain the
reputation of being excellent company for the remainder of your existence'
(p. 287). Hatherley is left with words rather than things which suggests an
estrangement from the 'real' world. This final image is thus in accord with
the idea of displacing, and so disempowering, the masculine. This is also
clear in the inference that the story teller is more likely to be Watson than
Hatherley.

The tale works through a series of displacements: from the city to the
country, from real to unreal (counterfeiting), from masculinity to symbolic
castration. It is these displacements which figure Holmes's own
displacement within the city. Debates about power are therefore developed
and expressed beyond their site of origin, even as Holmes asserts his grip
on a specifically metropolitan consciousness. Holmes is thus of the city,
but the reasons for his displacement from it can be related to the complex
gender issues of the time relating to the changes in London and the
emergence of female public spaces.

Holmes, mentally, seems to personify the city in terms which are familiar
from Simmel. Watson, for example, notes in 'The Resident Patient'
published in the *Memoirs of Sherlock Holmes* (1894) that Holmes 'loved to
lie in the very centre of five millions of people, with his filaments stretching
out and running through them, responsive to every rumour or suspicion
of unsolved crime'.[31] The problem with this image of a consciousness
situated in the centre of London is that it is one of a spider policing its
web which elsewhere in the *Memoirs*, in 'The Final Problem', is associated
with Professor Moriarty. Holmes says of Moriarty 'He has a brain of the
first order. He sits motionless, like a spider in the centre of its web, but
that web has a thousand radiations, and he knows well every quiver of
each of them'.[32] It is Moriarty who challenges Holmes for control of London,

it is a battle which pits the athletic Holmes against the unathletic Moriarty who:

> is extremely tall and thin, his forehead domes out in a white curve, and his two eyes are deeply sunken in his head. He is clean-shaven, pale, and ascetic-looking, retaining something of the professor in his features. His shoulders are rounded from much study, and his face protrudes forward and is forever slowly oscillating from side to side in a curiously reptilian fashion. (p. 472)

Yet, famously, this was Doyle's image of Holmes's intended nemesis. The tale suggests a doubling between Holmes and Moriarty and this distorted image of a degenerate masculinity physically represents Holmes's own decline as his authority becomes progressively erased. Like Moriarty, the danger is that Holmes 'pervades London [but] no one has heard of him' (p. 470).

Moriarty is explicitly associated with degeneration. Holmes informs Watson that Moriarty's mental (and moral) decline was because, 'the man had hereditary tendencies of the most diabolical kind. A criminal strain ran in his blood, which, instead of being modified, was increased and rendered infinitely more dangerous by his extraordinary mental powers' (p. 470–1). However, Holmes also operates beyond the normal moral constraints; in part this is suggested by his Bohemian lifestyle, but in this tale he also acknowledges that 'My horror at his [Moriarty's] crimes was lost in my admiration at his skill' (p. 471). Also, he evidences a sense that his own powers are in decline. He leaves a note for Watson written just before his final encounter with Moriarty, an encounter which he realises is likely to lead to his own death, and in the note he claims that 'my career had in any case reached its crisis, and ... no possible conclusion to it could be more congenial than this' (p. 480).

Ultimately the displacement of Holmes symbolically represents the marginalisation of a particular model of a masculine metropolitan consciousness. This is indicated by Holmes's defeat in London in 'A Scandal in Bohemia'. 'The Engineer's Thumb' also illustrates this displacement through images of symbolic castration and Holmes's failure to apprehend the culprits (his own disempowerment). This relocation of urban anxieties, and the inability to properly resurrect dominant masculine scripts can also be seen in Bram Stoker's *Dracula*.

Dracula

Dracula develops a series of tensions between London and Transylvania. On a political and economic level Transylvania is quite different from cosmopolitan London. Transylvania is associated with feudalism (the Count) rather than capitalism, with a rural peasant culture rather than a mercantile economy. Transylvania is also, at a more abstract level, characterised by irrationality, desire, disease, and the possibility of social decline (the servant-less Count seems, for Harker, to be somewhat impoverished). However, as we saw in Chapter 3, such attributes were also associated with London. London as a breeding ground for degenerates was a concern addressed by Andrew Mearns, W.T. Stead, and William Booth (amongst others). Transylvania thus functions as a projection of urban anxieties, and the defeat of the Count can therefore be understood as an attempt to purify the city.

In *Dracula* London is represented in pre-lapsarian and socially conservative terms. London generates wealth and celebrates commerce; characters are identified by their social positions and they know their correct place within these social hierarchies. Renfield functions as a key figure in bridging the human world and the vampire's world, and responses to his behaviour indicate just how important the maintenance of this class hierarchy is. Seward, for example, perceives Renfield's 'madness' in terms of his inability, perhaps refusal, to acknowledge social difference. Seward notes with some horror after a particular episode with Renfield that his 'attitude to me was the same as that to the attendant; in his sublime self-feeling the difference between myself and attendant seemed to him as nothing'.[33] Later Renfield 'proves' his sanity when he meets Seward, Godalming, Van Helsing and Morris and acknowledges their social importance by referring to them as 'You gentleman, who by nationality, by heredity, or by the possession of natural gifts, are fitted to hold your respective places in the moving world'. A claim which prompts Seward to believe 'that his reason had been restored' (p. 244).

The scenes in London also contain a series of encounters with largely helpful and deferential workmen who provide important clues relating to the whereabouts of the Count's fifty boxes of earth, which have been distributed across London to enable him to create a range of lairs. In *Dracula* there is very little sense of overt social unrest, rather it seems as though classes are (often unconsciously) united in ridding the city of the diseased figure of the Count. This fantasy of social cohesion is clearly at odds with the idea of a geopolitically divided city that breeds its own degenerates. The novel at one level moves beyond these anxieties by emphasising that the Count is an outsider to London. Many critics such as Daniel Pick and Jules Zanger have noted that the novel plays upon contemporary anti-Semitic anxieties concerning an invasion of Eastern

European Jews into London (an anxiety which, as we have seen, generated considerable anti-Semitic feeling at the time of the Whitechapel murders).[34] In this way, Stoker by characterising degeneration as an alien, foreign influence, can reassert some vague notion of national well-being (a fantasy of a united society) which can defeat such malign, diseased forces. That this is an external threat is underlined by Van Helsing's claim that 'to fail here is not mere life or death. It is that we become as him; that we henceforward become foul things of the night like him' (p. 237). However, as discussed in Chapter 1, *Dracula* compromises such apparent social clarity by suggesting that the British middle classes (as represented by Harker, and to some degree by Seward) are themselves in need of regeneration.

This identifies a central contradiction in the novel. The middle classes represent modernity, money, ambition and a sense of justice. However such a nebulous notion of a social and economic vision is unsustainable once individuals are isolated. Harker, alone in Castle Dracula, is a very different figure than that at the end of the novel as he plays his designated role in the destruction of the Count. The problem with vampirism is that it is too seductive and the fact that Harker is susceptible to its charms suggests *his* latent degeneracy. The Count will just not stay 'Othered'. Chapter 1 discussed this in relation to how Harker is made a 'man' by his encounter with Dracula. The paradox being that the Count represents a model of heroic manliness that he needs to emulate; in this way 'disease' is brought back into 'civilisation' in a way which is familiar from contemporary accounts of degeneration and London.

Nicholas Daly has argued that the novel does not so much indicate the presence of an anxiety about national decline, or fears relating to theories of degeneration, but rather uses the figure of the Count in order to indicate just how far the middle classes were assured of their power. Daly claims that:

> The group led by Van Helsing *are* the new men, an increasingly fraternal, or associationist, and in specific ways patriarchal group. The threat that ostensibly unties them is, so to speak, a back formation; and the woman in whose defence they claim to be working also provides them with the secretarial and other support services that sustain them. It is in this sense that we can speak of the text's *using* fear toward a particular end, rather than expressing it.[35]

In this way the vampire is, for Daly, merely a figure who is designed to inspire group loyalty. The bourgeoisie are thus able to consolidate their power through their battle with the vampire, a battle which necessarily requires them to function as a team.

This view of the novel tends to suppress the links between the Count and the vampire hunters, as at some level vampirism *is* an attractive option to them. However, it does acknowledge that the Count provokes the vampire hunters into becoming men of action. The Count provides a model of masculinity which the flaccid middle-class professional would do well to copy. As the Count tells Harker:

> We Szekelys have a right to be proud, for in our veins flows the blood of many brave races who fought as the lion fights, for lordship ... the Szekelys – and the Dracula as their heart's blood, their brains, and their swords – can boast a record that mushroom growths like the Hapsburgs and the Romanoffs can never reach. The warlike days are over. Blood is too precious a thing in these days of dishonourable peace; and the glories of the great races are as a tale that is told. (p. 28, pp. 29–30)

Such an issue might seem to take us beyond London, but the battle for social and moral ownership of London is central to the novel. However, as in the Sherlock Holmes tales, the intent is to assert order and rationality (or at least a bourgeois version of it) outside of London. Initially the battle for London concerns the discovery of the location of the Count's boxes; by systematically destroying them he would be unable to stay in the city. This takes place after the infection and subsequent staking of Lucy Westenra, which represents a defeat for the vampire hunters in London. However, after the Count is forced to leave London it would appear as though the national threat is averted. At an ostensible level it is no longer the decline of the whole nation which is at issue, but rather the health of Mina Harker. The Count is now the quarry rather than an empowered hunter. This final pursuit affects a double way of making 'men' of the flaccid bourgeoisie as it both removes the external threat of degeneration (the Count) and by turning them into men of action it removes the threatened internal source of degeneration. It seems as though 'healthy' manliness is restored by destroying 'unhealthy' manliness (even if, paradoxically, they have had to mimic it in order to destroy it).

The group are initially defeated in London, but they are able to assert their authority in this geographically displaced way. In some respects this is similar to Holmes's defeats in London and his attempts at imposing order in the Home Counties, attempts which are not always successful and which imply his inability to leave London behind. However *Dracula* addresses in a more emphatic (if equally unconscious) way the notion of racial, national, moral and sexual purity. These ambiguities can be refocused by looking at how Lucy Westenra represents issues relating to the city concerning the difficulty of distinguishing between the 'proper' and 'improper' woman. A cross-dressing woman who accosts him in the street might beat Holmes in London, but *Dracula* represents this conflict with an alternative version of a streetwalker.

Stoker uses Lucy Westenra's transformation as the 'bloofar lady' who preys on working-class children, in order to demonise a particular form of inverted motherhood, one in which she suckles children. The novel's celebration of 'normal' motherhood is clear elsewhere in the novel from Mina Harker's repeated associations with a virtuous maternalism. However, with Lucy Westenra we are returned to the issue of disguise which was also a concern of the Sherlock Holmes tales. When she is transformed into a vampire, Lucy appears as a grotesque parody of her earlier pure self. Seward notes, 'her eyes ranged over us. Lucy's eyes in form and colour; but Lucy's eyes unclean and full of hell-fire, instead of the pure, gentle orbs we knew' (p. 211). That Lucy has been transformed from 'proper' to 'improper' is emphasised throughout the pursuit and staking of Lucy. What is truly horrific to the vampire hunters is the transformation *not* the ostensible fact that she is vampire. On first seeing Lucy, Seward recounts 'we recognized the features of Lucy Westenra. Lucy Westenra, but yet how changed. The sweetness was turned to adamantine, heartless cruelty, and the purity to voluptuous wantonness' (p. 211). Later, when they have pursued her into her tomb, he notes: 'She seemed like a nightmare of Lucy as she lay there; the pointed teeth, the bloodstained, voluptuous mouth – which it made one shudder to see – the whole carnal and unspiritual appearance, seeming like a devilish mockery of Lucy's sweet purity' (p. 214). An early letter from Lucy to Mina recounts her three marriage proposals and suggests Lucy's latent desire for promiscuity, 'Why can't they let a girl marry three men, or as many as want her, and save all this trouble?' (p. 59). Although her transformation as the 'bloofar lady' results in her attacking children rather than men, it does formulate an implicit image of an unfit mother, whose carnal associations suggests a world of adult desire that indirectly refer to the corrupting influences of prostitution and child neglect (which is also implied by her attack on working-class children). To rid London of this streetwalker is to assert a now purified version of those streets, a possible transformation which is suggested in the changes to Lucy after she has been staked by Arthur: 'There in the coffin lay no longer the foul Thing that we had so dreaded and grown to hate that the work of her destruction was yielded as a privilege to the one best entitled to it, but Lucy as we had seen her in her life, with her face of unequalled purity' (pp. 216–17). The staking of Lucy is therefore part of an overall strategy of purifying London, a strategy made clear in the expulsion and subsequent destruction of the Count. This seems like an assertion of a now revived masculinity, one which claims 'mastery' over the city. However, *Dracula* is a thinly concealed fantasy of control, one in which such images of masculine control are increasingly associated with violence (the staking of Lucy), desire (Lucy's penetrative blood transfusions) and illegality (the bribing of locksmiths and officials in the pursuit of the Count). At some level the vampire hunters become monstrous in the process, and so the novel's ostensible search for purity and models of bourgeois 'decency' collapses under its inability to develop a coherent moral vision which keeps the degenerate at bay. After all when Harker looks in the mirror at Castle Dracula and expects to see the Count reflected in it, he sees only himself. So, in the end *Dracula* produces a fantasy of a purified London and a purified, non-degenerate masculinity which in the end it does not quite believe in.

All of the texts discussed here have been concerned with the city. Some more directly than others. Nevertheless what is clear from these narratives is that there existed a link between, often covert, debates about gender and the city in the period. These in part are related to a failure of a masculine claim on rationality to read the mysterious city in a cogent way. To read the city, or to rid it of its degenerates, is to exercise mastery over it and such mastery is linked to gender narratives. The work of Doyle and Stoker indicate how gender is reconsidered in the relationship between the city and the country (the Home Counties and rural Transylvania). In Doyle we can see how a certain kind of masculine, metropolitan consciousness becomes increasingly marginalised as London developed an economy which encouraged the breaking down of the distinction between the private home and the public market, and so created a female public sphere. With Stoker, the degenerate is imaged as an external danger whose defeat enables a provisional recuperation of the city, although ultimately one that is compromised by internally generated images of desire, illegality, and latent degeneracy. This helps to explain the fascination that some of these later texts evidence with a mobility that takes you beyond the city and yet is still tied to it.

London also provided the stage for Oscar Wilde's trials, where what was understood as constituting the dominant masculine script was scrutinised in a judicial context. Some aspects of these trials and how they relate to Wilde's writings will be discussed in Chapter 6.

Notes

1 Recent studies which explore this link include Joseph A. Kestner, *Sherlock's Men: Masculinity, Conan Doyle, and Cultural History* (Aldershot: Ashgate, 1997) and Diana Barsham, *Arthur Conan Doyle and the Meaning of Masculinity* (Aldershot: Ashgate, 2000). Barsham's book is also an exploration of how language-use in the texts works to either challenge or enshrine certain gender scripts. All subsequent references are to these editions, and are given in the text.

2 Thomas De Quincey, *Confessions of an English Opium Eater* (Harmondsworth: Penguin [1821] 1986) p. 196. All subsequent references are to this edition, and are given in the text.

3 Immanuel Kant, *The Critique of Judgement*, trans. James C. Meredith (Oxford: Clarendon [1790] 1986), see 'The Analytic of the Sublime', pp. 90–203.

4 Edmund Burke, *A Philosophical Enquiry into the Origin of our Ideas of the Sublime and Beautiful*, ed. Adam Phillips (Oxford: Oxford University Press [1759] 1998) p. 36.

5 Julian Wolfreys, *Writing London: The Trace of the Urban Text from Blake to Dickens* (Basingstoke: Macmillan, 1998) p. 104.

6 Catherine Belsey, *Critical Practice* (London and New York: Routledge, 1980) p. 114.

7 Robert Mighall, *A Geography of Victorian Gothic Fiction: Mapping History's Nightmares* (Oxford; Oxford University Press, 1999) p. 48. All subsequent references are to this edition, and are given in the text.

8 Deborah Epstein Nord, '"Vitiated Air" The Polluted City and Female Sexuality in *Dombey and Son* and *Bleak House*' in Andrew H. Miller and James Eli Adams (eds), *Sexualities in Victorian Britain* (Bloomington, IN and Indianapolis: Indiana University Press, 1996) pp. 38–59, p. 53.

9 Alison Milbank, *Daughters of the House: Modes of the Gothic in Victorian Fiction* (Basingstoke: Macmillan, 1992). Ellen Moers *Literary Women* (London: Women's Press, 1978). All subsequent references are to these editions, and are given in the text.

10 See Milbank, *Daughters*, p. 95.

11 Charles Dickens, *Bleak House* (Harmondsworth: Penguin [1853] 1985) p. 253. All subsequent references are to this edition, and are given in the text.

12 Wilkie Collins, *The Woman in White* (Harmondsworth: Penguin [1860] 1985) p. 47.

13 Georg Simmel, 'The Metropolis and Mental Life' in Donald N. Levine (ed.), *Georg Simmel on Individuality and Social Forms* (Chicago, IL: University of Chicago Press, 1971) pp. 324–39, 325. All subsequent references are to this edition, and are given in the text.

14 Rosemary Jann, 'Sherlock Holmes Codes the Social Body' in *English Literature History*, 57:3 (1990), 685–708, 693. All subsequent references are to this edition, and are given in the text.

15 Arthur Conan Doyle, 'The Man With the Twisted Lip' in *The Penguin Complete Sherlock Holmes* (Harmondsworth: Penguin [1930] 1981) pp. 229–44, p. 229. All subsequent references are to this edition, and are given in the text.

16 However here, despite this sense of moral disorientation (which is a source of horror in De Quincey's *Confessions*), London becomes a place where a man might effect an escape from bourgeois domesticity. To some degree this is De Quincey's ambition as well, although for him it turns into a series of troubling encounters.

17 Diana Barsham, *Meaning of Masculinity*, p. 128. There are some ambiguities here of course, because at one level St. Clair is represented as a reprehensible figure who has, however unwittingly, caused his wife distress (as well as defrauding the public). At another level, however, this also suggests a critique of bourgeois domesticity and middle-class forms of employment.

18 Franco Moretti, *Atlas of the European Novel 1800–1900* (London: Verso, 1998) p. 137. The quote from Loïc Ravenel is from his *Les Aventures Géographiques de Sherlock Holmes* (Paris: Découvrir, 1994), pp. 202–3, quoted at p. 137 in Moretti.

19 Arthur Conan Doyle, 'The Copper Beeches' from the *Adventures of Sherlock Holmes* (1892) in *The Penguin Complete Sherlock Holmes*, pp. 316–32, p. 323. All subsequent references are to this edition, and are given in the text.

20 Erika Diane Rappaport, *Shopping for Pleasure: Women in the Making of London's West End* (Princeton, NJ and Oxford: Princeton University Press, 2002) p. 5. All subsequent references are to this edition, and are given in the text.

21 Judith R. Walkowitz, *City of Dreadful Delight: Narratives of Sexual Danger in Late-Victorian London* (London, Virago [1992] 1998) p. 47. All subsequent references are to this edition, and are given in the text.

22 This is also implicit in Rosemary Jann's analysis of class.

23 There has been a tendency to see London as dominated by the masculine mood of men-only clubs. Roy Porter, for example, has claimed that, 'Clubs helped keep London a masculine city' in *London: A Social History* (Harmondsworth: Penguin, 2000) p. 342. Work such as that of Rappaport provides an important corrective to this.

24 Quoted in Rappaport, *Shopping for Pleasure*, p. 45. From Samuel L. Clemens, *A Tramp Abroad*, ed. Charles Neider (New York: Harper and Row, 1977) p. 290.

25 Arthur Conan Doyle, 'A Scandal in Bohemia' in *The Penguin Complete Sherlock Holmes*, pp. 161–75, p. 162. All subsequent references are to this edition, and are given in the text.

26 Holmes's Bohemian credentials are ones which correspond with his intellectual 'detachment' from society. However, the tale also suggests that Holmes cannot quite maintain a detachment when it comes to Adler. Also, in Simmel's terms, Holmes's logic can be seen as an internalisation of the logic of the market economy. Holmes's 'detachment' is therefore from

ideological forces (marriage, domesticity and so on), rather than the economics of that society.

27 It could be argued that, as Adler is only able to affect this by taking on a masculine guise that the streets exclude women. However, I am interested in how the performance suggests an infiltration of such masculine scripts, one which symbolically represents the taking over of the 'masculine' streets.

28 Arthur Conan Doyle, 'The Adventure of the Engineer's Thumb' in *The Penguin Complete Sherlock Holmes*, pp. 273–87, p. 274. All subsequent references are to this edition, and are given in the text.

29 Kestner, *Sherlock's Men*, p.79.

30 Kestner, *Sherlock's Men*, p. 80.

31 Arthur Conan Doyle, 'The Resident Patient' in *The Penguin Complete Sherlock Holmes*, pp. 422–34, p. 423.

32 Arthur Conan Doyle, 'The Final Problem' in *The Penguin Complete Sherlock Holmes*, pp. 469–80, p. 471. All subsequent references are to this edition, and are given in the text.

33 Bram Stoker, *Dracula* (Oxford: Oxford University Press [1897] 1996) p. 124. All subsequent references are to this edition, and are given in the text.

34 Daniel Pick, *Faces of Degeneration: A European Disorder, c.1848–c.1918* (Cambridge: Cambridge University Press [1989] 1996), see p. 173. Jules Zanger, 'A Sympathetic Vibration: Dracula and the Jews', *English Literature in Transition 1880–1920*, 34 (1991), 33–44.

35 Nicholas Daly, *Modernism, Romance and the Fin de Siècle* (Cambridge: Cambridge University Press, 1999) p. 46.

6

Performing masculinity: Wilde's Art

Oscar Wilde was convicted of the charge of gross indecency on 25 May 1895. Prior to this (between 3 April and 5 April 1895) he had attempted to prosecute Lord Queensberry for libel over Queensberry's accusation that Wilde was a 'somdomite' (sic). During his cross examination by Queensberry's defence counsel, Edward Carson, the following now famous exchange took place over the alleged homosexual content of *The Picture of Dorian Gray* (1891):

> *Carson*: The affection and love of the artist of Dorian Gray might lead an ordinary individual to believe that it might have a certain tendency?
> *Wilde*: I have no knowledge of the views of ordinary individuals.
> *Carson*: Have you ever adored a young man madly?
> *Wilde*: No, not madly. I prefer love – that is a higher form.
> *Carson*: Never mind about that. Let us keep down to the level we are at now.
> *Wilde*: I have never given adoration to anybody except myself. (Loud laughter)
> *Carson*: I suppose you think that a very smart thing?
> *Wilde*: Not at all.
> *Carson*: Then you have never had that feeling?
> *Wilde*: No. The whole idea was borrowed from Shakespeare, I regret to say – yes, from Shakespeare's sonnets.
> *Carson*: I believe you have written an article to show that Shakespeare's sonnets were suggestive of unnatural vice.
> *Wilde*: On the contrary I have written an article to show that they are not. I objected to such a perversion being put upon Shakespeare.[1]

The problem faced by Carson was how to make the novel give up its apparent homosexual content. Wilde successfully diverts the debate into an account of literary interpretation, one which elevates the higher feelings associated with Art which contrast with Carson's search for the novel's alleged, low (dirty) truth. The very double quality of the novel enables these exchanges to take place as Carson finds that the narrative works, seemingly simultaneously, on symbolic and literal levels; a double quality which suggests the presence of a covert strategy relating to sexual identity. However, the hidden symbolic narrative cannot be animated by a legal discourse which principally concerns itself with matters of fact, and Wilde is granted some intellectual mobility in this exchange, whereas Carson is compelled to work within the fact-based discourse of the law. That Wilde moves the debate back to Art seems to divert attention from the 'real' aspects of both the criminal case and the homosexual subtext of the novel. It is the status and function of Art which is significant because Wilde's Art contains the very thing which the diversion seems to conceal; namely the idea of an erotic presence. This presence can be usefully accounted for by an examination of his model of aesthetics.

Wilde's theory of Art is developed in his response to Platonic and Aristotelian conceptions of Art.[2] The notion of Art as realising an Ideal form, versus the notion of Art as self-realisation, has a political inflection in Wilde's theory of aesthetics. For him, Platonic Ideals suggest an adherence to pre-existing models of expression, ones which stifle the Artist's innovation (for Wilde they also, by analogy, suggest a wider commitment to moral and social convention). However, as in the reference to Shakespeare made above, to appropriate is not just to borrow, it is to rewrite. Art for Wilde is the place in which the Artist is realised, rather than the Art. In this way he works towards formulating a philosophy of Art which is also a philosophy of life. Such an argument about Art, which will be explored in some depth in this chapter, might seem to be an esoteric departure from the social and cultural arguments and prescriptions which have been explored throughout this book. However, Wilde's theory of Art contains within it a model of homosexuality which it both represents (through a theory of Camp which relocates his philosophy of aesthetics) and conceals (because, as he tells Carson, it is all 'just' about Art or representation).

As in the other examples discussed in this book, the central issue is one of visibility and invisibility. Wilde, by creating a secret gay identity was trying to make that identity visible to a gay culture and invisible to the dominant one. As we saw in Chapter 1, sexology suggests that gender scripts and desire are not *necessarily* related, but only conventionally or ideologically connected. In this way gender is performed and Wilde, who both concealed his desire and subverted gender scripts in the process, exploited the theatricality that the script provided.

In Wilde's writings the link between Art and the body also takes on a specific significance as he forges links between a dissident, criminal culture and a dissident intellectual and moral culture that he associates with images of Christ. Christ represents, in Wilde's version of him, a gay icon that gives back the moral respectability that the criminal trials had undermined. Christ, like the criminal, and especially like the homosexual criminal, is a martyr for society's ills. What this also indicates is how far Wilde is prepared to rewrite certain pre-existing narratives in order to develop his theory of identity politics. This is true not just in the use of Shakespeare or his version of Christ, it is also relevant to how his theory of Art, as a model of self-realisation, echoes certain theories of degeneracy which suggested that disease was latent (yet to be realised) in the body; a point to be returned to later in this chapter. Wilde also questioned the dominant masculine gender scripts while seemingly, at least until the trials, and despite his personal flamboyance, adhering to them.[3] This is another way of saying that Wilde's subversion of these narratives brings together all of the issues discussed in this book, in a new, and often self-consciously developed way by Wilde. However, ultimately Wilde, as we shall see, cannot quite get beyond certain conventional notions of gender identification.

Wilde has received considerable critical attention, and this chapter will outline a series of important stances on Wilde drawn from a range of relevant critics, before giving a close reading of *De Profundis* (published in 1905), *The Ballad of Reading Gaol* (1898), and *Dorian Gray*. As already suggested, one principal issue at the time which relates to masculinity and desire concerns visibility and invisibility, it is one which is addressed through Wilde's particular construction of Camp.

Camp

Thomas A. King has persuasively argued, in historicist terms, that the performative aspects of Camp challenge certain bourgeois prejudices concerning the existence of a unified and natural self.[4] Camp suggests an ontological absence which bourgeois culture cannot tolerate and this absence is consequently associated with deviance. Such absence is also tied to a failure of language whereby homosexuality becomes literally unspeakable, but is still representationally present via certain typically aristocratic poses. King argues that the seemingly impassive poses, with arms akimbo, struck by aristocrats in various paintings from the seventeenth century were meant to illustrate an aristocratic control over the emotions (and so emphasise their superior self-control, and thus right to rule); however, 'The bourgeoisie saw aristocratic affectation not as self-control, but as a dissembling of nature'.[5] Therefore posing came to be regarded as concealing a range of vices. For King, Camp represents the desire 'to reassert the primacy of performance beyond the epistemological privileging of the real or the ontological prejudice of identity' (p. 46). It becomes a gesture which opposes bourgeois notions of certainty and as such class and Camp are closely related. However, Moe Meyer takes this a step further by arguing that in Wilde's case Camp represents the construction of a new gay identity which even bourgeois culture cannot see.

Meyer notes that Wilde encountered a form of acting (which followed the training of Francois Delsarte) during his lecture tour of America in 1882. This mode of acting was putatively scientific in that it claimed to 'objectively' account for character in terms of performance. Meyer notes that: 'Delsarte was a semiotician whose science ... consisted of the classification and decoding of bodily inscriptions based on observations of human conduct in order to determine the causal correspondence between exterior signification and essential interiority'.[6] In this way a theatrical performance becomes an objective correlative for an inner life. What Wilde set out to do was to create, through Camp performance, this new identity. The performance would create a 'homosexual social identity' which would be understood as such by its performers, but not by the dominant culture (p. 82). This does not just relate to Wilde's way of conducting himself in public, but is also central to his artistic practice. The fundamental idea is that the artist controls the process of representation to the point (as in *Dorian Gray*) that the Art reflects the artist and not the artist's subject. This constructs a relationship of dominance in which the subject of the painting (such as Dorian Gray) loses control over the process of representation. The artist is the inscriber rather than the inscribed and this refers, to follow Meyer, to the ambivalent legal status of sodomy. This was because the law treated sodomy in terms of who took the penetrative, or 'active' role and who took the 'passive' role. The penetrator would not necessarily be associated with homosexuality whereas the 'passive' partner would. Meyer states that, 'The 'active' partner (inserter) in sodomy was thought to be guilty of a criminal act perhaps, but would not take on a social identity based on that sexual expression. In most cases, the active partner would continue to be perceived as heterosexual' (p. 89); which is reflected in the idea that in artistic production it is the model that plays the 'passive' role in relation to the artist.

So, for Wilde, posing enabled him to create and control a certain kind of artistic practice which was related to self-expression. It is because of this that Queensberry's accusation that Wilde was a 'posing sodomite' caused profound offence. It suggested that Wilde was the 'inscribed', the subject of a pose rather than its active agent and so implied that he took the 'passive' role in sodomy.[7] As Meyer notes, Queensberry claimed, when Wilde attempted to sue him for libel, that the near illegible handwriting on the visiting card actually said 'posing as a sodomite' a qualification which meant that Wilde only passed *as* a sodomite rather than was one.[8] However, although Wilde had accepted that Queensberry had actually meant that Wilde pretended to be a sodomite, nevertheless Queensberry's counsel had witness statements which corroborated the accusation that Wilde was indeed a 'sodomite'.[9] This meant that the issue of 'posing' became, in legal terms, a redundant nicety, even though it frustrated Carson's attempt to see through the narrative 'posing' of the novel. The trials explored these connections between sexual identity and what it was that Wilde was 'posing as', and the sheer weight of evidence from witnesses insured Wilde's inevitable conviction. This leads Meyer to claim that 'between the close of his libel suit against Queensberry on April 5, 1895 and the close of the State's case against him on May 25 ... The Homosexual was discursively produced' (p. 94). At last the homosexual was given visibility, although at some considerable cost.

So, Wilde turned the images of the dandified aristocracy into a new Camp identity, one which questioned the idea of the 'natural', an idea which was inherent in bourgeois notions of subjectivity. Meyer also claims, following the work of Jeffrey Weeks, that, 'Wilde was brought to trial within a context created by the dependence of the legal system upon the model of the Homosexual-as-type which had been established in and propagandized in the literature of sexology since the middle of the century' (p.95).[10] However, the crisis in the representation of masculinity that Wilde's trials so clearly illustrated was not quite so straightforward as this suggests.

Sexology

We saw in Chapter 1 that sexological claims concerning sexual orientation challenged any ideological claims that there was an essential link between 'masculinity' and heterosexuality. Havelock Ellis in *Studies in the Psychology of Sex*, Vol. II: *Sexual Inversion* (1897) argued that there was no necessary, natural link between gender identity and desire and provided a series of case histories which illustrated how 'masculine' homosexuals operated within apparently 'normative' gender scripts. Edward Carpenter in *The Intermediate Sex* (1908) had gone so far as to claim that apparent sexual orientation did not necessarily imply specific sexual activity; instead it generated homosocial bonds rather than homosexual acts. Otto Weininger in *Sex and Character* (1903), suggested that everyone was essentially bisexual and that homosexuality and heterosexuality were really just matters of degree rather than radically different from each other. Such sexological views conflicted with the position of degenerationists, such as Max Nordau, who sought to assert fundamental links between gender and sexual orientation. It is within the epistemological space provided by the sexologists that Wilde's writings *avant la lettre* operate.[11]

The debate about homosexuality during the period is usefully contextualised by Eve Kosofsky Sedgwick's critique in her *Epistemology of the Closet* (1991). In her reading of Nietzsche she raises the question of gender, one which radically problematises the idea of homosexual identity. She notes that, 'The question of how same-sex desire could be interpreted in terms of gender was bitterly embattled almost from the beginning of male homosexual taxonomy'.[12] Sedgwick develops the claims of George Chauncey and David Halperin in order to explain this. George Chauncey notes that, 'Sexual inversion, the term used most commonly in the nineteenth century, did not denote the same conceptual phenomenon as homosexuality. "Sexual inversion" referred to an inversion in a broad range of deviant gender behaviour'.[13] Sedgwick also quotes David Halperin who in *One Hundred Years of Homosexuality* (1989) claimed that the notion that, 'sexual object-choice might be wholly independent of such "secondary" characteristics, as masculinity or femininity never seems to have entered anyone's head until Havelock Ellis waged a campaign to isolate object-choice from role-playing and Freud … clearly distinguished in the case of the libido between the sexual "object" and the sexual aim'.[14]

Sedgwick's arguments about how Wilde relates to Christian notions of the body as fetish will be discussed later in this chapter, but first we will examine her response to sexological claims as it helps to position Wilde in relation to such theories and also to move him beyond them.

We can see that late nineteenth-century scientific attempts to construct objective models of homosexuality were challenged by a debate about gender. The male homosexual did not necessarily display feminine traits, and even if such traits were observed they would not have been understood as markers of homosexual orientation. It was because of this that Wilde was able to develop concealed homosexual identities in his writing. This is not to say, as discussed earlier, that his work is not without its Camp qualities, but rather that Campness functions as a form of archness in his writings which indicates the presence of a homosexual identity even as it conceals it. However, Sedgwick develops this idea of the self in disguise (or at least a self who has the potential to use disguise) to position Wilde in relation to a modernist aesthetic which itself playfully develops the idea that the self has a multiple, secret range of identities. In *Dorian Gray*, for example, Wilde constructs an image of the self which occupies a range of seemingly incompatible positions. In the novel the self reflects on itself and how it performs, without integrity, for others (which is as true for Dorian as it is for Lord Henry Wotton). In addition, other characters appear to exist as associated aspects of the same self. Also, the novel is 'obviously' about a hidden secret life that has links with sin and sexual secrets and yet it retains a moralising quality (relating to the consequences of Dorian's amorality) that problematises this. Additionally, it is the very aesthetics of the novel which complicate this issue of self and identity by introducing a typically Wildean model of performance and theatre. Sedgwick associates this with an uneasy modernist outlook in his work, uneasy because of its modernist prevarications about the nature of the self. She argues that, 'For Wilde, the progression from homo to same to self resulted at least briefly ... in a newly articulated modernist "self"-reflexiveness and antifigurality, antirepresentationism, iconophobia that struggles in the antisentimental entanglements of *Dorian Gray* and collapses in the sentimental mobilizations of *Reading Gaol*' (p. 161). It is Wilde's implicit connection with a modernist self-consciousness which is so important because it indicates how Wilde's aesthetic challenges the coherence of the prevailing notions of sexuality, gender and criminality. Sedgwick largely overlooks the significance of this challenge, but it is important to consider as it plays a central part in linking masculinity to criminality. It is criminalisation which imposes a simple bourgeois masculine script, one which 'outlaws' alternative identities and in this way dominant masculine scripts become reaffirmed itself even as they are attacked. Wilde provides an alternative way of challenging models of masculinity, one which draws attention to the provisional nature of masculinity by associating it (like Camp) with an unreal performance. To understand the nature of this challenge we need to consider Wilde's more overtly political writings, and how they suggest a link between masculinity and criminality.

Art and politics

The features that marked Wilde out as a degenerate were his Irishness, his sexuality, and his 'foreign', decadent art. However it is also the case that Wilde both adopts and adapts a language of degeneracy which complicates this picture of him. While it is true that he employed a language of degeneracy when making his appeal to the Home Secretary for early release, it was hardly a convincing argument.[15] What is of greater interest is Wilde's modification of this language of degeneracy because it lies at the heart of his artistic project. Michael Foldy in *The Trials of Oscar Wilde* (1997) acknowledges that Wilde's status as an artist was implicitly used to invoke a discourse of criminality at his trial.[16] He also makes the case that Wilde in 'The Soul of Man Under Socialism' (1891) argued that it was the criminal and the artist who manifested radical protests at the state of the world. The artist questioned the philistinism of the middle-classes and the criminal questioned the material inequalities of society.[17] Wilde therefore rewrites the degenerationists' view which linked criminality, and by association the artist, with a diseased sensibility. Foldy notes that, 'Contrary to the prevailing view, Wilde believed that a condition of chronic dissatisfaction with the status quo represented a sign of health in individuals, and by extension, a sign of health in society. Correspondingly, the 'will to rebel' was considered a public virtue since it almost always led to change and improvement in society' (*The Trials of Oscar Wilde*, p. 101). Foldy links this belief with Wilde's theatrical self-performances which celebrated a transgressive Campness that highlighted the theatricality, falseness and provisionality of cultural mores. Life becomes Art and Art becomes life, and this is not a simple or typically Wildean paradox, rather it argues the case that Art provides the space in which social change becomes inaugurated (one which is also articulated through Camp).[18] By making himself a living piece of Art he became an advert for the transgressive qualities of Art. So, the Art which was seen as socially suspect was used by Wilde in order to ask unsettling questions about the possibilities of social change.

As noted earlier, Wilde's theory of artistic practice was influenced by his response to ideas drawn from Aristotle and Plato. Foldy notes that Wilde was disdainful of the Platonic idea that Art should have some social use, that it should illustrate some aspect of morality. Whereas for Aristotle, Art was about the realisation of a thing's inherent form because it was about getting at a kind of truth to be found within form, one which transcends conventional moral obligations. For Wilde, Art also has links to a model of performance. As discussed earlier, it is associated with his construction of Camp. It is an idea of Art which therefore embraces the notion that the proper theatrical performance is based on the self-realisation of the actor rather than that of the character that they are playing (the good actor, like the good artist, therefore plays the 'dominant' role). In 'The Soul of Man Under Socialism' this appears in an account of Henry Irving's acting. He notes that Irving did not pander to the masses because: 'His object was to realise his own perfection as an artist, under certain conditions and in certain forms of Art. At first he appealed to the few: now he has educated the many'.[19] This might suggest that Irving's Art is honourable because it touches so many, but Wilde's wider point is that Irving has attempted to create, as Wilde does here, an appreciation of self-expression which is beyond ethics. He even goes so far in his essay to claim that 'There is this to be said in favour of the despot, that he, being an individual, may have culture, while the mob, being a monster, has none' (p. 1038). This is, of course, a somewhat elitist notion of cultural access although there are, as we shall see, other more internal problems in his theory of Art.

To summarise, Wilde valorises an Aristotelian feel for modes of perfection as the realisation of inherent form. This idea of an inner form struggling to manifest itself is central to Wilde's claims in 'The Soul of Man Under Socialism' concerning the importance of political self-realisation. However, it is also a model of development that implicitly echoes the idea of the covert presence of disease in models of degeneration. For degenerationists, the body contains a latent biological disposition which could develop a range of pathologies determined by its genetic legacy. The pathologised body thus realises itself through the presence of disease and this is echoed in Wilde's idea about artistic self-realisation. In this way, as suggested earlier, Wilde's work attempts a recuperation of degenerationist concerns about homoeroticism by subverting the language of disease and criminality that, from the work of Bénédict Augustin Morel in the 1850s onwards, had characterised the degenerate. By developing ideas from Aristotle, Wilde is able to critically incorporate a language of immanence and self-expression which would, in Nordau, be used to demonise him. This is not a coincidental echo on Wilde's part; we can see, for example, that Wilde's 'posing', his disguise, was in part dependent on his colonisation of certain dominant gender scripts (such as the image of the club-land gentleman). Wilde also adapts such scripts (via Delsarte's influence) in order to subvert, or 'perform' them. Art and masculinity are thus linked by Wilde, and his aesthetic theory simply extends this because it rests on a theory of latency which also makes links between Art (as self-realisation) and a new Camp masculinity (as a form of Art, or 'performance'). In this process the politics of contemporary theories of degeneration are flouted because they are translated into a theory of aesthetics that creates the 'decadent' Art that Nordau so reviled. Biology and Art are thus drawn into a strange (almost parodic) strategic alliance by Wilde and in order to appreciate this we need to examine how he represents the body.

What Wilde wants to disguise, and yet get back to, is the body (not as fact but as mystique). This is the body which resists power even as that power is imposed upon it (in imprisonment, literally) and in the resistance a form of knowledge, relating to the need for transgression, is produced. However, the attributes of this body need to be renegotiated as Wilde attempts to reclaim it from the degenerationists and settle on it a new authority which is related both to the possibility of transgression and the possibility of a homosexual poetics, one which is referenced through images of Christ.

The Christian body

In her discussion of the Greek and Christian models of the male body, Sedgwick argues that:

> Synecdochically represented as it tended to be by statues of nude young men, the Victorian cult of Greece gently, unpointedly, and unexclusively positioned male flesh and muscle as the indicative instances of 'the' body, of a body whose surfaces, features, and abilities might be the subject or object of unphobic enjoyment. The Christian tradition, by contrast, had tended to condense 'the flesh' (insofar as it represented or incorporated pleasure) as the female body and to surround its attractiveness with an aura of maximum anxiety and prohibition. (*Epistemology of the Closet*, p. 136)

For Sedgwick it is the case that Wilde runs these images together, and this implicitly reflects on Carson's inability to properly extract a model of 'deviant' desire in *Dorian Gray*. In part this is also because the ambivalences which surround the Christian body, its flesh and its vulnerability, imply the presence of a moral (theological) force that resists the attempt to 'debase' the body through association with perversion. Sedgwick argues that behind the fetishistic images of gay culture there lies this image of Christ's body. She argues of Catholicism that it, 'is famous for giving countless gay and proto-gay children the shock of the possibility of adults who don't marry, of men in dresses, of passionate theatre, of introspective investment, of lives filled with what could, ideally without diminution, be called the work of the fetish' (p. 140). Wilde's own flirtation with Catholicism is the obvious connection here.[20] Sedgwick goes on to link these images to that of Christ: 'presiding over all [representations of gay identity] are the images of Jesus. These have, indeed, a unique position in modern culture as images of the unclothed or unclothable male body, often in extremis and/or in ecstasy, prescriptively meant to be gazed at and adored' (p. 140). The problem here is one of ethics because for Wilde what is conventionally understood as ethical ties you into a world of, largely bourgeois, social responsibilities. An 'ethical' artist would therefore lose their polemical, crusading spirit. However, in keeping with how Wilde subversively worked within gender scripts and recuperated a language of degeneracy in his aesthetics, he reconstructed images of Christ's body in order to challenge conventional ethics.[21] Also, Christ's body was the subject of some gender contestation in the nineteenth century. James Eli Adams has noted how Christ's association with suffering and compassion suggested to some commentators that Christ possessed feminine virtues; while to other commentators, such as Charles Kingsley, this could be corrected through the practice of 'muscular Christianity'.[22]

Wilde's attempt to formulate an alternative version of masculinity is apparent in the way that he represents Christ, and Christ-like figures, in *De Profundis* and *The Ballad of Reading Gaol*. Such representations also reveal just how problematic Wilde's notion of masculinity is, and these texts will be examined here before turning properly to *Dorian Gray* (although the novel will be touched upon in the discussion of *De Profundis*). This might seem to be an unusual chronology to follow, but it is useful to address the connections between Christ, criminality, Art and social change at this point because they provide us with a way of reading the novel.

De Profundis

In *De Profundis* Wilde writes that: 'Christ's place indeed is with the poets. His whole conception of Humanity sprang right out of the imagination and can only be realised by it'.[23] Wilde's idea of a divine poet whose imagination contains within it a blueprint for social unity is one which develops the idea that a new form of ethical practice could, initially, be understood only as a version of the profane. Christ thus represents a not yet realised morality which links him to an artistic process that dramatises the possibility of social and intellectual change. This will lead Wilde to claim that, 'I had said of Christ that he ranks with the poets. That is true. Shelley and Sophocles are of his company' (p. 868). An atheist such as Shelley and a pre-Christian such as Sophocles can be associated with Christ because what is understood by Christianity is a brand of politics which could revitalise a decaying society (despite the associations with romantic radicalism or Athenian politicking).[24] The artist, like Christ, becomes truly transcendent because their significance is only understood after their time and this is indicated by their extreme individualism; or as Wilde puts it, 'Most people are other people. Their thoughts are some one else's opinions, their lives a mimicry, their passions a quotation. Christ was not merely the supreme individualist, but he was the first individualist in history' (p. 870). It is this line of argument which means that Dorian Gray cannot be seen as a new kind of profane quasi-Christian martyr. Dorian produces no new philosophy but rather exemplifies Lord Henry's attempts at social engineering, as Lord Henry notes, 'To a large extent the lad was his own creation'.[25] In this way Dorian is like Victor Frankenstein's creature, alienated from the world because he is misunderstood by other people. Dorian is a product whereas Christ is a producer (which also relocates the ideas of inscriber and inscribed, and penetrator and penetrated, discussed earlier in this chapter). In this way Dorian ultimately becomes bad, diseased and decaying Art because he is mere imitation. Innovation is to be found within transgression (such as challenging bourgeois notions of sexual propriety, for example) and not in the realisation of Platonic forms (because Dorian manifests Lord Henry's ideas, not his own). The question becomes how can this be linked to masculinity and criminality? In other words how do these associations indicate a crisis in masculinity?

Following Sedgwick, we can see that in the period the body of Christ represented a passive feminine body which had its place in a semi-erotic spectacle. This complex body (feminine but male) becomes in Wilde's writing the very thing which can revitalise masculinity even though it challenges conventional notions of the 'masculine'. This is, historically speaking, Wilde's essential paradox because Art, like Christ, can transform, but then so can criminality and criminality is linked, at least conventionally, to an idea of a pathologised masculinity. Wilde takes this apparently diseased masculinity and purifies it through suffering. Punishment, a vital aspect of criminality, is transformed into a positive force as it makes us Christ-like because we learn through suffering, so that Wilde can claim in his post-trial writings 'to have become a deeper man' which 'is the privilege of those who have suffered. And such I think I have become' (*De Profundis*,

p. 880). This 'Christian' element was implicit in Wilde's earlier writings and this new association with criminality is a development of them.

In *De Profundis* Wilde repeatedly occupies this Christ-like position and even suggests a variant in which his own body is displayed in public for mass execration. This was when Wilde was moved to Reading Gaol from London and was forced, with his guards, to wait for a train at Clapham Junction. Wilde was wearing prison dress at the time and this attracted much attention:

> Of all possible objects I was the most grotesque. When people saw me they laughed. Each train as it came up swelled the audience. Nothing could exceed their amusement. That was, of course, before they knew who I was. As soon as they had been informed they laughed still more. For half an hour I stood there in the grey November rain surrounded by a jeering mob. (p. 881)

However, for Wilde the growth of the spirit is dependent upon such moments of mortification, and consequently he replaces the physical body with a model of subjectivity which cannot be touched by either physical punishment or by humiliation. In this way the development of an inner life enables us to resist external, because social, condemnation. This pursuit of mystique also aligns him with the romantics as he searches for the 'Mystical in Art, the Mystical in Life, the Mystical in Nature' (p. 887), leading him to formulate a philosophy in which: 'Time and space, succession and extension, are merely accidental conditions of thought; the imagination can transcend them and move in a free sphere of ideal existences. Things also are in their essence of what we choose to make them; a thing is according to the mode in which we look at it' (p. 887). Here the tension is between an inner reality (the imagination) and a matter of perception (such as, for example, Wilde at Clapham Junction) that also, paradoxically, glosses Carson's problem concerning how to make the inner narrative speak.

What lies behind these ideas is a model of self-realisation which is developed through a theory of the imagination. The body ceases to have any real function other than to the extent that it is marked by signs of disease or pain, or touched by humiliation. Such perceptions are purely provisional for Wilde, as the 'real' identity is to be found within. This idea of leading a strange, secret, double life echoes the notion of a homosexual subtext in Wilde's work, which because of its very inner quality contains the 'real' truth. However, this also echoes ideas relating to masculinity and maleness. For Wilde, as it was for the sexologists, what you see is not what you get. The cultural signs of masculinity do not reveal the inner subject, their 'real' sexuality. Wilde thus develops sexological claims concerning the disjunction between gender behaviour and sexual orientation, because by introducing the model of a passive Christ-like body (one which reflects on the convict's disempowerment) he constructs an alternative version of masculinity. Wilde's trials were thus important because they indicate that Wilde performed as a figure caught within a matrix of conflicting masculine scripts which dramatised wider anxieties: about class, nation and Art. These other anxieties relate to how the seemingly normalising scripts of ethics, the law and of order were rendered unstable (denaturalised) by Wilde's personal and narrative performances.

At one level this all suggests the need for some form of conceptual escape from the disciplined body, some inner core which is not quite touched by disciplinary mechanisms or prescriptive notions of gender. For Wilde, a conventional model of masculinity does not provide a means of potential disguise for the homosexual male because it is a vehicle for social oppression precisely because it renders everyone the same. Gender scripts generalise male subjects and are therefore a great leveller for Wilde, and levelling tendencies are dangerous because they suggest the mob-like habits that horrify him so much at Clapham Junction. The criminal can thus become Christ-like because in their transgression lies the impulse for change which frees the individual from convention. It is these romantic, sentimental, but nevertheless highly politicised ideas, which are also developed in *The Ballad of Reading Gaol*. For Sedgwick: 'The squeam-inducing power of texts like *De Profundis* and *Reading Gaol* – and I don't mean to suggest that they are a bit the less powerful for often making the flesh crawl – may be said to coincide with a thematic choice made in each of them: that the framing and display of the male body be placed in the explicit context of the displayed body of Jesus' (*Epistemology of the Closet*, p. 148). However, in *Reading Gaol* it is not Wilde who occupies this position. Also the poem is much less certain than *De Profundis* about establishing this new model of masculinity, indeed the poem suggests that Wilde's model owes rather more to conventional notions of gender than at first appears.

The Ballad of Reading Gaol

Wilde's long poem opens with:

> He did not wear his scarlet coat,
>   For blood and wine are red,
> And blood and wine were on his hands

When they found him with the dead,
The poor dead woman whom he loved,
And murdered in her bed. (ll. 1–6)[26]

The poem places a sympathetic focus on the plight of the murderer who comes to be associated, implicitly, with Christ. The language of blood and wine here, while referring to a drunken murder also suggests the Eucharist. The murderer becomes the victim and is generalised into an everyman who reflects all of society's injustice. The 'horror' is not related to the murder but to the murderer's anticipated execution. Indeed what is truly horrific is the waiting itself. What becomes important is how Wilde sees in the man's plight a symbol for all kinds of loss; Wilde notes 'The man had killed the thing he loved,/And so he had to die.' (ll. 35–6). However:

Yet each man kills the thing he loves,
By each let this be heard,
Some do it with a bitter look,
Some with a flattering word,
The coward does it with a kiss,
The brave man with a sword! (ll. 37–42)

This claim for a symbolic pan-dimension to murder reveals just how much of an investment Wilde makes in the social and spiritual credibility of crime. The actual details of the specific killing are less important than the drama of the self, one which captures, in this instance, a general truth about the loss of love. This rarefied language also works to move beyond the body, here the dead body of the victim, because it suggests that we are all guilty of the same offence: 'For each man kills the thing he loves,/Yet each man does not die.' (ll. 53–4). The criminal's act is therefore made symbolic because it bestows on the murderer a peculiar dignity in which a quasi-Christian form of heroism is expressed through a temporary suffering in which he dies 'For each man'. The man is beyond normal suffering because he is beyond hope, but this dignity in the face of doom is again associated with an image of sacramental wine:

He did not wring his hands nor weep,
Nor did he peek or pine,
But he drank the air as though it held
Some healthful anodyne;
With open mouth he drank the sun
As though it had been wine! (ll. 115–20)

The physical world becomes turned into a model of bounty. However, this move towards a spiritual realm necessarily requires a repudiation of the body, not just the murderer's body, but also the body of the murdered woman. In this way the man's actions are merely a symptomatic act which function as a panacea for the other inmates who at the sight of him 'Forgot if we ourselves had done/A great or little thing,' (ll. 123–4). Like Christ he dies for them all, but this is not a neutral or equal sacrifice. Specifically the man dies in order to redeem men and this underlines how this crisis in masculinity is staged through a repudiation of the body. However, to move beyond the body is not quite the radical gesture that Wilde had suggested because here it is reliant on the destruction of the female. The assertion of sameness is thus dependent on a moment of difference, and this indicates the extent to which Wilde's sexual politics evidence hostility towards women. The murder of the woman merely becomes a pretext for a debate about brotherhood, heroism and the function of shared suffering. Wilde notes, after the man's execution:

> A prison wall was round us both,
> Two outcast men we were:
> The world had thrust us from its heart,
> And God from out His care:
> And the iron gin that waits for Sin
> Had caught us in it snare. (ll. 169–74)

The sense of abandonment is spiritual rather than physical. The body by this stage in the poem has become replaced by a space in which martyrdom is enacted.

So, for Wilde the gendered body inhabits a world of social perception and modes of punishment. To get beyond the body is to become Christ-like, it is to find a form of existence which is beyond conventional constructions of masculinity. This at least seems implicitly to be the conclusion in *De Profundis* and it is central to Sedgwick's argument. However, the image of Christ in Wilde's work is more complicated than this. In *Reading Gaol* the move beyond the male body is also a move predicated on the destruction of the female body. A version of masculinity becomes developed through the kinds of homosocial bonding which come through shared suffering. The poem, unconsciously, exposes the sexual politics at the heart of this denial of the male body, as it negates the physical 'signs' of gender only to replace such signs with a spiritual version of masculinity.

Wilde can never quite get beyond conventional gender politics after all because he cannot get beyond its binaries, but this confusion about gender illustrates one aspect of crisis within the culture of the time. To get outside of gender does not mean disposing of the body, it means renegotiating the possibility for social change and thus requires a way of rethinking the body's relationship to gender through the issue of desire. This is central to sexological claims about desire and gender because gender and same-sex desire, for example, do not necessarily correspond. Wilde has a similar view but develops an alternative strategy which actually rarefies a model of masculinity into a spiritual realm where it is both pure and unconstrained. In its own way it is an attempt to revitalise masculinity by turning Christ, or the criminal, into an icon for the male inner life. Such images are of course not, given the association with murder, particularly positive images of masculinity and although Wilde attempts to reclaim (or redeem) the criminal it only serves to reinscribe other, prevailing, models of gender construction.

So far the analysis has been confined to images of masculinity as developed through images of Christ in works of non-fiction (if *Reading Gaol* can be read as such). However, these images of persecution, transgression and death and their association with masculinity are common to many of the case histories explored in this book. The reiteration of this drama of masculinity is also staged within the Gothic of the time and although Wilde in *De Profundis* and *Reading Gaol* develops images relating to the horror of imprisonment they are not properly Gothic in any literary sense (despite the occasional reference to the grotesque). However, that Wilde sees his post-prison years through some Gothic touches is indicated by his adoption of 'Melmoth' as his pseudonym. It is, of course, *Dorian Gray* which relocates images of transgression and the double life within a Gothic idiom which seems to provide a natural home for such images. However, Wilde's later claims that the novel was one of his most moral works is revealing, it suggests that it retains a conventionality that, arguably, in some ways resolves the paradoxes that he would latter develop in *Reading Gaol*.[27] After an examination of the novel there will be a related exploration of a selection of Wilde's poems.

Dorian Gray *and the Gothic*

One of the central claims of this book is that by examining models of masculinity in the period we can isolate a specific narrative within the literature of the *fin de siècle* which illuminates how (in certain forms of social practice and medical discourse) masculinity becomes associated with disease, insanity and perversion. *Dorian Gray* provides an illuminating

example of this anxiety concerning the inversion of the status quo when
Lady Narborough says to Lord Henry Wotton:

'If we women did not love you for your defects, where would you all be?
Not one of you would ever be married. You would be a set of unfortunate
bachelors. Not, however, that that would alter you much. Nowadays all the
married men live like bachelors, and all the bachelors like married men.'
'Fin de siècle,' murmured Lord Henry.
'Fin du globe,' answered his hostess.
'I wish it were fin du globe,' said Dorian, with a sigh. 'Life is a great
disappointment'. (p. 196)

Lady Narborough's comically rendered account of the avoidance of marital
responsibilities conforms to contemporary concerns about an apparently
threatening *fin de siècle* climate of social change. In Wilde's novel these
images of social disarray reflect on the home, in which the end of the
family is also the end of the world. In a world of such domestic reversals,
the role of men becomes pivotal.

As we have seen, Wilde's novel was, during his trials, placed at the centre
of a debate concerning sexual morality which was suggested by reference
to Dorian's alleged double life. The claims for a double life are also to be
found elsewhere in Wilde's work; Bunburying in *The Importance of Being
Earnest* (1895) is, for example, a thinly veiled reference to other possible,
homosexual identities. However, *Dorian Gray* is more complex than such
claims about a double life admit, and despite its ironies, bon mots and
aperçus the novel also indicates that a life lived outside of bourgeois moral
codes becomes truly Gothic. However, even this is not without its
ambivalence.

The novel attempts to resolve an irreconcilable, because conflicting,
message; it suggests that one should question conventional notions of
morality, but not try to live a life free from moral constraints because then
all things become possible (including murder). The difficulty, therefore,
is knowing how to act ethically, or where to place moral limits. Famously,
Wilde attempted to divert attention from moral considerations in the
novel's prefatory claim that 'There is no such thing as a moral or an immoral
book. Books are well written, or badly written. That is all' (p. 3), although
elsewhere he would claim it as his most moral work. What appears to be
the real danger is that masculinity might itself be performative and this
(in terms of the moral frame of the novel) makes other identities possible
(such as Camp) while it simultaneously erases the world of moral
considerations which check excess. The essential, morally compromising
difficulty is related to Art and aesthetics, and it is Art which has connections

to masculinity and degeneracy in Wilde's broader vision. As discussed earlier, Wilde's support for an Aristotelian aesthetic endorses the idea of the presence of an inherent form waiting to be realised within the subject. This idea of immanence glosses those theories of degeneration which saw degeneracy as lurking in the body. Therefore, the paradox is that Wilde's work both questions models of masculinity while developing such questions in an aesthetic context which echoes the very demonisation of seemingly tainted masculinity that his work both questions and endorses. In this way it explains Wilde's paradoxes by other means. *Dorian Gray* is thus both a protest against moral and domestic restrictions on men, while also a critique of such a protest. It is both text and anti-text; a novel which erases, hides this message even in its very telling. As we have seen, it is for this reason that during Wilde's libel trial Carson tried to use the novel to generate evidence, only to find that the accusations concerning an illicit double life were easily countered by Wilde's assertion that it was a book that developed chaste ideas about love and beauty that had been inspired by Shakespeare's sonnets.

This strange doubleness of the text contains within it an image of a fatigued heterosexual masculinity (witness Lord Henry) that ultimately led commentators such as Nordau to allege that Wilde's work was a thinly veiled account of Wilde's own amorality. Nordau's *Degeneration* (1892) made the link between decadence and degeneracy which in essence was a demonisation of a complex form of homosexual identity. Complex because the issue of image-making and posing confused what was understood as 'real'. In addition the trials were highly theatrical affairs and Wilde's often theatrical performance in the witness box suggested that it was masculinity, and what was meant by that term, which was really on trial.

David Punter has noted that *Dorian Gray* shares a Gothic context concerning theories of degeneration which includes Stevenson's *Dr Jekyll and Mr Hyde* (1886), H.G. Wells's *The Island of Dr Moreau* (1896) and Stoker's *Dracula* (1897).[28] Punter argues that Wilde's unique contribution to anxieties about degeneration was in constructing the figure of the double in an aesthetic (rather than biological) context, and there is certainly a case to be made that the novel is a riposte to Walter Pater's model of the ideal life as a work of Art in his *Renaissance* (1873).[29] Indeed, the novel suggests that life cannot be lived in aesthetic terms as it removes the subject from a world of moral obligations. However, it also suggests that masculinity, as a mode of performance, becomes truly Gothic when it becomes debased Art; so that what is horrific for Dorian is that his faith in beauty is undermined by his associations with ugliness. However, although

Art is the key register for this decline it is one which glosses more scientifically expressed anxieties relating to degeneration. For Punter:

> Artifice is perhaps the key term: how much, if at all, do scientific and psychological discoveries help us to mould ourselves, and are the possible shapes into which they can project human life necessarily at all desirable. It is characteristic of Wilde's late romanticism that the means of moulding should be not science but the art of painting, but the tenor of the metaphor is the same: is there anything we can do with this knowledge, on the one hand of our myriad-mindedness and on the other of our proximity to the beasts, which will be other than harmful? (p. 7)

Punter notes that 'The answer of the 1890s was unanimous: No' (p. 7); but what is interesting is that this argument can move us beyond images of a demonised, theatrical and performative image of degenerative masculinity and take us into the realm of science. Wilde's 'late romanticism' might seem to take him beyond a scientific context but actually it suggests that he merely extends romantic ideas in another way.

This idea of science and Art helps to underline the distinctions which Wilde makes between knowledge and feeling. This distinction valorises feelings above empirical knowledge and is linked to the kinds of superficial depoliticising of gender to be found in *De Profundis* and *Reading Gaol*. The Gothic body is thus one which was, in the period, closely related to ideas about science and masculinity. What it means to be a man and how one might account for it needs to be explained through Wilde's representation of science.

Wilde science

> … the nineteenth century has gone bankrupt through an over-expenditure of sympathy, I would suggest that we should appeal to Science to put us straight. The advantage of the emotions is that they lead us astray, and the advantage of Science is that it is not emotional. (*Dorian Gray*, p. 47)

Lord Henry's appraisal of the *fin de siècle* foreshadows, typically given his controlling presence in the novel, Dorian's subsequent fascination with science. Dorian's studies range across a series of intellectual systems none of which he, characteristically, commits to; so that:

> for a season he inclined to the materialistic doctrines of the *Darwinismus* movement in Germany, and found a curious pleasure in tracing the thoughts and passions of men to some pearly cell in the brain, or some white nerves in the body, delighting in the conception of the absolute dependence of the

spirit on certain physical conditions, morbid or healthy, normal or diseased. (p. 147)

Dorian's familiarity with theories which reflect on degeneracy is ironic but also suggestive of a kind of consciousness which, paradoxically, lacks self-awareness. For Dorian all analytical systems are false because they are hostile to life, so that 'no theory of life seemed to him to be of any importance compared to life itself' (p. 147). This romantic position inevitably overlooks the fact that Dorian is the product of Lord Henry's musings on beauty. His model of life is therefore associated with artificiality, with performance, and this is the painful truth which Dorian confronts at the end of the novel. However this view of science has a special, anti-romantic, place elsewhere in Wilde's writings. The key figure here would appear to be Keats. In 'The Garden of Eros' Wilde argues that in this new scientific age:

> Methinks these new Actaeons boast too soon
>   That they have spied on beauty; what if we
> Have analysed the rainbow, robbed the moon
>   Of her most ancient, chastest mystery,
> Shall I, the last Endymion, lose all hope
> Because rude eyes peer at my mistress through a telescope! (ll. 235–40)[30]

There is also a hint of Shelley here in the image of a memorialising of lost, or eroded worlds. Science takes life out of life, and reduces the 'Garden' to a set of scientific calculations. What is at issue is a debate about 'humanity' staged within the 'inhumanity' of science:

> What profit if this scientific age
>   Burst through our gates with all its retinue
> Of modern miracles! Can it assuage
>   One lover's breaking heart? What can it do
> To make one life more beautiful, one day
> More godlike in its period? but now the age of Clay. (ll. 241–6)

Humanity is a complex notion in Wilde's work because Dorian exists as a product of Lord Henry's philosophy; what is 'natural' is therefore at the centre of the debate about 'humanity' in the novel. Also, arcadia cannot be reclaimed as even it is touched with hints of danger. 'Magdalen Walks', a poem which celebrates the bounty of nature, closes on an image of 'The kingfisher' who 'flies like an arrow, and wounds the air' (l. 20).[31] Eden cannot be reclaimed in this postlapsarian *fin de siècle* world. As Wilde notes in 'Humanitad':

Somehow, the grace, the bloom of things has flown,
And of all men we are most wretched who
Must live each other's lives and not our own
For very pity's sake and then undo
All that we lived for – it was otherwise
When soul and body seemed to blend in mystic symphonies. (ll. 418–23)[32]

The relationship between body and soul is what is at stake in Dorian's brief adherence to a range of different knowledges. Perhaps more significantly such pessimism also compromises the idea of a Christ-like return, one which revises Wilde's notion of the preacher-like poet whose unique understanding of the world can lead to its transformation. Here, such a revitalisation becomes impossible. Also, science is associated with institutional authority in *Reading Gaol* in the image of the Doctor, where we, the other unconvicted murderers do not have 'To put on convict-clothes,/While some coarse-mouthed Doctor gloats, and notes/Each new and nerve-twitched pose,' (ll. 74–6). The execution of the murderer therefore becomes divested of some of its glamour 'The Doctor said that Death was but/A scientific fact' (189–90) as the man's plight becomes divorced from its symbolic function.

In Punter's argument, Wilde uses science symbolically to the degree that such ideas relating to degeneration become translated into a theory of aesthetics; it implies a relationship between science and Art that conceals a narrative about gender, because, as we have seen, Wilde takes over the language of degeneracy in his theory of Art. This bringing together of apparently incompatible worlds (such as science and Art) is also a characteristic of Wilde's poetry. The poems also bring together seemingly different (if non 'scientific') worlds, which blurs distinctions between masculine and feminine through symbolic images of the hermaphrodite where feminine rose petals and masculine ivory are brought together in a reworked, postlapsarian image of arcadia. In 'Fantaisies Décoratives' Wilde writes of how:

With pale green nails of polished jade,
  Pulling the leaves of pink and pearl,
  There stands a little ivory girl
Under the rose-tree's dancing shade. (ll. 33–6)[33]

This image, through its association with Wilde's infamous celebration of green as a gay marker, suggests the possibility of a hidden other world. The image of petals and ivory is also developed in 'Canzonet' where a more pessimistic image is used to suggest a thwarted desire:

Hylas is dead,
Nor will he e'er divine
    Those little red
Rose-petalled lips of thine.
    On the high hill
No ivory dryads play,
    Silver and still
Sinks the sad autumn day. (ll. 25–32)[34]

It is also Dorian Gray who combines these symbolic qualities and this suggestion of the hidden homosexual narrative in the novel can be made clear by seeing Lord Henry's influence over Dorian as an echo of that between Victor Frankenstein and the creature; a dynamic which is discussed by Sedgwick.

The construction of the self, its artificiality, is the starting point for a pursuit for the meaning of identity, one which in *Dorian Gray* is translated into an image of soul-searching. Sedgwick has written extensively of this type of image in *Between Men* (1985) and in the *Epistemology of the Closet* claims that Nietzsche's emphasis on a 'heroics of embodiment':

> provides an exemplar for the Gothic-marked view of the nineteenth century as the Age of Frankenstein, an age philosophically and tropologically marked by the wildly dichotomous play around solipsism and intersubjectivity of a male paranoid plot – one that always ends in the tableau of two men chasing one another across a landscape evacuated of alternative life or interest, toward a climax that tends to condense the amorous with the murderous. (p. 163)

Science therefore functions as a trope for the construction, and concealment, of identity. In *Frankenstein* men make themselves men through science, but it does not quite work like this in Wilde. For Wilde, science reads the signs of physical life but it has no metaphysic and so fails to read character. This means that Wilde collapses all the systems which should anchor, or explain, identity. In *Dorian Gray* identity is artificial, a matter of influence. In some respects this corresponds to Wilde's idea that gender is merely performed. However, the novel condemns the idea of artificiality by asserting that such a performance is staged outside of the dominant moral codes and leads, ultimately, to self-destruction rather than self-realisation.

Dorian Gray returns to a moral conventionality in which Dorian is horrific because he becomes bad Art. What is striking about Dorian is that above all he is a product of a covert policy of social engineering. There is nothing natural about him at all. He is a theatrical production who becomes the bad (ugly) art that he detests. That Dorian is seen in such terms is clear from Lord Henry's musings concerning matters of influence in which character 'becomes an echo of someone else's music' (p. 23). Dorian is moulded from Lord Henry's philosophy of the self, one which encourages the breaking of all forms of moral obligations and ties. To demonise Dorian is to undo such a philosophy and yet it is Lord Henry's philosophy, one which emphasises Lord Henry's self-realisation through others, which is to blame.

With *Dorian Gray* we turn full circle. The novel suggests that performance is not enough, although Wilde cannot replace it with anything more profound. These tensions and paradoxes are not resolved in Dorian's death, because they are also displaced onto other characters such as Hallward and Lord Henry. Desire and its relationship to gender are, however, problematised as Dorian's death represents the inability to be authentic (because his feelings are an aping of Lord Henry's) and the failure to be artificial (because he ceases to represent Art). Ultimately the novel suggests the presence of a disjunction between inner and outer lives, one which cannot, as in sexology, be properly resolved no matter how hard Wilde works towards constructing a new form of pseudo-Christian, Camp, identity politics.

Also there is an argument, although admittedly a non-chronological one between *De Profundis, Reading Gaol,* and *Dorian Gray* which suggests that Wilde returned to the issue of masculinity in a variety of different ways.[35] *De Profundis* suggests the possibility of innovation through its recuperation of a Christ-like body. *Reading Gaol* unconsciously (accidentally) questions the link between this recuperated masculine body and criminality, because it all rests on the relegation of the murder of the woman, and so re-inscribes prevailing notions of gender superiority. *Dorian Gray,* perhaps more consciously, reasserts a conventional moral system that also suggests the such gender innovation is not without its problems.

What is striking about Wilde is how he works within particular dominant narratives, relating to degeneration, gender, and religion (Christ's body), in order to subvert them. This subversion is also an act of recuperation in which gender becomes turned into performance, the politics of degeneration becomes transformed into an aesthetic philosophy of self-realisation, and Christ comes to personify the necessity of 'criminal' transgression. Ultimately, Wilde cannot quite establish a new masculine identity. However, Wilde in *Dorian Gray, De Profundis* and *The Ballad of*

Reading Gaol runs together arguments about criminality, identity, Art and sexuality in ways which reveal just how unstable the term 'masculine' was at the time.

Notes

1 From Richard Ellmann, *Oscar Wilde* (Harmondsworth: Penguin, 1987) p. 422.
2 See Wilde's 'The Critic as Artist' in *The Complete Works of Oscar Wilde*, ed. G.F. Maine (London: Collins, 1992) pp. 948–98. See also Michael Foldy, *The Trials of Oscar Wilde: Deviance, Morality, and Late-Victorian Society*, (New Haven, CT and London: Yale University Press, 1997) pp. 110–16 for a relevant discussion of Wilde's aesthetics and how the idea of a Platonic Ideal influenced Wilde's sexual preference for young men. All subsequent references are to this edition, and are given in the text.
3 That is to say that Wilde's frequenting of clubs and his fondness for all-male company, did not imply homosexuality.
4 See also Foldy, *Trials of Oscar Wilde*, pp. 101–3.
5 Thomas A. King, 'Performing "Akimbo" Queer pride and epistemological prejudice' in Moe Meyer (ed.), *The Politics and Poetics of Camp* (London: Routledge, 1994) pp. 23–50, p. 25. All subsequent references are to this edition, and are given in the text.
6 Moe Meyer, 'Under the Sign of Wilde: An Archaeology of Posing' in Meyer (ed.), *Politics and Poetics of Camp*, pp. 75–109, p. 80.
7 See Meyer, 'Under the Sign', p. 90.
8 Ibid., p. 91.
9 The argument whether Wilde was the active or passive agent seemed to be irrelevant during the trials as they focused, *inter alia*, on the legality of his procuring young men.
10 Meyer is here reworking a claim from Jeffrey Weeks's 'Movements of Affirmation: Sexual Meanings and Homosexual Identities' in *Radical History Review*, 20 (1979), 164–79, 167.
11 Wilde's conviction took place before these works were published and I am therefore not suggesting that he self-consciously developed their ideas, rather that sexology identified and explored the presence of a disjunction between desire and its relationship to gender which Wilde was also responding to.
12 Eve Kosofsky Sedgwick, *Epistemology of the Closet* (London: Harvester Wheatsheaf, 1991) p. 134. All subsequent references are to this edition, and are given in the text.
13 George Chauncey, Jr., 'From Sexual Inversion to Homosexuality: Medicine and the Changing Conceptualization of Female Deviance', *Salmagundi*, 58–9 (Fall 1982–Winter 1983), 114–25, 124, cited in Sedgwick, *Epistemology of the Closet*, pp. 157–8.

14 David Halperin, *One Hundred Years of Homosexuality* (New York: Routledge, 1989) p. 16, cited in Sedgwick, *Epistemology of the Closet*, p. 158. Alan Sinfield in *The Wilde Century: Effeminacy, Oscar Wilde and the Queer Moment* (London: Cassell, 1994), takes issue with how Freud's invariably unexamined ideas about gender condition his argument about sexuality (see pp. 162–7). The reason for this is because the Oedipus complex rests on a gender distinction and consequently gender is central to Freud's model of identity (p. 167). However, these are the kinds of historical parameters within which Freud should be seen. While Sinfield is happy to claim that we should not dehistoricise Wilde and read his work as possessing a covert queer presence he nevertheless debunks Freud and the sexologists as applying a 'false' model of identity, which does require a moment of critical retrospection.

15 The letter was written on 2 July 1896, in it he claims, via Lombroso and Nordau, that he suffers from a form of 'sexual madness' and that the degenerationist link between the artifice of life and madness also relates to him; as such he should be pitied rather than punished. PRO reference HO 45/24514.

16 Foldy, *The Trials of Oscar Wilde*, p. 97.

17 Ibid., p. 100.

18 See Ibid. Foldy refers to this as Wilde's 'ontological aesthetic' (p. 102).

19 Oscar Wilde, 'The Soul of Man Under Socialism', in *The Complete Works*, ed. G.F. Maine, pp. 1018–43, p. 1035. All subsequent references are to this edition, and are given in the text.

20 For an argument which links Wilde's interest in Catholicism with his fascination with Freemasonry and his trials, see Marie Mulvey Roberts, 'The Importance of being a Freemason: the trials of Oscar Wilde' in Tracey Hill (ed.), *Decadence and Danger: Writing, History and the Fin de Siècle* (Bath: Sulis Press, 1997), pp. 138–49.

21 There is also a complexity here concerning whose body is represented in this way? Dorian is not quite a martyr, and because he is the product of Lord Henry's 'philosophy' he lacks an essential radical edge. However, in reality there is a debate about the construction of identity which does address this concern with the body, and it is in the debate, rather than in any obvious personification, that the idea of Christ's body is located.

22 James Eli Adams, *Dandies and Desert Saints: Styles of Victorian Masculinity* (Ithaca, NY and London: Cornell University Press, 1995) p. 8. See pp. 107–47 for an account of Kingsley.

23 Oscar Wilde, *De Profundis* in *The Complete Works*, ed. G.F. Maine, pp. 853–88, p. 868. All subsequent references are to this edition, and are given in the text.

24 Arguably Shelley's atheism is granted a particular ethical character to the degree that it challenged an ethical orthodoxy.

25 Oscar Wilde, *The Picture of Dorian Gray* (Harmondsworth: Penguin, 1985) p. 65. All subsequent references are to this edition, and are given in the text.

26 Oscar Wilde, 'The Ballad of Reading Gaol' in *The Complete Works*, ed. G.F. Maine, pp. 822–39. All subsequent references are to this edition, and are given in the text.

27 Richard Ellmann discusses Wilde's claims that *Dorian Gray* was 'too moral' in *Oscar Wilde*, p. 303.

28 David Punter, *The Literature of Terror* (London and New York: Longman, 1996) Vol. 2, pp. 1–26. All subsequent references are to this edition, and are given in the text.

29 The relevant part of Pater's *The Renaissance* (Oxford: Oxford University Press, 1986) ed. Adam Phillips, is the Conclusion, see pp. 150–3.

30 Oscar Wilde, 'The Garden of Eros' in *The Complete Works*, ed. G.F. Maine, pp. 701–8.

31 Oscar Wilde, 'Magdalen Walks' in *The Complete Works*, ed. G.F. Maine, pp. 730–1.

32 Oscar Wilde, 'Humanitad' in *The Complete Works*, ed. G.F. Maine, pp. 780–90.

33 Oscar Wilde, 'Fantaisies Décoratives' in *The Complete Works*, ed. G.F. Maine, pp. 795–6.

34 Oscar Wilde, 'Canzonet' in *The Complete Works*, ed. G.F. Maine, p. 797.

35 There is a case to be made that if the texts were critically read in a different order with *Dorian Gray* first, then *Reading Gaol* followed by *De Profundis* then it could be claimed that Wilde was growing in confidence about this new, Christ-like identity. However, I feel that this would be misleading because this suggests that Wilde simplifies his argument rather than intellectually develops it. A more plausible case, I feel, is to be made that Wilde returns to these ideas in rather different ways, and that considered as a whole they indicate different perceptions of the same problem rather than a refinement of them.

Conclusion

In this book I have sought to make a contribution to a range of different knowledges including accounts of masculinity, our understanding of the *fin de siècle*, the relationship between literature and science, and scholarship on the Gothic. In some respects this might seem to be an overly ambitious project, although it is held together by an understanding of how we discuss literary texts and scientific knowledge in culturally contextualised ways.

The range of issues and case histories which I discuss help to develop our understanding of the constructions of masculinity during the period. Such constructions, although staged in different literary, quasi-scientific, or strictly medical contexts, are united by a shared concern that the middle-class male had become susceptible to moral decline and physical disease. Different writers address this in different ways. For Samuel Smiles, for example, the loss of a masculine middle-class mode of gentlemanly behaviour would lead to economic, political, and national decline. However, Wilde embraced the possibility of an alternative type of gender politics with some enthusiasm. This is really another way of acknowledging that although there exists some shared perception relating to the erosion of certain masculine scripts, for some writers this was a liberation rather than a cause for concern.

Writing on the *fin de siècle* has typically emphasised the idea that the period was characterised by crisis. However, as the example of Wilde suggests, there is a difference between provoking a crisis and seeing in it the opportunity for new forms of expression. Also, as I have suggested throughout, this notion of crisis was, in substantial part, self-generated. This is not to claim that such an economically and socially privileged group of middle-class professions somehow self-destructed for obscure reasons, rather it is to acknowledge that a process of self-reflection on their procedures and practices generated some uncomfortable truths. As we saw in the case of the Whitechapel murders, one of the peculiarities was that a medical gaze seemingly encountered itself in the guise of a murderous autopsy. Also, as Treves's account of Merrick testifies, the anxiety was that the 'normal' and the 'abnormal' could become conflated and so implicate medicine as the producers of pathology (as we saw in 'A Cure for Nerves') rather than as the guardians of health. In this way, I have attempted a reassessment of how notions of crisis at the *fin de siècle*, specifically in relation to masculinity, were generated.

I have also constructed an argument which at various points, and at different levels of engagement, concerns the relationship between science and literature. This relationship is often an indirect one because science and literature are produced in different literary and epistemological contexts. Nevertheless it is clear that there are points of convergence between them, and although I acknowledge their respective contexts, a covert alliance is formed out of these shared cultural preoccupations. This is not to say that such contexts can be simply collapsed into each other, but rather to claim that a relationship did exist between how the Gothic influenced a certain medical language (such as Treves's) and how images of science influenced the Gothic (as in *Jekyll and Hyde* and *Dracula*). In addition, as we saw in the press reports during the Whitechapel murders, the distinction between the literary and the scientific was somewhat blurred at the time; or at least it was in a certain kind of popular imagination that the – largely non-broadsheet – press was reaching out to.

However, it is also important to note that although one should exercise some caution in relating literary and scientific texts to each other, an additional issue is that neither the scientific nor the literary contexts constitute, at least in the examples referred to in this book, a coherent body of work. Science is working at different levels of explicitness and objectivity across the texts. In some respects this is clear in the difference between the scientific ambitions of the sexologists and the work of Max Nordau, a journalist, novelist and playwright, who attempted in *Degeneration* to apply scientific concepts to cultural texts. Indeed as I briefly discussed in Chapter 1, Nordau's model of degeneration was attacked for its lack of scientific rigour by such figures as H.G. Wells, William James and George Bernard Shaw. Also, the claims for scientific certainty are obviously more exact in the autopsy reports of the Whitechapel murder victims, than say in the often subjective case histories to be found in Havelock Ellis's *Studies in the Psychology of Sex*. To some degree it is perhaps unfair to relate the quite different disciplines of sexology and post-mortem science to each other, as they are obviously making different claims on truth. Nevertheless, it is also important to acknowledge that the science explored here does not constitute a unified discourse, despite a shared interest in the issue of gender.

Gender is engaged with in different ways across the texts that I have discussed. The sexologists, for example, were explicitly examining this issue whereas it is unconsciously generated in the instance of the autopsy reports. This sense of diversity also applies to the literary culture. Stevenson, Stoker, Doyle and Wilde have quite different aesthetic and political ambitions. *Dracula*, for example, treats the New Woman in a reactionary way, and this conservative attitude towards gender is also clear in the representation of masculinity. The novel argues the case that by making Jonathan Harker a 'man' the middle classes can overcome the threat of degeneration although, as we have seen, the compromising and seemingly unconscious paradox is that in order to effect this the vampire hunters have to become more, not less, like the Count. *Jekyll and Hyde* is arguably more deliberate in its construction of a paradox which is articulated through the figures of Jekyll and Hyde. Although Hyde appears to be the central Gothic character, there is also the suggestion that it is middle-class professionals such as Jekyll and Utterson who lead empty, dislocated and alienated Gothic lives. Like *Dracula*, the novella suggests a paradoxical way of overcoming such associated images of degeneration. The middle classes lack the vitality that Hyde possesses, and although he is represented as a figure who infiltrates their world he is also represented, at least ostensibly, as a gentleman and so emphasises the inherent 'horrors' of bourgeois life. Stevenson does not attempt, as Stoker does, a way of overcoming this pessimism, and by closing on a moment of uncertainty (about whether Jekyll has killed Hyde, or Hyde has killed Jekyll), he is able to maintain the tensions between Jekyll and Hyde without resolving them.

Wilde's Gothic is of a different order: founded on aesthetics rather than biology. The irony is that *Dorian Gray*'s implicit message, that life cannot be lived in aesthetic terms, was overlooked at Wilde's trials where an emphasis was placed on the novel's alleged immorality. However, the novel does not really celebrate the possibility of a supposed immoral decadence, and by representing Dorian as the product of Lord Henry Wotton's philosophy the text suggests Dorian's fundamental emptiness, which in some respects echoes the emptiness of Jekyll. Dorian's double is a painting, but its representation of a morally disfigured inner life reflects on how Dorian's apparent social graces create a particular kind of ugliness, just as Jekyll's putative adherence to bourgeois notions of respectability generates horror from within.

What also unites these accounts of masculinity is the issue of class. Throughout this book I have emphasised that it is the male middle-class subject (and his gender scripts) who became peculiarly susceptible to pathologisation. Even Treves's account of Merrick tells us more about Treves than it does about either Merrick's illness or what his life had really been like. Treves, by turning Merrick into a mock Dandy, not only feminises Merrick but also bestows social mobility upon him; underlined by Merrick's introduction to people of considerable social standing (including the Prince and Princess of Wales). This dressing-up of Merrick by Treves is in its own way an attempt to 'normalise' the pathological, even as its effects suggest that the normative scripts (Merrick as a 'gentleman'), have become pathologised.

This issue of class cannot be separated from gender. As we saw in Hutchinson's *Syphilis*, it is the condition of the middle-class client which concerns him most. Such patients are responsible for the transmission of the disease, but Hutchinson emphasises the need for discretion in dealing with such a patient's wife. In effect the presence of the disease becomes a secret between the doctor and his client. The middle-class male may therefore be susceptible to disease, but a veneer of respectability is asserted. However, as all the examples in this book testify, yet again the middle-class male is associated with pathology, and this link suggests quite profound anxieties relating to the exercise of social and economic power. This was an idea that was central to Smiles's notion of the gentleman in *Self-Help*. For Smiles true economic and political power is to be found in the middle classes, and yet these are the classes which, seemingly, are subjected to the possibility of moral and physical dissipation.

Smiles's male subject is a divided one, torn between the demands of their body and social duty. What is so interesting about Smiles's argument is that far from seeing this divided male subject as posing a problem, it is turned into an opportunity to exercise self-restraint (self-help) in the interests of class power, and consequently of a national authority. Self-restraint would not, so Smiles and after him Charles Kingsley claim, possess any virtue if it were not exercised in the interests of a greater, depersonalised and abstract, social good. The obvious conundrum is that this process of depersonalisation in its own way implies the presence of something pathological and corrupting that lies at the centre of the body politic of a nation which could demand such self-sacrifice.

In their own ways the issues and case histories which I have explored are all founded on the paradox of asserting an abstract notion of the good (whether that be ethically understood, or related to an idea of professional competence) which is dramatically at odds with some version of an 'inner' life (expressed either as 'desire', or as an awkward professional self-reflection, as in many of the medical narratives discussed here). However, this is not to assert some vague notion of essentialism that exists independently, and somehow more authentically, outside of the dominant, controlling, class and gender scripts; rather, it is to acknowledge that such an 'inner' life needs to be scrutinised in cultural rather than psychoanalytical terms. This, finally, takes us back to *Jekyll and Hyde*, because Stevenson explicitly raises this question of a divided, real and unreal self, but refuses to sanction the idea that such a division exists. I referred to this passage at the beginning of Chapter 1, but I think that it is worth restating here. Jekyll informs us that: 'Though so profound a double-dealer, I was in no sense a hypocrite: both sides of me were in dead earnest: I was no more myself when I laid aside restraint and plunged in shame, than when I laboured, in the eye of day, at the furtherance of knowledge or the relief of sorrow and suffering'.[1] This version of the subject is in many ways quite different to that of Smiles and Kingsley's. This later subject is not trying to suppress latent biological urges in the interests of society, rather such a model of subjectivity suggests that instability lies at the very core of the male subject just, so the novella suggests, as this replicates the wider social and political instabilities that reflect the tensions to be found in representations of class power. The social self and the private self are therefore negated as Stevenson paradoxically, and highly problematically, creates an image of a self united in its very division.

Stevenson's oxymoron is represented in different way in all the narratives discussed here and its presence provides us with an insight into the ambivalence with which class power and gender authority was expressed. The *fin de siècle* seemingly brought these pre-existing tensions to a climax and it is notable that no other period quite gives us such a rich array of case histories as Merrick's, the Whitechapel murders, and Wilde's trials; case histories which dovetail with theories of degeneration and sexological accounts of subjectivity. All of these narratives underline just how important it is to put the history back into theories of the self and so avoid the essentialist trap.

Notes

1 Robert Louis Stevenson, *The Strange Case of Dr Jekyll and Mr Hyde* (1886) in *The Strange Case of Dr Jekyll and Mr Hyde and Other Stories*, ed. Jenni Calder (Harmondsworth: Penguin, 1984) p. 81.

Bibliography

Adams, James Eli, *Dandies and Desert Saints: Styles of Victorian Masculinity* (Ithaca, NY and London: Cornell University Press, 1995).

Barsham, Diana, *Arthur Conan Doyle and the Meaning of Masculinity* (Aldershot: Ashgate, 2000).

Begg, Paul, Martin Fido and Keith Skinner (eds), *The Jack the Ripper A–Z* (London: Headline, 1996).

Belsey, Catherine, *Critical Practice* (London and New York: Routledge, 1980).

Bland, Lucy and Laura Doan (eds), *Sexology in Culture: Labelling Bodies and Desires* (Cambridge: Polity, 1998).

Bland, Lucy and Laura Doan (eds), *Sexology Uncensored: The Documents of Sexual Science* (Cambridge: Polity, 1998).

Booth, Charles, *Life and Labour of the People of London* (London: Macmillan [1889] 1892).

Booth, William, *In Darkest England and the Way Out* (1890) from Sally Ledger and Roger Luckhurst (eds), *The Fin de Siècle: A Reader in Cultural History c.1880–1900* (Oxford: Oxford University Press, 2000).

Botting, Fred, *Gothic* (London: Routledge, 1996).

Bristow, Joseph, 'Symond's History, Ellis Heredity: *Sexual Inversion*' in Lucy Bland and Laura Doan (eds), *Sexology in Culture: Labelling Bodies and Desires* (Cambridge: Polity, 1998).

Bronfen, Elisabeth, *Over Her Dead Body: Death, Femininity and the Aesthetic* (Manchester: Manchester University Press, 1992).

Brooke, Emma, *A Superfluous Woman* (New York: Cassell, 1894).

Burke, Edmund, *A Philosophical Enquiry into the Origin of our Ideas of the Sublime and Beautiful*, ed. Adam Phillips (Oxford: Oxford University Press, [1759] 1998).

Butler, Josephine, 'The Garrison Towns of Kent', *Shield*, 9 May 1870 cited in Judith R. Walkowitz, *City of Dreadful Delight: Narratives of Sexual Danger in Late-Victorian London* (London: Virago, 1992).

Carpenter, Edward, *The Intermediate Sex: A Study of Some Transitional Types of Men and Women* (London: Swan Sonnenschein, 1908). Edition cited from Lucy Bland and Laura Doan (eds), *Sexology Uncensored: The Documents of Sexual*

Science (Cambridge: Polity, 1998).

Chamberlain, J. Edward, 'Images of Degeneration: Turnings and Transformation' in J. Edward Chamberlain, and Sander L. Gilman (eds), *Degeneration: The Dark Side of Progress* (New York: Columbia University Press, 1985).

Chamberlain, J. Edward and Sander L. Gilman (eds), *Degeneration: The Dark Side of Progress* (New York: Columbia University Press, 1985).

Chauncey, George Jr., 'From Sexual Inversion to Homosexuality: Medicine and the Changing Conceptualization of Female Deviance', *Salmagundi*, 58–58 (Fall 1982–Winter 1983), 114–45.

Clemens, Samuel L., *A Tramp Abroad*, ed. Charles Neider (New York: Harper and Row, 1977).

Collins, Wilkie, *The Woman in White* (Harmondsworth: Penguin, [1860] 1985).

Cooper, Alfred, *Syphilis* (London: Churchill, 1895).

Curtis, L. Perry Jr., *Jack the Ripper and the London Press* (New Haven, CT: Yale University Press, 2001).

Daly, Nicholas, *Modernism, Romance and the Fin de Siècle* (Cambridge: Cambridge University Press, 1999).

De Quincey, Thomas, *Confessions of an English Opium Eater* (Harmondsworth: Penguin, [1821] 1986).

Dickens, Charles, *Bleak House* (Harmondsworth: Penguin, [1853] 1985).

Dijkstra, Bram, *Idols of Perversity: Fantasies of Feminine Evil in Fin-de-Siècle Culture* (Oxford: Oxford University Press, 1986).

Dollimore, Jonathan, 'Perversion, Degeneration, and the Death Drive' in Andrew H. Miller and James Eli Adams (eds), *Sexualities in Victorian Britain* (Bloomington, IN and Indianapolis: Indiana University Press, 1996).

Doyle, Arthur Conan, *A Study in Scarlet* (1887) in *The Penguin Complete Sherlock Holmes* (Harmondsworth: Penguin, [1930] 1981).

——*The Sign of Four* (1890) in *The Penguin Complete Sherlock Holmes.*

——'A Scandal in Bohemia' from the *Adventures of Sherlock Holmes* (1892) in *The Penguin Complete Sherlock Holmes.*

——'The Adventure of the Engineer's Thumb' from the *Adventures of Sherlock Holmes* (1892) in *The Penguin Complete Sherlock Holmes.*

——'The Copper Beeches' from the *Adventures of Sherlock Holmes* (1892) in *The Penguin Complete Sherlock Holmes.*

—— 'The Man With the Twisted Lip' from the *Adventures of Sherlock Holmes* (1892) in *The Penguin Complete Sherlock Holmes.*

——'The Final Problem' from the *Memoirs of Sherlock Holmes* (1894) in *The Penguin Complete Sherlock Holmes.*

——'The Resident Patient' from the *Memoirs of Sherlock Holmes* (1894) in *The Penguin Complete Sherlock Holmes.*

Ellis, Havelock, *Man and Woman: A Study of Human Secondary Sexual Characteristics* (London: A. & C. Black, 1894) in Lucy Bland and Laura Doan (eds), *Sexology Uncensored: The Documents of Sexual Science* (Cambridge: Polity, 1998).

——*Studies in the Psychology of Sex*, Vol. II: *Sexual Inversion* (Philadelphia: F.A. Davis,[1897] 1915) cited in Lucy Bland and Laura Doan (eds), *Sexology Uncensored: The Documents of Sexual Science*.

——*Affirmations* (London: Constable, [1898] 1929).

Ellis, Kate Ferguson, *The Contested Castle: Gothic Novels and the Subversion of Domestic Ideology* (Urbana and Chicago, IL: University of Illinois Press, 1989).

Ellmann, Richard, *Oscar Wilde* (Harmondsworth: Penguin, 1987).

Evans, Stewart P. and Keith Skinner (eds), *The Ultimate Jack the Ripper Sourcebook: An Illustrated Encyclopedia* (London: Constable, 2001).

Fleenor, Juliann (ed.), *The Female Gothic* (Montreal: Eden Press, 1983).

Foldy, Michael, *The Trials of Oscar Wilde: Deviance, Morality, and Late-Victorian Society* (New Haven, CT and London: Yale University Press, 1997).

Foucault, Michel, *The History of Sexuality: An Introduction*, Vol. 1, trans. Robert Hurley (Harmondsworth: Penguin, [1976] 1984).

Frayling, Christopher, 'The House that Jack Built: Some Stereotypes of the Rapist in the History of Popular Culture' from Sylvana Tomaselli and Roy Porter (eds), *Rape* (Oxford: Blackwell, 1986).

Freud, Sigmund., 'The "Uncanny"' in *Art and Literature: Jensen's Gradiva, Leonardo Da Vinci and Other Works*, in Vol. 14 Penguin Freud Library, trans. James Strachey, ed. Albert Dickson (Harmondsworth: Penguin, 1985).

Gilman, Charlotte Perkins, *The Yellow Wallpaper* (London: Virago, [1892] 1990).

Gilman, Sander L., '"Who Kills Whores?" "I Do," Says Jack: Race and Gender in Victorian London' in Sarah Webster Goodwin and Elisabeth Bronfen (eds), *Death and Representation* (Baltimore, PA and London: Johns Hopkins University Press, 1993).

Goodwin, Sarah Webster and Elisabeth Bronfen (eds), *Death and Representation* (Baltimore, PA and London: Johns Hopkins University Press, 1993).

Grand, Sarah, *The Heavenly Twins* (New York: Cassell, 1893).

——*The Beth Book* (London: Heinemann, 1897).

Greenway, Judy, 'It's What You Do With It That Counts: Interpretations of Otto Weininger' in Lucy Bland and Laura Doan (eds), *Sexology in Culture: Labelling Bodies and Desires* (Cambridge: Polity, 1998).

Grenfell, Wilfred, *A Labrador Doctor: The Autobiography of Sir Wilfred Grenfell* (London: Hodder and Stoughton, [1920] 1931).

Hake, Egmont, *Regeneration: A Reply to Max Nordau* (London: Archibald Constable, 1895).

Hall, Lesley A., '"The Great Scourge": Syphilis as a Medical Problem and a Moral Metaphor, 1880–1916', at http://homepages.primex.co.uk/~lesleyah/grtscrge.htm

Halperin, David, *One Hundred Years of Homosexuality* (New York: Routledge, 1989).

Halstead, D.G., *Doctor in The Nineties* (London: Christopher Johnson, 1959).

Hendershot, Cyndy, *The Animal Within: Masculinity and the Gothic* (Ann Arbor, MI: University of Michigan Press, [1998] 2001).

Hill, Tracey (ed.), *Decadence and Danger: Writing, History and the Fin de Siècle* (Bath: Sulis Press, 1997).

Howell, Michael and Peter Ford, *The True History of the Elephant Man* (Harmondsworth: Penguin, 1980).

Hughes, William, *Beyond Dracula: Bram Stoker's Fiction and its Cultural Context* (Basingstoke: Macmillan, 2002).

Hurley, Kelly, *The Gothic Body: Sexuality, Materialism, and Degeneration at the Fin de Siècle* (Cambridge: Cambridge University Press, 1996).

Hutchinson, Jonathan, *Syphilis* (Cassell: London, [1887] second edition, 1909).

Ibsen, Henrik, *Ghosts* (1881) in *Ghosts and Other Plays* (Harmondsworth: Penguin, 1964).

James, William, review of *Degeneration* in *Psychological Review*, 2 (May 1895), 289–90.

Jann, Rosemary, 'Sherlock Holmes Codes the Social Body' in *English Literature History*, 57:3 (1990) 685–708.

Kant, Immanuel, 'The Analytic of the Sublime' in *The Critique of Judgement*, trans. James C. Meredith (Oxford: Clarendon, 1986 [1790]), pp. 90–203.

Kestner, Joseph A., *Sherlock's Men: Masculinity, Conan Doyle, and Cultural History* (Aldershot: Ashgate, 1997).

King, Thomas A., 'Performing "Akimbo" Queer pride and epistemological prejudice' in Moe Meyer (ed.), *The Politics and Poetics of Camp* (London: Routledge, 1994).

Kingsley, Charles, 'Great Cities and Their Influence for Good and Evil' (1857) in *Sanitary and Social Lectures and Essays* (London: Macmillan, 1880).

——'The Science of Health' (1872) in *Sanitary and Social Lectures and Essays*.

——'The Tree of Knowledge' (1880) in *Sanitary and Social Lectures and Essays*.

Lankester, Edwin, *Degeneration: A Chapter in Darwinism* (London: Macmillan, 1880).

Le Bon, Gustave, 'The Mind of Crowds', in *The Crowd: A Study of the Popular Mind* (London: T. Fisher Unwin, 1896).

Ledger, Sally and Roger Luckhurst (eds), *The Fin de Siècle: A Reader in Cultural History c.1880–1900* (Oxford: Oxford University Press, 2000).

Lewis, Matthew, *The Monk* (Oxford: Oxford University Press, [1796] 1992).

Loomba, Ania, *Colonialism/Postcolonialism* (London: Routledge, 1998).

McHugh, Paul, *Prostitution and Victorian Social Reform* (London, Croom Helm: 1980).

Mearns, Andrew, *The Bitter Cry of Outcast London: An Inquiry into the Condition of the Abject Poor* (1883) in Sally Ledger and Roger Luckhurst (eds), *The Fin de Siècle: A Reader in Cultural History c. 1880–1900*.

Merrick, Joseph, 'The Autobiography of Joseph Carey Merrick', reproduced in Michael Howell and Peter Ford, *The True History of the Elephant Man* (Harmondsworth: Penguin, 1980).

Meyer, Moe (ed.), *The Politics and Poetics of Camp* (London: Routledge, 1994).

——'Under the Sign of Wilde: An Archaeology of Posing' in Moe Meyer (ed.),

The Politics and Poetics of Camp (London: Routledge, 1994).

Mighall, Robert, *A Geography of Victorian Gothic Fiction: Mapping History's Nightmares* (Oxford: Oxford University Press, 1999).

Milbank, Alison, *Daughters of the House: Modes of the Gothic in Victorian Fiction* (Basingstoke: Macmillan, 1992).

Miles, Robert, *Ann Radcliffe: The Great Enchantress* (Manchester: Manchester University Press, 1995).

——(ed.), 'Female Gothic Writing', special issue of *Women's Writing: the Elizabethan to Victorian period, Triangle*, 1:2 (1994).

Miller, Andrew H. and James Eli Adams (eds), *Sexualities in Victorian Britain* (Bloomington, and Indianapolis, IN: Indiana University Press, 1996).

Moers, Ellen, *Literary Women* (Women's Press: London, 1978).

Moretti, Franco, *Atlas of the European Novel 1800–1900* (London: Verso, 1998).

Mulvey Roberts, Marie, 'The Importance of being a Freemason: the trials of Oscar Wilde' in Tracey Hill (ed.), *Decadence and Danger: Writing, History and the Fin de Siècle* (Bath: Sulis Press, 1997).

Nord, Deborah Epstein, '"Vitiated Air" The Polluted City and Female Sexuality in *Dombey and Son* and *Bleak House*' in Andrew H. Miller and James Eli Adams (eds), *Sexualities in Victorian Britain* (Bloomington and Indianapolis, IN: Indiana University Press, 1996).

Nordau, Max, *Degeneration* (Lincoln, NE and London: University of Nebraska Press, [1895]1993).

Pankhurst, Christabel, *The Great Scourge and How to End It* (London: E. Pankhurst, 1913).

Pater, Walter, *The Renaissance*, ed. Adam Phillips (Oxford: Oxford University Press, 1986).

Pick, Daniel, *Faces of Degeneration: a European Disorder, c.1848–c.1918* (Cambridge: Cambridge University Press, [1989] 1996).

Porter, Roy, *London: A Social History* (Harmondsworth: Penguin, 2000).

Punter, David, *The Literature of Terror*, Vols 1 and 2 (London and New York: Longman, 1996).

Radcliffe, Ann, 'On the Supernatural in Poetry', *New Monthly Magazine*, 16 (1826) 145–52.

Rappaport, Erika Diane, *Shopping for Pleasure: Women in the Making of London's West End* (Princeton, NJ and Oxford: Princeton University Press, 2002).

Reynolds, G.W.M., *The Mysteries of London* (London: George Vickers, 1846).

Sedgwick, Eve Kosofsky, *Between Men: English Literature and Male Homosocial Desire* (New York: Columbia, 1985).

——*Epistemology of the Closet* (London: Harvester Wheatsheaf, 1991).

Shaw, George Bernard, *The Sanity of Art: An Exposure of the Current Nonsense about Artists Being Degenerate* (London: New Age Press, 1908).

Shelley, Mary, *Frankenstein: or The Modern Prometheus* (Harmondsworth: Penguin, 1985).

Showalter, Elaine, *Sexual Anarchy: Gender and Culture at the Fin de Siècle*

(Harmondsworth: Viking, 1990)

Simmel, Georg, 'The Metropolis and Mental Life', in Donald Levine (ed.), *Georg Simmel on Individuality and Social Forms* (Chicago, IL: University of Chicago Press, 1971).

Sinfield, Alan, *The Wilde Century: Effeminacy, Oscar Wilde and the Queer Movement* (London: Cassell, 1994).

Smiles, Samuel, *Self-Help: With Illustrations of Conduct and Perseverance* (London: John Murray, [1859] 1877).

Smith, Andrew, *Gothic Radicalism: Literature, Philosophy and Psychoanalysis in the Nineteenth Century* (Basingstoke: Macmillan, 2000).

Somerville, Siobhan B., 'Scientific Racism and the Invention of the Homosexual Body' in Lucy Bland and Laura Doan (eds), *Sexology in Culture: Labelling Bodies and Desires* (Cambridge: Polity, 1998).

Spongberg, Mary, *Feminizing Venereal Disease: The Body of the Prostitute in Nineteenth-Century Medical Discourse* (Basingstoke: Macmillan, 1997).

Stallybrass, Peter and Allon White, *The Politics and Poetics of Transgression* (London: Methuen, 1986).

Stead, W.T., 'The Maiden Tribute of Modern Babylon' (1885) in Sally Ledger and Roger Luckhurst (eds), *The Fin de Siècle: A Reader in Cultural History c.1880–1900* (Oxford: Oxford University Press, 2000).

Stevenson, Robert Louis, *The Strange Case of Dr Jekyll and Mr Hyde* (1886) in *The Strange Case of Dr Jekyll and Mr Hyde and Other Stories*, ed. Jenni Calder (Harmondsworth: Penguin, 1984).

Stoker, Bram, *Dracula* (Oxford: Oxford University Press, [1897] 1996).

Tomaselli, Sylvana and Roy Porter (eds), *Rape* (Oxford: Blackwell, 1986).

Tosh, John, *A Man's Place: Masculinity and the Middle-Class Home in Victorian England* (New Haven, CT and London: Yale University Press, 1999).

Treves, Frederick, 'A Case of Congenital Deformity', *Transactions of the Pathological Society of London*, xxxvi (March 1885) 494–8.

——*The Elephant Man and Other Reminiscences* (London: Cassell, 1923).

Walkowitz, Judith R., *City of Dreadful Delight: Narratives of Sexual Danger in Late-Victorian London* (London: Virago, 1992).

Weeks, Jeffrey, 'Movements of Affirmation: Sexual Meanings and Homosexual Identities', *Radical History Review*, 20 (1979).

Weininger, Otto, *Sex and Character* (New York: AMS Press, [1903] 1906).

Wells, H.G., 'Zoological Retrogression', *Gentleman's Magazine*, 271 (1891) 246-53.

——*The Island of Doctor Moreau* (London: Pan, [1896] 1975).

Wilde, Oscar, 'The Garden of Eros' in *The Complete Works of Oscar Wilde*, ed. G.F. Maine (London: Collins, 1992).

——'Humanitad' (1881) in *The Complete Works of Oscar Wilde*, ed. G.F. Maine.

——'Magdalen Walks' (1881) in *The Complete Works of Oscar Wilde*, ed. G.F. Maine.

——'Fantaisies Décoratives' (1887) in *The Complete Works of Oscar Wilde*, ed. G.F. Maine.

——'Canzonet' (1888) in *The Complete Works of Oscar Wilde*, ed. G.F. Maine.

——'The Decay of Lying' (1889) in *The Complete Works of Oscar Wilde*, ed. G.F. Maine.

——'The Critic as Artist' (1890) in *The Complete Works of Oscar Wilde*, ed. G.F. Maine.

——'The Soul of Man Under Socialism' (1891) in *The Complete Works of Oscar Wilde*, ed. G.F. Maine.

——*The Picture of Dorian Gray* (Harmondsworth: Penguin, [1891] 1985).

——*The Importance of Being Earnest* (1895) in *The Complete Works of Oscar Wilde*, ed. G.F. Maine.

——*The Ballad of Reading Gaol* (1898) in *The Complete Works of Oscar Wilde*, ed. G.F. Maine.

——*De Profundis* (1905) in *The Complete Works of Oscar Wilde*, ed. G.F. Maine.

Wilde, W.R., 'Medico-Legal Observations upon the Case of Amos Greenwood', *Dublin Quarterly Journal of Medicine & Science*, 27 (1858) 51–87.

Wolf, Leonard, *Annotated Dracula* (London: N. Potter, 1975).

Wolfreys, Julian, *Writing London: The Trace of the Urban Text from Blake to Dickens* (Basingstoke: Macmillan, 1998).

Zanger, Jules, 'A Sympathetic Vibration: Dracula and the Jews', *English Literature in Transition 1880–1920*, 34 (1991) 33–44.

Index

Note: individual works can be found under authors' names.

Lightning Source UK Ltd.
Milton Keynes UK
UKOW06f0843301216

291064UK00020B/226/P